The Metamorphoses of Ancient Myths

Małgorzata Budzowska / Burç İdem Dinçel /
Jadwiga Czerwińska / Katarzyna Chiżyńska (eds.)

The Metamorphoses of Ancient Myths

Bibliographic Information published by the Deutsche Nationalbibliothek
The Deutsche Nationalbibliothek lists this publication in the Deutsche Nationalbibliografie; detailed bibliographic data is available in the internet at http://dnb.d-nb.de.

Library of Congress Cataloging-in-Publication Data
A CIP catalog record for this book has been applied for at the Library of Congress

Cover image: © Maksim Šmeljov / Fotolia.com

This Publication was financially supported by the Chair of Classics and the Institute of Romance Studies of the University of Lodz.

Printed by CPI books GmbH, Leck

ISBN 978-3-631-67372-0 (Print)
E-ISBN 978-3-653-06632-6 (E-Book)
E-ISBN 978-3-631-70224-6 (EPUB)
E-ISBN 978-3-631-70225-3 (MOBI)
DOI 10.3726/978-3-653-06632-6

© Peter Lang GmbH
Internationaler Verlag der Wissenschaften
Frankfurt am Main 2017
All rights reserved.
Peter Lang Edition is an Imprint of Peter Lang GmbH.

Peter Lang – Frankfurt am Main · Bern · Bruxelles · New York · Oxford · Warszawa · Wien

All parts of this publication are protected by copyright. Any utilisation outside the strict limits of the copyright law, without the permission of the publisher, is forbidden and liable to prosecution. This applies in particular to reproductions, translations, microfilming, and storage and processing in electronic retrieval systems.

This publication has been peer reviewed.

www.peterlang.com

Contents

Acknowledgements 7

List of contributors 9

Małgorzata Budzowska and Burç İdem Dinçel
Introduction. *The Work of Myth* within the *Work on Myth* 13

Part I *Work on Myth* within Antiquity

Jadwiga Czerwińska
Myth in Greek Drama of Classical Greece in the Light of Scholia 27

Katarzyna Chiżyńska
Greek Myths in the *Hypotheseis* of Tragedy of the Classical Period 41

Françoise Lecocq
The Palm Tree, the Phoenix and the Wild Boar: Scientific and Literary Reception of a Strange Trio in Pliny the Elder (*Natural History* 13, 42–43) and in *Satyricon* (40, 3–8) 55

Cíntia Martins Sanches
Seneca's *Phoenissae*: Anger and the Myth of Oedipus 79

Damian Pierzak
Is Pelias a Mistake for Aeson? Towards a New Interpretation of Cicero's *De senectute* 23, 83 89

Hanna Zalewska-Jura
Mythical Motifs in Early Byzantine Epigrams 103

Part II Modern and Postmodern *Work on Myth*

Olympia Tachopoulou
Ancient Tragedy in Seferis' Poetry: From Existential Historicism to Philosophical Existentialism 113

Tomasz Kaczmarek
Yvan Goll and Ancient Legacy in His Work 133

Anna Zaorska
Myths as "Collective Experiences" in the German Democratic Republic
on the Example of Chosen Works by Heiner Müller 147

Rossana Zetti
The Re-staging of *Antigone* in Twentieth-Century Europe:
an Irish Example 159

Magdalena Hasiuk
"As if he was not a grandson but the child of the Greeks":
Wajdi Mouawad's Dialogue with Antiquity 179

Stephen Wilmer
Greek Tragedy as a Window on the Dispossessed 191

Małgorzata Budzowska
Death in Theatre. Between Word and Image 207

Burç İdem Dinçel
The Tragic Burst of Laughter in Theodoros Terzopoulos'
Prometheus Bound 235

Index 257

Acknowledgements

This volume is the result of the painstaking efforts of many people, including contributors, reviewers, editors as well as the organisers of the second edition of the international conference *Reception of Ancient Myths in Ancient, Modern and Postmodern Culture* that took place at the University of Lodz in Poland in November 2015. The conference was organised by the Laboratory of Reception of Greek Literature, which is a part of the Chair of Classical Philology, working in cooperation with the Chair of Romance Studies. Editors of the volume would like to warmly thank the reviewers (prof. Mercedes Aguirre – Complutensa University of Madrid, Spain; dr Barbara Bibik – Nicolaus Copernicus University, Toruń, Poland; dr hab. Agnieszka Dziuba – Catholic University of Lublin, Poland; dr Özlem Hemiş – Istanbul University, State Conservatory, Turkey; dr Laura Jansen – University of Bristol, England; dr Panayiota Mini – University of Crete, Greece; prof. Krzysztof Narecki – Catholic University of Lublin, Poland; dr hab. Ewa Osek – Catholic University of Lublin, Poland; dr Joanna Pypłacz – Jagiellonian University Library, Kraków, Poland; dr Benjamin Eldon Stevens – Trinity University, San Antonio, USA; prof. Jerzy Styka – Jagiellonian University, Kraków, Poland), who through a double-blind process provided critical insight into the essays presented in this book.

List of contributors

Małgorzata Budzowska – Assistant Professor at Classics Faculty, University of Lodz in Poland. She was awarded her PhD by the University of Lodz, Classics Faculty, and MA by the Institute of Contemporary Culture (theatre and drama theory) at the same university. Her book *Phaedra – Ethics of Emotions in the Tragedies of Euripides, Seneca and Racine* (Peter Lang 2012) considers intertextual correlations between three plays which adapted the myth of Phaedra in relation to the theory of unrestraint (*akrasia*) by Aristotle. She is a co-editor of the volume *Ancient Myths in the Making of Culture* (Peter Lang 2014). Currently, she is involved in two research projects: *Reception of Ancient Myths of Mediterranean Culture in Polish Theatre of the Twenty-first Century* and *Ancient Drama and Theatre in the Works of Scholiasts*, both funded by the National Science Centre in Poland.

Jadwiga Czerwińska – Full Professor at the University of Lodz, chief editor of *Collectanea Philologica*, member of The Committee on Ancient Culture of the Polish Academy of Sciences (PAN), The Classical Association, The Centrum Latinitatis Europae, The Scientific Committee of Łódź (ŁTN), The Scientific Committee at KUL (Catholic University of Lublin), The Polish Philological Committee (PTF), the scholar of Hardt Foundation, Vandoeuvres-Genève, and The Lanckoronski Foundation. Interested in Greek theatre and drama (mainly Euripides), Greek philosophy and the reception of Antiquity in Italian culture. Author of many articles, including Polish and Italian monographs about the works of Euripides. For her achievements, she was awarded, *inter alia*, with the medal of The Commission of National Education. She was also prized by the Polish Ministry of Science and Higher Education.

Katarzyna Chiżyńska – Assistant Professor at University of Lodz (Poland), Chair of Classical Philology. PhD (2012) in Classical Literature (*Scholia Medicea in Aeschyli "Persas" – Translation and Commentary*), MA (2007) in Cultural Studies (theatre), MA (2005) in Classical Philology. Current research project: *Ancient theatre and drama in the light of scholia* (National Science Centre). Her research concerns ancient scholars' works and poetics of ancient drama.

Burç İdem Dinçel – PhD candidate in Drama at Trinity College Dublin. He has published extensively on Theatre and Translation Studies and taught courses on twentieth-century theatre, theatre movements, traditional Turkish theatre, as well as the history of Turkish theatre. He is the author of *Last Tape on Stage in Translation: Unwinding Beckett's Spool in Turkey*.

Magdalena Hasiuk – Tutor at the Polish Academy of Science, Institute of Art in Warsaw, lecturer at The National Academy of Dramatic Art in Warsaw, author of the book *'Cruelly Strange Side' of the World. About the Prison Theatre* (2015) and numerous academic articles published in Polish and international journals and joint publications. She is also the author of more than seventy theatre reviews and the translator of the book by Jacques Lecoq *Poetic Body* (2011).

Tomasz Kaczmarek – Associate Professor at the University of Lodz in the Department of Romance Philology, Doctor of Humanities of Paris IV (Sorbonne). His research interests include mainly French and Italian literature of the twentieth century, especially in the area of drama and avant-garde theatre in Europe in the first half of the twentieth century. He is the author of three monographs on the work of Henri-René Lenormand, French theatre from the perspective of the expressionist aesthetics and anarchy in the French theatre. His works have been published in such magazines as *Folia Litteraria Romanica, Zagadnienia Rodzajów Literackich, Etudes Romanes de Brno, Echos des Etudes Romanes, Cahiers Octave Mirbeau, Contributi, Quaderni Italo-Ungheresi, L'Avant-Scène*, as well as in numerous collections of post-conference proceedings.

Françoise Lecocq – Maître de Conférences in Latin, University of Caen Normandy (France). She specialises in myths, mainly of the phoenix and Europa, and the image of Rome. Her study of the phoenix has included its literary and symbolic evolution from ancient Egypt till the end of the Roman Empire in Ovid, Pliny the Elder, Lactantius, Claudian, in various genres (poetry, history, natural history, novel, religious texts) and themes (politics, aromatics, gender, iconography, the making of the myth); she has also inventoried some of its contemporary metamorphoses. She studied Europa's medieval metamorphoses in texts and representations (*Moralized Ovid*, the Sybil Europa), as well as Europa's modern sculptures. She has also studied the image of Rome, from Antiquity to contemporary times, both as an abstract entity (*dea Roma*), and as an architectural and symbolic legacy (Pantheon, plaster models of the city). Her other works concern Erasmus' *Adagia* and the book on the fish of the *Hortus Sanitatis*.

Cíntia Martins Sanches – PhD student of Literature from São Paulo State University (UNESP) in Brazil (FAPESP's scholarship); MA in Literature from UNESP/Brazil (CAPES' scholarship); BA in Language and Literature (Portuguese/Latin/English) from UNESP/Brazil; BA in Social Communication – Journalism from Union of Faculties of the Great Lakes in Brazil.

Damian Pierzak – earned his PhD from the University of Silesia in Katowice, Poland, in December 2015 upon the approval of his thesis on Greek myth in

Cicero's *Speeches*. His scientific interests include Cicero, Roman rhetorical theory, and *scholia* on Ciceronian orations. He has published several articles on ancient poetry and rhetoric.

Olympia Tachopoulou – has taught Modern Greek literature as Visiting Lecturer at the University of Cyprus and as Adjunct Lecturer at the Hellenic Open University, University of Crete and Open University of Cyprus. She has worked as a researcher for the Institute for Mediterranean Studies (FORTH) and has been involved in a research project of Nikos Kazantzakis Museum. She is currently teaching as Adjunct Lecturer at Open University of Cyprus and Hellenic Open University. Her book *Modernist Primitivism: Aspects of Surrealism in the Poetry of Nikos Engonopoulos* (2009) investigates the influence of primitive art and non-Western cultures on the aesthetics of Surrealism. Her research interests include classical reception, the history of Greek Surrealism, literary theory and the interdisciplinary study of literature, ethnography and art.

Stephen Wilmer – Professor Emeritus and former Head of the School of Drama, Film and Music at Trinity College Dublin, and a Research Fellow at the International Research Center "Interweaving Performance Cultures" at the Freie Universität Berlin. Recent publications include ed. (with Audrone Zukauskaite) *Resisting Biopolitics: Philosophical, Political and Performative Strategies* (Routledge 2016), *Deleuze and Beckett* (Palgrave Macmillan 2015) and *Interrogating Antigone in Postmodern Philosophy and Criticism* (Oxford UP, 2010). He also recently edited a special number of *Nordic Theatre Studies* on "Theatre and the Nomadic Subject" (2015).

Hanna Zalewska-Jura – Associate Professor, University of Lodz, Chair of Classical Philology. Research interests: ancient Greek literature, archaic Greek epics, archaic Greek monody, the satyr play, Greek epigram, the theory of translation. Selected bibliography: *Wątki i elementy mityczne w epigramach „Antologii Palatyńskiej"* (*Mythological Motives and Elements in the Epigrams of* Greek Anthology), Ossolineum, Wrocław 1998, *W rytmie sikinnis. Studium nad warstwą aluzji i podtekstów w greckim dramacie satyrowym* (*In the Rhythm of Sikinnis. Study on Allusion and Overtones in Greek Satyr Play*), Wyd. UŁ 2006; *Pro Bessarione poeta*, "Studia Ceranea" V, 2015.

Anna Zaorska – Assistant at the University of Lodz, Chair of Literature and Culture of Germany, Austria and Switzerland. MA at the University of Lodz, (Master's thesis: *Image of a Women in the Drama of Gotthold Ephraim Lessing*), PhD at the same university, Chair of Literature and Culture of Germany, Austria and Switzerland (PhD dissertation: *"My crimes are born from love". The Medea*

Myth in German Literature). DAAD scholarship at University of Bielefeld and Free University of Berlin. Research focus: myth in literature, the Age of Enlightenment.

Rosana Zetti – graduated *magna cum laude* in Classical Literature from Università degli Studi di Milano (Italy), where she studied Greek and Latin literature and language, Greek and Roman history, classical philology, philosophy and linguistics. She studied for a semester at the University of Toulouse (France) within the Erasmus Exchange Program. She completed her MA in Classics at the University of Edinburgh (Scotland), where she is currently working on her PhD project supported by the School Doctoral Scholarship. Her research interests include Greek literature and language, philology, theatre studies and theory of reception. She focuses on the reception of Sophocles' *Antigone* in the twentieth-century Europe, and her study aims to clarify the ideologies and contexts which have produced several renewed versions of *Antigone* in this century.

Małgorzata Budzowska[*] and Burç İdem Dinçel[**]

Introduction.
The Work of Myth within the *Work on Myth*

Dwelling upon mythopoetic practices of human beings, the present volume intends to investigate different cases of myth reoccupation *qua* myth (re)creation. By lending a close ear to Hans Blumenberg, who recognizes the *work on myth* (*Arbeit am Mythos*) as "the ongoing reworking of inherited mythical materials, which is the only form and the only way in which we know myth", and the *work of myth* (*Arbeit des Mythos*) as "the essential and original function and accomplishment of myth as such" (1985: 112), we can consider the cycle of myth reworkings (*works on myth*) as a sort of mythopoetic praxes attempting to create new "faces" of old myths, in effect, performing, to varying degrees, the essential *work of myth*.

Elaborating on the essence of the *work of myth*, Blumenberg proffers the notion of *significance* (*Bedeutsamkeit*) to expose the nature and function of mythical knowledge gained by humans.[1] Remaining convinced that "myths do not answer questions as philosophical theories do, but they make questions non-posed",[2] he notices that:

> Significance is the form in which *the background of nothing* [*des Nichts*], as that which produces anxiety, *has been put at a distance*, whereby, without this 'prehistory,' the function of what is significant remains uncomprehended, though present. For *the need for significance is rooted in the fact that we are conscious of never being definitively exempted from the production of anxiety*. (Blumenberg 1985: 110; emphases added)[3]

---

[*] University of Lodz, Poland.
[**] Trinity College Dublin, Ireland.
[1] "No one will want to maintain that myth has better arguments than science; no one will want to maintain that myth has martyrs, as dogma and ideology do, or that it has the intensity of experience of which mysticism speaks. Nevertheless it has something to offer that even with reduced claims to reliability, certainty, faith, realism, and intersubjectivity still constitutes satisfaction of intelligent expectations. The quality on which this depends can be designated by the term significance [*Bedeutsamkeit*], taken from Dilthey." (Blumenberg 1985: 67)
[2] Observation provided by Stefan Klemczak in regard to Blumenberg's reflections (Klemczak 2005: 63).
[3] Cf. also: "Significance is one of the concepts that can be explained but cannot, in the strict sense, be defined. Heidegger associated it, together with 'involvement,' with the

The *work of myth* takes place mainly in the space of the symbolic imaginary and it is a process of the euphemization of reality. As Gilbert Durand indicates, in the contemporary scientistic world this process is connected with the procedure of re-mythisation, since science can create only the "relationships" between humans and things, while affective and imaginary myths are able to connect humans with each other (Durand 1986: 133). Every culture is more or less an effective alloy of myth and rationality,[4] while myth is considered as the dynamics of imagination, *imaginaire en devenir*, remaining constantly *in statu nascendi*. Then, myth can be graspable and understood only in its *terminus ad quem*, in the moment when the *work of myth* is finished only for its particular, always temporary, version, it means, within the specific *work on myth*.[5] However, although myth represents an aggregate of its versions, it never reaches an end, it is always prone to be surrounded by the multiplicity of additions. These incidental appendices can take the form of incorporations, extensions, augmentations, supplements, deformations, transformations, and so on. The adroitness of their application seems to be an evidence of creativity while myth is "re-occupied"[6] within these inventive actions. Being occupied by the new aesthetical trends in order to express current ethical concerns, myth is subject to the process of *mythopoesis* that protects it against solidification into an icy canon. This procedure of myth re-creation (*work on myth* qua *work of myth*) appears to stem from the "intrinsic need for rebellion" (Blumenberg 1985: 551) as being a sign of originality, a countersignature of an artist who *occupies* and *appropriates* a well-known text of culture as myth appears.

Myth as the most locally determined genre (Goody 2010) needs to be compatible with present, with the current experience of community to perform its sublimating and familiarizing function. Locality and temporality become determinants that affect the mythical core and adapt it to the current needs of individual societies. Creation of myth within a piece of art is always connected, consciously or not, with the previous manifestations of the same *mythos* (word-plot-content) within different systems of signs. The transcendence of a myth is the process of a

---

'worldhood' of the world, and thus with the assemblage of being-in-the-world, from which objects, as 'present at hand' with their properties, must first be detached before one can bring to them a theoretical interest that is no longer subjectively 'owned.'" (Blumenberg 1985: 68)

4   Cf. Laprée and Bellehumeur 2013: 267: "En réalité, toutes les cultures et tous les systemes de pensée (les cosmogonies, les théories scientifiques, les idéologies…) sont des alliages plus ou moins efficaces de mythe et de raison calibrés de façon variable."
5   Cf. Klemczak 2005: 54.
6   Using Blumenberg's notion of myth *re-occupation* (*Umbesetzung*) (1985).

transtextual work which aims, firstly, at decoding the systems of signifying practices peculiar to a particular time and space, and, subsequently, at creating a new set of signs according to the techniques and methods distinctive for a specific field of art. The climax of this procedure, however, is reached in the act of reception that becomes an extension of *mythopoesis*, since recipients filter the communicated set of signs through their personal structure and gain its understanding in their own individual ways.

Emphasizing the apotropaic function of myth creation and re-creation, Blumenberg deems the Graeco-Roman literature as an advanced form of the *work of myth*:

> Both phenomena, that of the elimination of monsters from the world and that of the transitional forms on the way to the human *eidos* [form, figure], must have to do with myth's function of producing distance from the quality of uncanniness. The mental schema of distance still rules the Greeks' concept of theory as the position and attitude of the untroubled observer. *In its purest embodiment, in the attitude of the spectator of Greek tragedy, this schema paves the way for the conceptual history of "theory."* (Blumenberg 1985: 117; emphasis added)

As such, *corpus* of ancient myths, dynamically developed by the oral tradition, became a repository of topics and motifs for Greek tragedy that shed light on the then current concerns of Greek culture. Mimetic diegesis of myth performed on stage improved its semantic scope within the present and actualised mythical universal *semper ubique* into current *hic et nunc*. Stage mediation of myth in ancient Greek theatre provided the final, albeit temporary, version of myth that was a product of the creative process of myth transformation. Ancient Greek playwrights employed mythical tissue to construct new plots in accordance with the tragic idea they wished to evolve. This process of reworking of the old myths performed an intertextual creative mimesis when the mythical core existed in the overriding plan and was subject to transmutation into a specific dramatic plot. Choosing to associate this artistic method with adaptation, Linda Hutcheon points out that

> Part of this pleasure (…) comes simply from repetition with variation, from the comfort of ritual combined with the piquancy of surprise. Recognition and remembrance are part of the pleasure (and risk) of experiencing an adaptation; so too is change. (Hutcheon and O'Flynn 2013: 4)

This remark captures the essence of the reworkings of myths within the specific context of ancient Greek theatre that allowed these well-recognized cultural materials to transmutate into new forms of expression, thereby bringing the main reason for spectating them on stage. This issue is analysed from a metatextual perspective in two essays presented in the first part of this volume. Jadwiga Czerwińska reflects on the question of mythical transmutations in Greek tragedy on the basis of scholia, critical commentaries that investigated all changes implemented by poets. Similarly, Katarzyna Chiżyńska analyses the *hypotheseis* to Greek tragedies, which could be described as summaries of ancient dramas written by ancient and medieval scholars and researchers. Both articles scrutinise the form and content of these first scientific analyses of the phenomenon of myth reception within Antiquity. The so-called "mythological" scholia are considered as metatexts inclined to provide an overview and archive the mythical motifs and their transformations, at the same time providing remarkable analytical and evaluative notices.

Corresponding scientific-like perspective towards transformations of mythical imaginary in ancient times is presented in the encyclopaedic work of Pliny the Elder, *Historia Naturalis*, which is the object of inquiry in Françoise Lecocq's essay, where she meticulously explores the images of "the strange trio" – palm tree, phoenix and boar – examining the presence of these mythical figures/motifs in the symbolic imagination of Roman culture saturated by Egyptian and Arabic influences. Such an extended overview emphasises the important notion of Roman civilization that evolved in the background and under the influence of many other abundant cultures, creating a multicultural melting pot also in the space of the symbolic imaginary. In this cultural context, various myths and their elements from the West, South, and East, enriched by the North Celtic contributions, worked together transforming old myths into new ones.

Intertextual reception of myths within Antiquity, regarded as a creative *work on myth*, is studied in three essays exploring different literary genres. Two of them investigate works of Latin literature, which was developed in the overwhelming shadow of its Greek precedent. Cintia Martins Sanches tracks intertextual relationships between Greek tragedy and Latin drama epitomised by Seneca's work. This well-researched area is further explored by the analysis of Seneca's *Phoenissae*, a play which survived only in fragments and which is a creative compilation of two Greek tragedies (Euripides' *Phoeanissae* and Sophocles' *Oedipus at Colonus*), and as such exemplifies the re-occupation of Labdacides' myth by connecting two previously separated threads in one dramatic plot. Furthermore, Sanches makes important references to Senecan philosophical treatises, since the Roman philosopher wrote his dramas as negative moral *exempla* to disseminate his stoic ethics. This specific employment of ancient myths in ethical musing reflects the distinctive usage of myths in Latin ethical works. Philosophical *work on myth* allowed authors to provide case studies supporting their theoretical considerations. The second essay, by Damian Pierzak, inspects the prominent example of a similar procedure regarding Cicero's treatise *De senectute*. Analysing the question of senility, the ancient thinker applied the myth of Medea's magical skill of human rejuvenation, making essential changes in the well-known mythical story. Pierzak minutely explores the rich scholarship concerning these changes, which can be seen as mistakes or as an intentional act of myth adaptation. Yet, the most absorbing aspect of the essay is the interpretative examination of Cicero's work itself, offering some fresh remarks about Pelias/Aeson's mythical confusion thereof. The last work probing into the reception of myths in Antiquity is the essay by Hanna Zalewska-Jura, who studies early Byzantine epigrams. Intriguingly, Zalewska-Jura discusses several epigrams to inquire into the issue of resistance to the employment of old pagan myths in order to spread new Christian ideology. This study searches the significant area of intellectual and artistic actions being in opposition to the ideological involvement of myths transformed to be useful tools in religious or political propaganda. The analysis underlines that the *work on myth* in the Byzantine period, dominated by Christian ideology, was the perfect epigonic way to cultivate Hellenistic artistry of myth transformation.

The second part of the volume brings together essays focused on modern and postmodern reception of ancient myths in the fields of literature and theatre. This area of expertise is defined within classical reception studies,[7] which signify the research approach focusing both on source (ancient) and target (modern) culture. Significantly, this kind of research, performing comparative and con-

---

7   There is an extensive theoretical and methodological background for reception studies in general. It was initiated by the anti-positivist ideas of Russian formalism, which focused, however, only on study of functionality of poetic language and internal structure of the work, and therefore interpretation was determined by *intentio operis*. This approach was continued by New Criticism (American formalism), which stressed disinterest in the author's intention. The essential change of perspective was introduced by Wolfgang Iser, whose reader-response theory underlined the significance of *intentio lectoris*. This theory was developed by Hans Robert Jauss, who formulated the Rezeptionstheorie, seeing as crucial the relationship between process of production and process of reception. The emphasised idea of reciprocal *intentio auctoris* and *lectoris* became developed by the Marxist approach in literary studies, which pointed out the importance of contexts of both processes. This approach was then improved by Hans-Georg Gadamer who indicated that the meaning of the work is shaped by historical determinants (Cf. Propp 1968; Jakobson 2000; Warren 1943; Iser 1972, 1978; Jauss 1970, 1977, 1982; Gadamer 2004). There are also some theoretical and methodological studies relevant for classical reception scholarship, the most important of them being: Martindale and Thomas 2006; Hardwick and Stray 2008; Hardwick and Harrison 2013.

textual analysis, zooms in on the double track relationship between the source work and the work adapting the source, and between cultural background of the source and target culture. Since in classical reception studies crucial significance belongs to context, the main explorations concentrate on these cultural phenomena, which evoke the analysed piece of art. It is worth accentuating that reception studies prioritise the target work and its cultural context over the source. This approach inevitably leads to revision of meanings, searching for contexts that were forgotten or went unrecognized, finding new meanings of source work noticeable only from the perspective of rewriting the work. Therefore, classical reception studies center upon mainly on refigurations, re-contextualisations, criticism, redefinitions – in general, on change. Then, the matter of these studies consists of artistic and intellectual processes involved in selection, imitation and adaptation of texts of ancient culture, in which there is a train of transtextual procedures. Moreover, the contexts of these creative processes are analysed along with exploring goals and functions of the process of reception. As its *conditio sine qua non*, the reconstruction of the system of values and its signs, consistent with *hic et nunc* of the reception process, needs to be performed. Considering the act of reception in terms of reworking it is bound to be seen as a procedure of intercultural and intertemporal translation set in a specific spatiotemporal context of *hic et nunc*.

As such, classical reception studies explore the reworkings of ancient sources, regarded as creative processes of reinterpretation being simultaneously transtextual processes of reception[8] which, from both reciprocal perspectives, express a specific "contesting" tribute to the source work, a homage sharing oedipal jealousy and adoration (Horton and McDougal 1998: 8). Therefore, reworking – seen as a "non derivative derivation" (Hutcheon and O'Flynn 2013: 9) – exposes its double nature of derivative and original product, as well as of an interpretative process of source work and a creative process of new work. Within this conception of reworking, researchers should restrain themselves from perceiving the rewritten work as secondary, especially – as it seems – when both source and target work employ myths. As it was explained above, the *work of myth* takes place in the space of symbolic imagination, which exploring universal phenomena of human life, impregnates collective imagination by *semper ubique mythos*. In the following processes of its re-occupation, the *work of myth* is repeated and translated into *hic et nunc* circumstances of the present. These *works on myth* have a double nature – derivative and original – when mythical index meets its incidental ap-

---

8   Cf. Hutcheon 2013.

pendices.[9] This Derridian supplement can be deeply embodied in mythical tissue of rewriting the work, and its exposure and analysis proves to be the main task of the researcher.

> Making a circle, or rather arranging centripetal spiral, the researcher is able to touch the crucial meaning, since s/he has a chance to reach the semantic essence of studied phenomenon. However, the experience of this "zero point" remains incomplete, if it will be limited to the textual level, it means, to signs analysed structurally or semantically, while ignoring the fields belonging to myth. (Sosień 2003: 12; translation M.B.)

Given the fact that the main carriers of myths in Antiquity were dramatic works, staged or written,[10] the second part of the volume explores dramatic poetry and stage productions in the context of aesthetical and conceptual, reciprocally employed, reception of myths. Two authors investigate the aesthetic issues in regard to reception of Greek tragedy in dramatic poetry. Olympia Tachopoulou analyses the dramatic nature of Giorgos Seferis' poetry with its transparent evocations to ancient tragedy and myths. Her essay presents different poems, tracing the notion of the tragic both in its form and content within the background of modernism and existentialism respectively. Tachopoulou paves the conceptual alley further in order to examine the recontextualisation procedure of myth employed to analyse the political realities of Seferis' times. The idea of the tragic, considered from the aesthetic and ethical perspectives, becomes the central issue in the essay by Tomasz Kaczmarek, who uses the case study of Yvan Goll's dramas to investigate the implicit traces of ancient legacy. This intriguing probe proves how ancient myths and ways of their expression can resonate with new forms of artistic manifestations. Within this approach, Kaczmarek tries to establish the receptive link between Attic tragedy and postdramatic theatre in its harbinger form of modernist avant-garde. Ancient myth expressed by the Greek notion of the tragic is then analysed as reworked by expressionistic and surrealistic means of dramatic poetry.

Reception of ancient myths in terms of their ability to diagnose and express the political and societal concerns of *hic et nunc* is the matter of study of the four subsequent essays. Two of them examine the involvement of ancient myths in indirect depicting of current politics in dramas. Anna Zaorska takes Heiner Müller's plays as case studies to show the procedure of confusing the communist censorship by using mythical masks. Interestingly, Müller constructed the highly innovative, postmodern form for his dramas and with this aesthetic act of resistance rewrote ancient mythical stories, employing heroic figures as masks for real

---

9 Cf. Wachowski 1993.
10 Cf. Buxton 2013.

political figures. Zaorska's essay analyses all these issues using as case studies *Philoctetes* and *The Horatian* plays in relation to political events in the communist GDR. Similar approach can be found in the article by Rossana Zetti, who considers the political involvement of Antigone's myth by exploring the tragic events of Civil War in Ireland. The mythical mask of resistance against the state is analysed here as reworked by two Irish playwrights, Tom Paulin (*The Riot Act*) and Brendan Kennelly (*New Version of Antigone*). Being clearly derivative and, at the same time, original, these two rewritings of the ancient myth recontextualise mythical figures and plots, while the essence of the tragic remains unchanged, in order to emphasise the perpetual nature of human behaviour. Zetti's study configurates the links between mythical masks and real events of Irish Civil War, examining the language and structure of the plays in question.

The next two essays are focused on the more global, societal issue of emigration and exile, and the ways in which artists explore it through the notion of ancient myths in their dramatic versions. Magdalena Hasiuk describes the artistic attitude of the Lebanese playwright Wajdi Mouawad, emphasizing the link between personal experience of the author, being an exile in Canada, and his dramatic work. The essay examines the play *Scorched* to expose the tragedy of women being imprisoned during the Civil War in Lebanon. The contemporary context of the plot is analysed in relation to the myth of Oedipus, since both the content of the play revealing litanies of crimes, and its form of investigation to find the parents, call Sophocles' version of the Oedipus' myth to mind. Nevertheless, what seems to be the most intriguing is the interpretative path that leads the author to the notion of the tragic in Mouawad's work influenced by the Sophoclean poetics and his artistic transformation of myths. The main topic studied here is human cruelty existing between citizens of the same nation, within the family of the same state. Ancient Greek myths are especially prone to uncover the experience of civil war, as a result of which the state order becomes destroyed and society has to face the time of cruel fratricide struggles to find and sacrifice a scapegoat, and try to forgive each other, as was thoroughly studied by René Girard (1979; 1986). The war experience of refugees, who are forced to leave their countries to save their lives, is another topic extensively explored by myths. Stephen Wilmer focuses in his essay on the most recent phenomenon of Middle Eastern and African refugee wave in Europe, which caused not only political turbulences, but mainly the crisis of values and human rights. On the basis of the ancient Greek notion of hospitality, which was a kind of moral duty connected with suppliant's rights, the author draws on Elfriede Jelinek's *Die Schutzbefohlenen* as an emblematic case of the *work on myth* to comment on the current events in Europe. Furthermore, next to the analysis of the dramatic works considering the above indicated issues, with special focus put on Marina Carr's *Hecuba*, Wilmer provides several examples of theatre productions of Jelinek's play that involved professional actors and refugees. This study exposes the *work of myth* concerning the most basic human rights. Significantly, when performed on the theatre stage, the play becomes art which through visible things enables one to intuitively feel and imagine that which is invisible (Suzuki 2012: 97). In this particular case, through visible bodies, faces, the heard voices of refugees and their tragedy embodied by the actors' play, spectators are able to imagine and, consequently, feel and understand the commonly invisible tragedy of the dispossessed people.

Bearing in mind that the process of reception, as outlined above, can also be connected with transcoding actions when the system of communicated signs is changed and source text of culture is translated into different fields of art, the remaining essays in the volume concentrate on modern theatre practices staging ancient tragedy to explore mythical *semper ubique* in contemporary *hic et nunc*. Małgorzata Budzowska looks at the issue of stage re-presentation in regard to the most unpresentable phenomenon – death. Ancient myths are deeply involved in considering the experience of death, since it is an uncanny occurrence in human life. However, showing death on stage in ancient theatre was restricted by aesthetic rules as defined by Aristotle and Horace. In relation to the ancient rule of *decorum*, the essay presents a comparison between ancient and contemporary aesthetics of staging death. Within this approach, the question of visualizing the symbolic mythical imagination is discussed on the basis of a number of case studies of theatre productions. And finally, Burç İdem Dinçel recapitulates the chief concerns of the volume by bringing into focus the theatre praxis of Theodoros Terzopoulos. By concentrating on the director's reworking of Aeschylus' *Prometheus Bound* for the transcultural Promethiade Project (2010), Dinçel aims to shed further light at once on the aesthetics that governs the production, and the dynamics that underwrites the project, both of which, in essence, provide fertile grounds to explore the mimetic aspects of *mythopoesis*.

The edited collection of essays aims at presenting various approaches to the issue of the *work of myth* within the *work on myth*. To study different transmutations of ancient myths in Antiquity and beyond, researchers should be encouraged to investigate the deep structures of myths which very often disclose their presence in works of art implicitly. No matter how significant archiving work is, it seems that classical reception research with respect to myths has to avoid a simple overview of figures, motifs and plots, a kind of registry of repeated topics; in other words, it has to escape from intertextual archiving.[11] The subtle nature of mythical redundancies, comparable with probabilistic nature of quantum physics (Durand 1986: 87), does not allow to unambiguously indicate the direction in which a myth follows. Nonetheless, it is possible to track the dynamics of its derivations and to try to extract its temporary meanings: "Redundancies, fluctuations, metamorphoses, or even temporary disappearance of particular forms belong to the same, continual, great process: process of creation of meanings." (Jasionowicz 2003: 27; translation M.B.). The process of creation of meanings is the creative gesture of the *work of myth* within the artistic process of creation of artwork, that is, in fact, in the *work on myth*. Considering human culture as "the production and the exchange of meanings – 'giving and taking of meaning' – between the members of a society or group" (Hall 1997: 2), intertextual renarrations of myth should be regarded as a process of exchanging meanings.

References:

Abramowska, Janina. 1992. „Serie tematyczne". In *Między tekstami. Intertekstualność jako problem poetyki historycznej*. Ed. by Jerzy Ziomek. Janusz Sławiński Włodzimierz Bolecki, Warszawa: PWN.

Blumenberg, Hans. 1985. *Work on Myth*. Trans. by Robert M. Wallace, Cambridge: MIT Press.

Buxton, Richard. 2013. *Myths and Tragedies in their Ancient Greek Contexts*. Oxford: Oxford University Press.

Durand, Gilbert. 1986. *Wyobraźnia symboliczna*. Trans. by Cezary Rowiński, Warszawa: PWN.

Gadamer, Hans G. 2004. *Truth and Method*. Trans. by Joel Weinsheimer and Donald G. Marshall, London: Continuum.

Goody, Jack. 2010. *Myth, Ritual, and the Oral*. Cambridge: Cambridge University Press.

Girard, René, 1979. *Violence and the Sacred*. Trans. by Patrick Gregory, Baltimore: The Johns Hopkins University Press.

Girard, René, 1986. *The Scapegoat*. Trans. by Yvonne Freccero. Baltimore: The Johns Hopkins University Press.

Hall, Stuart. 1997. Introduction. In: *Representation. Cultural Representations and Signifying Practices*. Ed. by Stuart Hall, London: Sage. 1–11.

---

11 Cf. Jasionowicz 2003: 23, Abramowska 1992: 60–61.

Hardwick, Lorna and Christopher Stray (eds.). 2008. *A Companion to Classical Receptions*. Maldon and Oxford: Blackwell.

—.and Stephen Harrison (eds.). 2013. *Classics in the Modern World. A Democratic Turn?* Oxford: Oxford University Press.

Horton, Andrew. McDougal, Stuart Y. (eds.). 1998. *Play it again, Sam. Retakes on remakes*. Berkeley: University of California Press.

Hutcheon, Linda and Siobhan O'Flynn. 2013. *A Theory of Adaptation*. London and New York: Routledge.

Iser, Wolfgang. 1972. 'The Reading Process: A Phenomenological Approach'. In *The Implied Reader: Patterns of Communication in Prose Fiction from Bunyan to Beckett*. Baltimore: Johns Hopkins University Press.

—.1978. *The Act of Reading: Theory of Aesthetic Response*. London and New York: Routledge.

Jakobson, Roman. 2000. "On Linguistic Aspects of Translation". In *The Translation Studies Reader*. Ed. by Lawrence Venuti, London and New York: Routledge. 113–118.

Jasionowicz, Stanisław. 2003. „Intertekstualność w świetle badań nad wyobraźnią twórczą". In *Intertekstualność i wyobraźniowość*. Ed. by Barbara Sosień, Kraków: Universitas.

Jauss, Hans R. 1970. *Literaturgeschichte als Provokation*. Frankfurt: Suhrkamp.

—.1977. *Ästhetische Erfahrung und literarische Hermeneutik*. Munich: Fink.

—.1982. *Towards an Aesthetic of Reception*. Brighton: Harvester.

Klemczak, Stefan. 2005. „Szaleństwa prób definiowania mitu". *Studia Religiologica. Zeszyty Naukowe Uniwersytetu Jagiellońskiego* MCCLXXXIII. 38: 45–63.

Laprée, Raymond and Christian R. Bellehumeur. 2013. *L'imaginaire durandien. Enracinements et envols en terre d'Amérique*. Québec: Presses de l'Université Laval.

Martindale, Charles and Richard F. Thomas (eds.). 2006. *Classics and the Uses of Reception*. Maldon and Oxford: Blackwell.

Nussbaum, Martha. 2010. *Not for Profit: Why Democracy Needs the Humanities*. Princeton and Oxford: Princeton University Press.

Propp, Władimir. 1968. *Morphology of the Folktale*. Trans. by Laurence Scott, Austion: University of Texas Press.

Sosień, Barbara. 2003. „Hipoteksty, teksty, mity, czyli o współistnieniu metod". In *Intertekstualność i wyobraźniowość*. Red. Barbara Sosień, Kraków: Universitas.

Suzuki, Tadashi. 2012. *Czym jest teatr?* Trans. by Anna Sambierska. Wrocław: The Grotowski Institute.

Wachowski, Jacek. 1993. *Dramat-mit-tradycja. O transtekstualności w polskiej dramaturgii współczesnej.* Poznań: Acarus.

Warren, Robert P. 1943. "Pure and Impure Poetry". *The Kenyon Review* vol 5. no. 2: 228–254.

Part I
Work on Myth within Antiquity

Jadwiga Czerwińska*

Myth in Greek Drama of Classical Greece in the Light of Scholia[1]

Abstract: Relationships between myth and tragedy are particularly absorbing for researchers, considering the fact that dramatic plots were commonly based on mythical stories. Ancient playwrights employed traditional myths, however, they transformed them in order to develop their own creative intentions; in other words, they adapted myths to the logic of tragic drama. This procedure was extensively commented upon by ancient scholiasts. Scholia, considered as scientific literature, provide a significant research material to study the employment of myths by playwrights. In this article, the main analysis concerns two scholia (scholion from *Scholia vetera ad Sophoclis Oedipum Tyrannum*, line 8, and scholion from *Scholia vetera ad Sophoclis Ajacem*, line 1a), which epitomise the nature of commentaries regarding the relationships between myth and drama. These two commentaries deliver a lot of interesting remarks about myths, their usage by the poet, and the significance of incipits of tragedy in exposition of dramatic plots, which can be confirmed also in the case of other ancient playwrights. As such, scholia constitute a valuable source of knowledge about the ancient art of playwriting.

Keywords: Greek tragedy, scholia, myth

Greek dramas are commonly known mainly from preserved texts, which constitute the predominant material for their multifaceted interpretation, as well as research in dramatic arts, and the phenomenon of myth and its application by individual poets, which is of particular interest to this study. Nevertheless, *scholia* (Greek: σχόλιον – "comment", Latin: *scholion*) can also be a plentiful source of analysis of such phenomena.

Scholia were created "above all around the texts written by the most prominent authors, especially poets. They are usually the judgements of commentary wisdom represented by various scholars in different historical periods: Alexandrian, Byzantine, Carolingian or Renaissance" (Małunowiczówna 1960: 210). Structurally, scholia have a predefined construction, as emphasised by Małunowiczówna, who states that "they usually consist of a lemma, i.e. a

---

* University of Lodz, Poland.
1 This article is part of the research project *Ancient theatre and drama in the works of scholiasts*, funded by the National Science Centre (decision No. DEC-2012/07/B/HS2/01475).

word (a set of words or a sentence) derived from the original text and its explanations (shorter or longer). It sometimes happens that the lemmas themselves were successively changed and 'corrected' by copyists" (*ibid.*), which means that mistakes occasionally appear in their writing. Thus, while lemmas may contain some inaccuracies, it is significantly more "reliable to rely on the text of the commentary itself, since it is much less exposed to modifications" (*ibid.*). Therefore, "we will take it as a rule that the commentator had, in front of him, the text which his explanations suggest, but not necessarily the text which is located in the lemma" (*ibid.* 211).

Scholia were developed as early as in Antiquity, but also in later centuries, and above all in the Middle Ages. These critical metatexts were inserted between the lines (*scholia interlinearia*) and on the margins (*scholia marginalia*) of classical dramas, and then written down and published as separate collections of scholia. Due to the information they contain, it is difficult to overestimate their literary and historical value. They comprise a wide spectrum of linguistic, metrical, historical, geographical and mythological issues, whose purpose is to provide explanation to the lines commented on within dramas and the related circumstances.

The significance of the information conveyed by scholia is confirmed in the brilliant dissertation *Scholia Medicea in Aeschyli Persas* by Katarzyna Chiżyńska, who emphasises in her work the meaning of ancient commentaries for research on ancient texts, stating that:

> Despite the thematic variety of scholia, two elements can be distinguished which determine the information presented by the scholiast. The first one is the content of the work commented on [...]. The second element is the literary form [...], an example of which is [...] *scholia* related to the poetics of tragedy and the language of drama.
> The collection of Medicean commentaries contains remarks which facilitate the reading of tragedy, and it also provides useful information for researchers of various branches of science, who may be less interested in the literary work itself. These commentaries are a wealthy source of information, valuable to philologists researching e.g. the history and theory of literature (*cf. sch.* 65, 181) or linguistics (*cf. sch.* 420). Numerous remarks in the scholia are also of great value to the representatives of auxiliary sciences of classical studies such as historians (*cf. sch.* 769), archaeologists (*cf. sch.* 666), religion experts (*cf. sch.* 628) as well as ethnologists and anthropologists (*cf. sch.* 39). (Chiżyńska 2012: 256)

Out of the immensely rich collection of commentaries to Greek dramas drawn up by scholiasts, I would like to present selected examples which are related to some aspects of myths used by Greek tragic poets.

First, let us have a look at the *scholia vetera* to *Oedipus Tyrannus* by Sophocles. The scholiast comments on line 8 (Sophocles 1912) which takes the following wording: ὁ πᾶσι κλεινὸς Οδίπους καλούμενος. In literal translation this means: "I, Oedipus, who enjoys fame among all", whereas in the literary translation it becomes: "I, Oedipus renowned by all" (Jebb 1887). Having quoted the lemma "I, renowned by all", the scholar explains: "renowned by all (because of virtues) or since people talk about him all the time". The commentary that follows reads: "It is obvious that the name itself of the person enouncing the prologue explains a lot, and at the same time the audience wishes to learn about (the presented version of) Oedipus's fate". Having stated this, the scholiast adds: "Not immediately does (scilicet Sophocles) lead us to the source of knowledge, but he reveals [it] gradually and appropriately, at the right moments". In this rather lapidary comment by the scholiast we find three extremely interesting observations: the first relates to the myth itself; the second regards the manner in which it was used by the poet; the third concerns the gradual introduction of the audience into the complexities of the plot.

Let us ponder over the first issue, which the scholiast signalled by writing: "the name of the person announcing the prologue explains a lot itself". A perfect – and yet quite ironic – comment to this is the statement by Antiphanes, a comedy poet, who in a visibly sarcastic manner presents the difference between tragedy and comedy, stating that:

μακάριόν ἐστιν ἡ τραγῳδία	Now Tragedy's a lucky sort of art.
ποίημα κατὰ πάντ', εἴ γε πρῶτον οἱ λόγοι	First the house knows the plot before you start;
ὑπὸ τῶν θεατῶν εἰσιν ἐγνωρισμένοι,	You've only to remind it. 'Oedipus'
πρὶν καί τιν' εἰπεῖν. ὥσθ' ὑπομνῆσαι μόνον	You say, and all's out-father Laïus,
δεῖ τὸν ποιητήν. Οἰδίπουν γὰρ ἂν μόνον	Mother Jocasta, daughters these, sons those,
φῶ, τἄλλα πάντ' ἴσασιν. ὁ πατὴρ Λάιος,	His sin, his coming punishment. Or suppose
μήτηρ Ἰοκάστη, θυγατέρες, παῖδες τίνες,	You say 'Alcmaeon'; in saying that, you've said
τί πείσεθ' οὗτος, τί πεποίηκεν. ἂν πάλιν	All his sons too, how he's gone off his head
εἴπῃ τις Ἀλκμέωνα, καὶ τὰ παιδία	And killed his mother, and how Adrastus next
πάντ' εὐθὺς εἴρηχ', ὅτι μανεὶς ἀπέκτονεν	Will enter, exit, and re-enter, vexed.
τὴν μητέρ', ἀγανακτῶν δ' Ἄδραστος εὐθέως	Then, when a playwright's tired of his play
ἥξει πάλιν τ' ἄπεισι.....	And simply can't find any more to say,
ἔπειθ' ὅταν μηδ' ν δύνωντ' εἰπεῖν ἔτι,	As easy as winking up goes the trapeze,
κομιδῇ δ' ἀπειρήκωσιν ἐν τοῖς δράμασιν,	And everyone's content with what he sees.
αἴρουσιν ὥσπερ δάκτυλον τὴν μηχανήν	We Comic writers have more claimant needs;
καὶ τοῖς θεωμένοισιν ἀποχρώντως ἔχει.	There's all to invent, new names, new words, new deeds,
ἡμῖν δὲ ταῦτ' οὐκ ἔστιν, ἀλλὰ πάντα δεῖ	Prologue, presuppositions, action, ending.
εὑρεῖν, ὀνόματα καινά, τὰ διῳκημένα	While Peleus now, or Teucer if he missed
πρότερον, τὰ νῦν παρόντα, τὴν καταστροφήν,	One of these details wouldn't be offending,
τὴν εἰσβολήν. ἂν ἕν τι τούτων παραλίπῃ	If Chremes, say, or Pheidon does he's hissed.
Χρέμης τις ἢ Φείδων τις, ἐκσυρίττεται.	
Πηλεῖ δὲ ταῦτ' ἔξεστι καὶ Τεύκρῳ ποιεῖν.	

In the quoted fragment (fr. 191) of his comedy entitled *Poiesis* (Poetry),[2] Antiphanes – with a clear inclination – ridicules the secondariness of tragedy to comedy. In his opinion, tragic poets only use already exiting myths, whereas comedy poets, as he boastfully emphasises, put a substantial poetic effort and invention into creating their own, brand new literary work. Undoubtedly, this caricaturally sketched picture, just like any caricature, contains a grain of truth. Here, Antiphanes manages to express a principally characteristic feature of both tragedy and comedy: tragedy, while referring to a myth, spoke in a language which the audience of that time was familiar with, whereas comedy created a new stage reality. However, Antiphanes' statement – just as any statement that is a simplification of a multifaceted and complex issue – contains a certain inaccuracy related to the creativity of comic and tragic authors: not everything in comedy is exclusively the poet's invention, in much the same way as not everything in tragedy is merely the recreation of the existing myth. Even ancient Greek comedy willingly finds inspiration in mythological threads,[3] as well as motifs and characters that appeared in tragedies, whereas tragedy, especially the Euripidean, liked to invent "prologue, presuppositions, action, ending" (τὰ διῳκημένα πρότερον, τὰ νῦν παρόντα, τὴν καταστροφήν, τὴν εσβολήν), which means that, to a certain extent, it matched the description of comedy, as stipulated by Antiphanes (Czerwińska 2004: 19–20).

---

2 English translation of the Antiphanes' fragment is based on the edition: Edmonds 1959.
3 According to Srebrny, the mythological parody in Attic comedy originates from Doric farce, although it is also possible that those kinds of motifs had appeared in indigenous pre-Attic comedy. "The titles and fragments of the lost works prove that among the works by ancient Attic comedy writers there were some that constituted a parody of a myth; certainly, this was not, however, a general trend: it would be more appropriate to assume that it was typical of parodic and mythological motifs to be intertwined in threads whose axis was the then current satire – political, related to contemporaneous currents of thought, literary or artistic. Mythological parody introduced to the Attic stage the cosmic characters of gods and heroes, such as Hermes in *Peace*, Iris, Prometheus, Poseidon, Heracles and the 'barbaric god' of the Triballians in *The Birds*" (Srebrny 1955: 16). Analysis of the role of myth in Aristophanes's comedy is performed by Turasiewicz (1997: 33–52), who discusses, among other things, the relationship between myth and cult, and its reflection in comedy, e.g. in *The Acharnians*, where we can find a description of a phallic cult procession (Turasiewicz 1997: 33), as well as the ideas of the myth as a compositional dominant, the myth in the decorative role, and the transformation and syncretism of myths. He also focuses on the issue of new mythology and the creation of myths (Turasiewicz 1997: 42 ff.) and new deities (Turasiewicz 1997: 49 ff.).

Both statements – made by the scholiast and Antiphanes – bring a significant piece of information on the subject of myth, namely that it constituted the fabric of the plot in tragedy. This was not always so, since tragic poets – although extremely rarely – happened to use historical events too.[4] Nevertheless, the principle remained unchanged: the myth was the fabric of tragedy (Nestle 1901: 6 ff.), and by its means the idea of tragic drama was created.

And why was it so? First of all, this stood in accordance with the literary tradition dating back to the times of Homer, whose works, "in Greece, gained the respectable reputation of patterns to be followed, not only in terms of aesthetics, but also as complete explanations of the world of humans and gods" (Szlezák 1997: 46). Secondly, as noticed by Lengauer, "myths tell us a lot about people and their standing in the world, about the human condition, nature and fate" (Lengauer 1994: 19), which means they posses both a theological and anthropological value (Lengauer 1994: 20). At the same time, one must not forget that in the ancient classical culture there developed a tendency to "transfer the ideological content of the myth into temporary reality" (Jaeger 2001: 328). Myth refers to the issues of a historical, socio-political and religious nature, whereas poetry that utilises it becomes a direct translator and guide in life (Jaeger 2001: 20). Therefore, "even in the post-Homeric period, the myth retains its meaning as an inexhaustible source of poetic creation" (*ibid.*).

Here, two issues appear: the first one is related to myth in the poetic message of tragic poets, and the second one is connected with the reception of the myth by the audience. Let us begin with the first issue by posing the following question: did myth, as a traditional fabric of tragedy, not limit the poets in their creative invention and expression? Knowing Greek tragedy, we can wholeheartedly state that it did not. As it is rightly claimed by Kitto:

---

4   There were some exceptions to the principle of using myth to construct the plot layer of tragedy in Greek theatre. These are, for instance, the tragedies by Phrynichus – *The Capture of Miletus* and *The Phoenissae* (*Phoenician Women*), and *The Persians* by Aeschylus. The fact that the tragedies presented historical events does not mean, however, that the poets strived to create a "documentary theatre". On the contrary, they mythologised history by using it in the same manner as mythological contents, i.e. through individual events in the *hic et nunc* layer (here and now) they attempted to reach the universal dimension of *semper ubique* (always and everywhere). Kitto makes a very apt observation on this issue, when referring to Aeschylus he writes that "he operated historical content/material with the same ease with which dramatists use myth […], in order to eradicate everything that does not stand in accordance with dramaturgic intent and to emphasise everything that is important" (1997: 42).

> Limitation [...] does not engender poorness, but increases intensity. This certain 'limitation' of tragic poets 1) stimulated their imagination in order to present a well-known myth and its characters in an innovative fashion; 2) motivated them to search for a new sense and meaning of the staged play and to use it to create a new tragic idea; 3) became a challenge that their creativity had to face while reinterpreting myths and, at the same time, inspired them to enter into discussion with the hitherto prevailing tradition. (1997: 35)

And thus, as Barbara Sosień puts it: "myth in its absolutely original shape does not exist, since it is the entirety of its various versions, mutations and subsequent 'updates'" (2003: 16–17). It is then quite justifiable to state that all creative processes that myths underwent in the Greek literary tradition are processes that could be described with the term *in statu nascendi* (in the nascent state). This is predominantly connected with the fact that there were no canonical versions of myths; instead, there were only those which had been conveyed by the previous literary tradition. Therefore, Greek tragic poets could freely work on the myths they used in their dramas, with the purpose of making them suit their creative intent. This also refers to the whole network of meanings that were assigned to the versions of myths they created and which constituted the plot layer of their dramas.

Let us focus now on the second signalled issue: the reception of the myth by the audience. Did the audience not find it dull to watch plays based on recurring myths? As a side note, it is worth mentioning that, for instance, the myth of the House of Atreus or the myth of Labdacus appeared on numerous occasions in the works of all three greatest tragic poets. The audience's reaction is best illustrated with an anecdote in which one of the spectators, while waiting for the performance to begin, asks another spectator if the poet could tell them anything new about Orestes. This humorous remark may show the extent to which the new interpretation of a myth by these poets was looked forward to. This is also confirmed by the aforementioned remark written by the scholiast in reference to line 8 of *Oedipus Tyrannus*. As can be seen from the comment, having heard the name Oedipus in the prologue, a spectator wishes to learn about the version of his fate presented in this particular play. Therefore, it can be stated that returning to the same mythological motifs and characters captured the audience's attention and kept them interested, as well as that it rendered the audience's sensitivity to any subtleties within the text and its staging, since they contained specific ideas or thoughts that the poet wished to convey; thus, the audience interpreted the meaning of the drama, focusing on all the allusions, hints and signs made by the author.

Undoubtedly, this proves how watchful the audiences of ancient plays were. The analysis of the texts of tragedies confirms that "the listener remembers the text they heard once quite easily and for long. The spoken word lingers in the memory of the audience", as noticed by Axer (1991: 13), who also adds that "it is not about the listener remembering what was said, but [...] how it was formulated" (1991: 13). This means that – with this type of reception of theatrical plays – the audience was capable of registering any proposed variants of myths that were staged. Spectators perfectly perceived all mythological innovations introduced by poets and interpreted the meaning they carried.

In this regard, Sosień's remark is quite apt: "a myth always opens to another myth, facilitating the interpretation of its new variation" (2003: 17). Therefore, literature is replete with "countless myths and their variations [...] as a configuration of structures that submit to logical analysis and classification [...], as constellations of mythems and mythologems, i.e. fundamental ontological and epistemological questions which are answered satisfactorily neither by religious systems nor by logical ones" (Sosień 2003: 17). And thus, "myth is not merely a simplistic repetition" (Jasionowicz 2003: 26).[5] And it had never been so in Greek theatre and the whole of Greek culture.

The divagations on the subject of myth made so far in this article, which started from the scholiast's comments, prove that these ancient commentaries offer a much broader scope and meaning, despite referring to individual literary works. In a synthetic manner, they describe certain phenomena and principles of dramaturgical art which are used universally, and not only in reference to a specific work commented on by the scholiast. On the contrary, the information contained in scholia illustrates the principles of the poetics of tragedy, which were developed and applied by tragic poets of the time. For this reason, it constitutes such a fascinating and educative reading material.

Working with the texts of Greek dramas, we naturally realise that the aforementioned formal principles inevitably underwent modifications. It is then quite rightly noted by Kitto, that "the form of a play is only determined by its main idea" (1997: 8), and that "we can only hope to explain the form and style of individual plays or collections of plays if, by any means, we succeed in revealing the concept of tragedy which is incorporated in them" (ibid.). Therefore, it is the concept of tragedy that determines the construction of a play and all its remaining constituents, including the manner in which the *dramatis personae* are created, the fashion in which the plot is carried out, and the type and content of the incipits.

As far as the incipits are concerned, *scholion* 1a within *Scholia vetera in Sophoclis Ajacem* offers a very interesting testimony. While explaining the situation at

---

5 Cf. Durand 1996: 87.

the very beginning of the play, the scholiast quotes the following expression from the first line ὦ παῖ Λαρτίου as the lemma, indicating the presence of Odysseus on stage, to whom these words are addressed by the goddess Athena delivering the prologue. From the text of the *scholion* that follows this fragment we learn that Odysseus is alarmed, since he is afraid – as claimed by the scholiast – that "he may be harmed by the enemy", i.e. by Ajax, the protagonist of the play. The scholiast also suggests that "the actor [who plays Odysseus] should look around as if he were afraid that he may be spotted". This means that the commentator gives hints that might be useful to the actor, thus creating a type of stage direction for the text of the tragedy.

Later, the *scholion* contains an information which can be recognized as crucial, since it includes a significant remark on the type of the incipit. The commentator states that "all the most vital assumptions of the play (πάντα δὲ τὰ τῆς ὑποθέσεως συνεκτικὰ) are divulged at the beginning". Then, the scholiast precisely stipulates what he has in mind by writing "to whom the speech is addressed, what the *skene* depicts, and what actions Odysseus takes". In order to emphasise the gravity of his words, in the final part of the comment the scholiast repeats his earlier thought, practically opting for the same wording: "The most vital constituents of the play (τὰ τῆς ὑποθέσεως συνεκτικὰ) must already be introduced at its very beginning".

Obviously, the principle formulated by the scholiast does not refer exclusively to the tragedy that he is commenting on. It is both applied and finds its confirmation in all the preserved dramas of the most prominent Greek tragic poets. At the beginnings of their plays, i.e. in the prologues,[6] they provide the audience with information that is important for the development of the initial exposition of the work. Not only do the incipits[7] they create introduce the plot performed on stage,

---

6 According to the theory of poetics by Aristotle (Aristotle 1966), the prologue is a compositional or quantitative constituent of tragedy (*Poet.* 1452b 15–16), which he defines in the following manner: "A prologue is the whole of that part of a tragedy which precedes the entrance of the chorus" (*Poet.* 1452b 19). The character of a prologue and its function in the structure of drama are discussed by George Maximilian Anthony Grube in the chapter entitled *Prologues and Epilogues* (1961: 63–79).

7 The literature on the subject of incipits in literary works is very rich and profound, and includes numerous publications in the field of literary studies. Their main focus is on the organisation of time and space. Among the most prominent publications, it is worth to mention the following works: Sławińska (1988), Ubersfeld (2002), Próchnicki (2003: 158–183), Bartoszyński (1987: 158–183), Buczyńska-Garewicz (2003), Głowiński (1977), Lewicki (1974: 93–103), Kurek (2003), Petach (1945). The issue of stage space is discussed by Wiles (2012).

but they also provide the audience with a detailed presentation of the settings, time and, as far as it is possible, the *dramatis personae*.

Such an initial exposition of the play is particularly important in the dramatic plays of Euripides and is connected with the fact that he was keen on implementing in his works bold mythological innovations. When altering the traditional versions of myths, he obviously had to signal the changes to the audience. And yet, that is not all, as the tragic poet uses incipits not only to present his *dramatis personae* and their modified genealogies (*Hecuba*). Occasionally, it is of great importance to him to define more precisely the setting of the play and, in particular, the character of the setting where the action is about to take place.

The example of the above is perfectly illustrated by *Iphigenia in Tauris*, whose prologue contains information on the detailed location of the stage building and the description of its macabre appearance. Behind the *orchestra* the audience can see the façade of the great temple of Artemis of the Taurians whose finial is "red with blood" (l. 73), and "decorated" with horrible trophies: skulls and remains of humans sacrificed to the goddess (l. 74). In front of the temple there is an altar "that drips with the slaughter of Hellenes" (l. 72). In his attempt to reconstruct the scenography of the play, Vincenzo Di Benedetto (1997: 139) makes an assumption that the architectural elements mentioned in the text may really have been placed on the facade, whereas the victims' heads were in all probability represented by rows of hanging masks.

The information included in the initial exposition of the discussed play, and the drastic and detailed description of the space where the events take place in particular, are justified by the direction in which the plot of *Iphigenia in Tauris* is developed. Thus, the conclusion can be drawn that it was not a coincidence that Euripides and other tragic poets paid such attention to the incipits to their dramas, which is also distinctly emphasised by the scholiast. Their importance is also recognized by today's theatre researchers. Anne Ubersfeld states that "if there is anything significant that we owe to the structural analysis, it is, for sure, the meaning it attributes to the beginning, the *incipit*, from the very first signs around which the later ones are organised. The beginning of each theatrical text is full of hints on the time" (2002: 157), but also on the space and the *dramatis personae* in the play.

The analysed scholia contains one more remark which may turn out to be interesting in the context of the discussed issues. In the *scholion* to line 8 of *Oedipus Tyrannus* we read: "Not immediately does (scilicet Sophocles) lead us to the source of knowledge, but *he reveals [it] gradually and appropriately, at the right moments*" (emphasis added). The scholiast's comment, referring to Sophocles' *Oedipus the King*, is fully justified by the tragic idea and the resulting structure of the tragedy, where individual constituents of the plot were successively revealed in the course of the action, i.e. there was a sequence of events that led to the tragic finale.

In the case of *Hecuba*[8] by Euripides, however, the circumstances are different to what is described by the scholiast. In its prologue, where the first one to speak is the Ghost of Polydorus, followed by the female protagonist, the poet gives a detailed summary of the events that are about to happen. In the first part of the prologue, they are announced by the Ghost of the late Polydorus whose speech contains information on earlier events (l. 1–30), i.e. the ones that had occurred before the beginning of the play. Next, he mentions current issues (l. 30–34) and finally – which, for us, is most interesting and surprising at the same time – he also discusses the events to come (l. 35–44). They will later be confirmed by Hecuba's prophetic dream in which her deceased son, Polydorus, reveals her the as-yet-unknown future. "By using anticipation at the very beginning of the play, Euripides deprives the audience of the thrill and emotion related to sudden twists in the plot. At the same time, however, he forces spectators to watch the play with distance, which is necessary to appropriately read the sense and meaning of the whole drama" (Czerwińska 2013: 69),[9] where the poet's attention is focused upon the poetic description of the θυμός phenomenon as a constituent immanently incorporated into ἀνθρώπεια φύσις. This, in turn, results in him leading the audience to the discovery of the tragic idea of the drama through the analysis of θυμός and the mechanisms that govern it.

The above presented divagations, which were based only on two *scholia* by ancient commentators, and just a few examples of tragedies, prove what rich content they constitute. Being nothing more than just an outline of the subject matter, the present article shows that comments preserved in scholia are as important for the comprehension of Greek tragedies as the texts of the dramas themselves. Scholiasts performed a deep and profound analysis of each line in plays, and their comments, despite being made in the margins, constitute an invaluable source of information for scholars and researchers, not only on individual works by Greek tragic poets, but also on the performing art, including language, staging and the poetics of drama.

---

8   Regarding this issue cf. Czerwińska 2013: 45–190.
9   Cf. Kitto 1997: 262, 203.

Language: Scholiasts noticed peculiar expressions and phrases, explaining them as clear as possible; they jotted down their observations on the specific character of language used by individual authors, as well as the meter they used and the neologisms and metaphors the authors developed.

Staging: Scholiasts did not focus exclusively on the text of the drama itself. On the contrary, while commenting on it, they strived, as accurately and precisely as possible, to sketch the stage conditions, the actors' movements and gestures, appropriate behaviour matching the words they uttered, the relationships between various characters and their accurate representation on stage.

Principles of poetics of drama: When making all those observations, scholiasts noticed and noted down some inaccuracies related to the poetics of drama, and at the same time they attempted to develop formal principles thereof.

Thus, thanks to scholiasts we have access to an extremely valuable, or even priceless material that helps us better understand texts of tragedies, their staging and dramaturgical techniques.

Translated by Konrad Brzozowski

References:

Aristotle. 1966. *Aristotle's Ars Poetica*. Ed. by Rudolf Kassel. Oxford: Clarendon Press.

Axer, Jerzy. 1991. *Filolog w teatrze*. Warszawa: PWN.

Bartoszyński, Kazimierz. 1987. „Problem konstrukcji czasu w utworach epickich". In *Problemy teorii literatury*. Ed. by Henryk Markiewicz, Wrocław. 158–183.

Buczyńska-Garewicz, Hanna. 2003. *Metafizyczne rozważania o czasie*. Kraków: Universitas.

Chiżyńska, Katarzyna. 2012. *Scholia in Aeschyli Persa – opracowanie, przekład i komentarz*. PhD diss. Łódź.

Czerwińska, Jadwiga. 2004. „Fantastyka i baśniowość w *Alkestis* Eurypidesa". In *Thaleia. Humor w antyku*. Ed. by Gościwit Malinowski. „Classica Wratislaviensia" XXIV: 18–33.

Czerwińska, Jadwiga. 2011. „Co nam zostało z teatru antycznego?" In: *Dylematy dramatu i teatru u progu XXI wieku*. Lublin: Wydawnictwo Katolicki Uniwersytet Lubelski. 179–212.

Czerwińska, Jadwiga. 2013. *Innowacje mitologiczne i dramaturgiczne Eurypidesa*. Łódź: WUŁ.

Di Benedetto, Vincenzo and Enrico Medda. 1997. *La tragedia sulla scena. La tragedia greca in quanto spettacolo teatrale*. Torino: Einaudi.

Durand, Gilbert. 1996. „Perennité, dérivations et usure du mythe". In *Champs de l'Imaginaire*, textes réunis par D. Chauvin. Grenoble: ELLUG. 81–107.

Edmonds, John M. 1959. *The Fragments of "Attic Comedy" After Meineke, Bergk, and Kock: Augm., Newly Ed. with Their Contexts, Annot., and Completely Translated Into English Verse*. Leiden: Brill. Vol. II.

Głowiński, Michał. 1977. *Porządek, chaos, znaczenie*. Warszawa: PIW.

Grube, George M. A. 1961. *The drama of Euripides*. London: Methuen.

Jaeger, Werner. 2001. *Paideia*. Trans. by Marian Plezia, Henryk Bednarek. Warszawa: Fundacja Aletheia.

Jasionowicz, Stanisław. 2003. „Intertekstualność w świetle badań nad wyobraźnią twórczą". In *Intertekstualność i wyobraźniowość*. Ed. by Barbara Sosień. Kraków: Universitas. 21–33.

Jebb, Richard (ed.). 1887. Sophocles. *The Oedipus Tyrannus of Sophocles*. Ed. by Sir Richard Jebb. Cambridge: Cambridge University Press.

Kitto, Humphrey D.F. 1997. *Tragedia grecka. Studium literackie*. Trans. by Janusz Margański. Bydgoszcz: Homini.

Kurek, Marcin. 2003. *Powieść totalna*. Wrocław: Wydawnictwo Uniwersytetu Wrocławskiego.

Lengauer, Włodzimierz. 1994. *Religijność starożytnych Greków*. Warszawa: PWN.

Lewicki, Zbigniew. 1974. „Problem czasu w powieści Faulknera". *Litteraria* VI 93–103.

Małunowiczówna, Leokadia. 1960. *Wstęp do filologii klasycznej wraz z metodologią pracy umysłowej i naukowej*. Lublin: Towarzystwo Naukowe KUL.

Nestle, Wilhelm. 1901. *Euripides der Dichter der griechischen Aufklärung*. Stuttgart: Kohlhammer.

Petsch, Robert. 1945. *Wessen und Formen des Dramas*. Halle: M. Niemeyer.

Próchnicki, Włodzimierz. 2003. „Czas, przestrzeń, literatura: ustalenia i uściślenia". In *Problemy teorii dramatu i teatru*, t. I: *Dramat*. Ed. by Janusz Degler. Wrocław: Wydawnictwo Uniwersytetu Wrocławskiego. 158–183.

Sławińska, Irena. 1988. *Odczytywanie dramatu*, Warszawa: PWN.

Sophocles. 1912. Vol 1: *Oedipus the king. Oedipus at Colonus. Antigone*. Trans. by F. Storr. The Loeb classical library. London, New York: William Heinemann Ltd.; The Macmillan Company.

Sosień, Barbara. 2003. „Hipoteksty, teksty, mity". In *Intertekstualność i wyobraźniowość*. Ed. by Barbara Sosień. Kraków: Universitas. 9–34.

Srebrny, Stefan. 1955. *Wstęp*. In Arystofanes, *Wybór komedii*. Trans. by Stefan Srebrny, Warszawa: Instytut Wydawniczy.

Szlezák, Thomas A. 1997. *Czytanie Platona*. Trans. by Piotr Domański, Warszawa: Wydawnictwo Instytutu Filozofii i Socjologii Polskiej Akademii Nauk.

Turasiewicz, Romuald. 1997. *Funkcja mitu w komedii Arystofanesa*. „Prace Komisji Filologii Klasycznej PAU" 25: 33–52.

Ubersfeld, Anne. 2002. *Czytanie teatru I*. Trans. by Joanna Żurowska. Warszawa: PWN.

Wiles, David. 2012. *Krótka historia przestrzeni teatralnych*. Trans. by Łukasz Zaremba, Warszawa: PWN.

Katarzyna Chiżyńska*

Greek Myths in the *Hypotheseis* of Tragedy of the Classical Period[1]

Abstract: The article focuses on the ancient Greek *hypotheseis*, i.e. summaries of ancient dramas, written by ancient and medieval scholars and researchers. The first part of the article presents the nature of *hypotheseis* as a meta-textual characteristic of the ancient drama. The analysis scrutinises the form, structure and substantive content of summaries. The differences between *hypotheseis* and various dramatic genres are also discussed. The second part of the article brings examples of selected summaries of ancient Greek tragedies in which the themes from the most popular myths were used. This rendered it possible to analyse the similarities and differences between individual *hypotheseis* related to the same mythical story, e.g. the myth on the House of Atreus. In the course of the analysis, it was possible to demonstrate what constituents of the plot and action individual authors of summaries considered most significant, what traits of mythical heroes they perceived as worth mentioning, and what was their personal attitude towards any given poet. The analysis of the constituents exposed by the authors of *hypotheseis* can also comprise an attempt to interpret the story presented by the poet.

Keywords: ancient Greek tragedy, ancient Greek theatre, ancient Greek myths, *hypothesis*

Part I.

The Greek word *hypothesis*, in its almost unaltered form, entered most of Indo-European languages (cf. English: *hypothesis*, German: *Hypothese*, Czech: *hypotéza*, French: *hypothèse*, Spanish: *hipótesis*). The majority of modern languages have taken only one meaning of the Greek term, namely "assumption", "supposition", "intent" or "intention", ignoring the second range of meaning: "subject", "topic", "content", "plot" and eventually "theatrical play".

Moreover, in the ancient times the word *hypothesis* (Latin: *argumentum*) meant a specific meta-textual literary form, the purpose of which was to summarise, and sometimes even discuss, any given literary work. Although all *hypotheseis* were written for a similar purpose, they differ in form and length, as they contain vari-

---

* University of Lodz, Poland.
1 This article is part of the research project *Ancient Theatre and Drama in the Works of Scholiasts*, funded by the National Science Centre (decision no. DEC-2012/07/B/HS2/01475).

ous types of information. These differences stem from the fact that *hypotheseis* were created over a long time, their authors used miscellaneous styles, and discussed various types of texts. The best-known preserved Greek summaries refer to the works of ancient dramatists and individual books within Homer's epic poems.

The *hypotheseis* of classical Greek tragedies are some of the most interesting extant drama meta-texts. They provide modern researchers with a great amount of information, not only on the plots of the discussed works and mythical stories, but also on literary criticism of the period, theatrical practice, and the ancient poets themselves.[2] Another interesting aspect is that a single play can have several *hypotheseis* written in different cultural periods by different researchers, which translates into a variety of summaries.

Summaries began to be written in the Antiquity (the majority were produced in the Hellenistic period). Later, they were drafted by the Byzantine scholars, who often remained anonymous. The oldest author of summaries known by name was Aristotle's student, Dicaearchus of Messana (c. 350 – c. 285 BC), who is credited with writing a whole collection of summaries entitled Ὑποθέσεις τῶν Εὐριπί δου καὶ Σοφοκλέους μύθων (*Summaries of the Plots of Euripides and Sophocles*). When compared to other *hypotheseis*, however, Dicaearchus' works differ in their form, since they resemble modern summaries for school pupils, as they were, in all likelihood, drafted to eliminate the necessity of reading the dramas themselves.

To describe such collections of summaries, which were independent of the main texts of tragedies, the term *epitome* (Dickey 2007: 32) was frequently applied. The most recognized author of *hypotheseis* was the major scholar of the Royal Library of Alexandria, Aristophanes of Byzantium (c. 257 – c. 180 BC).[3] There are numerous summaries signed by Aristophanes, but it is not certain whether he was their original author.[4] While working in the Ancient Library of Alexandria,

---

2 Translations of *hypotheseis* into modern languages are rarely published in print. Therefore, few people realise that it was the summaries that influenced the standard practice of inserting into dramatic works meta-texts, such as the *didascalium* or the list of *dramatis personae*. Hypotheseis also provide us with a great amount of information on the history of ancient theatre.
3 In about 200 BC, Aristophanes of Byzantium held the office of the head librarian of the Library of Alexandria. Traditionally, Aristophanes is credited with the invention of the accent system used in Greek texts and setting the colometry of lyrical texts, which were customarily written stychometrically, i.e. in the same manner as prose. Aristophanes is also thought to be responsible for the preparation of editions of dramas whose text was divided into lines and stanzas.
4 More information on the *hypotheseis* by Aristophanes of Byzantium is available in Herschell 1901: 287–298.

Aristophanes of Byzantium prepared various editions of texts by Greek authors, including tragedies, and each play was prefaced with his foreword. It is assumed that the preserved Aristophanean *hypotheseis* are the remnants of these forewords. In the Middle Ages, the most significant author of summaries of classical dramas was Demetrius Triclinius (c. 1280–1340).[5] The great majority of extant summaries, however, are anonymous. Allegedly, their texts were written by Byzantine scholars, who compiled and abridged the *hypotheseis* prepared by earlier researchers (Dickey 2007: 32).

Regardless of the authorship and time of their writing, all types of *hypotheseis* to classical dramas share a similar structure and contain comparable information. In the longest and most complete summaries, the following data can be found:

- the description of events preceding the time of the beginning of the plot (in the case of tragedies and satirical drama, mythical events are quoted, whereas in comedies, which did not use myths, the presentation includes fictional events imagined by the author of the drama and described in the prologue);
- the descriptions of plot and action (usually much more detailed for comedies than for tragedies, since mythical stories – on which the plots of tragedies were customarily based – were commonly known, whereas stories told in comedies were the inventions of the authors);
- comments in the form of stage directions, describing the movement on stage, the characters' behaviour and the organisation of the theatrical space;
- the information on the composition of the chorus;
- the information on the character enouncing the prologue (authors use the term προλογίζει);
- the description of the setting (customarily, the authors of *hypotheseis* depict what can be seen on the *skene*, using the following words: ἡ μὲν σκηνὴ τοῦ δράματος ὑπόκειται ἐν... or ἔστιν ἡ μὲν σκηνὴ τοῦ δράματος...);
- the list of *dramatis personae* (Greek: τὰ τοῦ δράματος πρόσωπα);
- the date of the staging (the year and the Olympiad) as well as the name of the *archon* in charge (a commonly used wording is ἐδιδάχθη τὸ δρᾶμα ἐπὶ ἄρχοντος...);

---

5   Demetrius Triclinius pioneered the realm of scholia, analysing the metrical structure of texts by Aeschylus, Sophocles and Euripides. An important part of his linguistic activity was also the preparation of editions of ancient texts, onto which he would inscribe lections from older manuscripts and comments drafted by other scholiasts. Presumably, he is responsible for the extant manuscript of the most ancient variants of nine plays by Euripides.

- the name of the *choragus* (an Athenian citizen appointed by the *archon* and responsible for the preparation of the chorus in dramatic productions);
- the information on the results of the dramatic competition during which the play was staged (authors of *hypotheseis* precede the name of the winning poet with the adjective πρῶτος);
- the names of all poets taking part in the competition;
- the information whether any given myth was used in another drama by a different poet (the information is given exclusively in reference to tragedies; authors of *hypotheseis* only took into account the works by the three most prominent classical poets: Aeschylus, Sophocles and Euripides; when any given myth was used only in the discussed tragedy, the author of the *hypothesis* would write the following comment: παρ' οὐδετέρωι κεῖται ἡ μυθοποιία);
- the titles of plays included in the tetralogy (in the case of tragedy);
- the information on the feast during which the play was staged (in the case of comedy, authors of *hypotheseis* indicated the Dionysia or the Lenaia);
- the explanation of the title of the play;
- the name of the author of the *hypothesis*;
- information whether the texts of the play had survived until the *hypothesis* was written down (authors of *hypotheseis* most frequently use the note οὐ σῴζεται).

What is also of importance, particularly as far as the criticism of the texts is concerned, is the fact that the researchers who wrote summaries used quotations from different dramas. Therefore, a *hypothesis* on one drama often contains interesting information on another drama, which also happens to be quite helpful in determining the correct version of texts of extant dramas and in learning more about fragments of lost plays.[6]

The historical and literary passion of Hellenistic and Byzantine scholars was the main reason for which *hypotheseis* of ancient works were drafted. Nevertheless, summaries were also written for educational purposes, as proven by the presence of some *hypotheseis* among the works by Byzantine rhetoricians (e.g. Johannes Logothetes or Gregorius Corinthius). The tradition of writing a *hypothesis* for this purpose has survived until today. The necessity to draft a summary increases the level of the reader's concentration, which in turn facilitates the process of memorizing it. Thus, the preparation of *hypotheseis* also served the purpose of learning more about ancient dramas and of bequeathing the stories told by clas-

---

6   The majority of information that can be found in the contents of *hypotheseis* can also be traced in *scholia*. A selection of thematically organised comments by scholiasts can be found, for instance, in Nünlist 2009.

sical Greek poets to future generations. Besides the poets' biographies, the extant *hypotheseis* most frequently constitute part of the scholia – critical comments authored by ancient Byzantine and mediaeval scholars. Scholiasts' main purpose was to discuss, and occasionally to evaluate, any given work of literature, which in consequence facilitated its reading. More often than not, the information to be found in *hypotheseis* can be also traced in the wording of individual comments. Scholia are divided by periods in which their collections were compiled into *scholia vetera* (of the Hellenistic period – the earliest and, thus, the most valuable) and into *scholia recentiora* (later and created in the Byzantine period).[7]

As far as the content and the text format are concerned, *hypotheseis* are divided into three main categories: narrative, descriptive and learned (van Rossum-Steenbeek 1998: 1–39). Narrative *hypotheseis* are most commonly written in the past tense, and draw the reader's attention to the presentation of the mythical story told by the poet in the play, which makes them similar to summaries of mythographic works.[8] When compared with the works of mythographers, how-

---

7   Due to the great amount of miscellaneous information included in the comments, scholia are an exceptionally valuable source of knowledge for modern researchers. What makes the study of the collections of scholia particularly difficult, though, is the fact that it is unworkable to determine their authors, which in turn also renders it impossible to specify the time in which they were written. A once written comment may have been altered and abridged on numerous occasions by successive researchers and copyists. The contents of various comments written in different centuries were mixed up when scholiasts copied older scholia into younger manuscripts or complemented a text from one volume with information contained in another.

8   Even though classical Greek tragedy was inseparably related to myth, there were some exceptions to the rule. Two tragedies based on historical, not mythological, events were written by Phrynichus (6th-5th century BC), the predecessor of Aeschylus. Only one history-based tragedy has been preserved: *The Persians* by Aeschylus. And yet, even in *The Persians*, which tells the story of the Greek victory in the Persian Wars, the poet mythologises the presented events. The story described in the play possesses the features of a myth: Xerxes' defeat is a punishment for his *hybris*, whereas the Athenian leader is called Alastor – the avenger spirit. (Cf. West 1990). The two extant *hypotheseis* to *The Persians*, from the collections of *scholia vetera* and *recentiora*, do not differ substantially from summaries of mythological plays. The description of the mythical story is substituted with the depiction of historical events and some biographical information on the Persian king Darius. Neither of the authors found it necessary to discuss more explicitly the uniqueness of the theme in *The Persians*. It can also be alleged that the reason for the information being abandoned is that the story presented in the play does not differ in its nature from myths. The authors of the summaries of *The Persians* offer a great amount of historical and literary data informing the reader that Phrynichus'

ever, narrative *hypotheseis* are written in a simpler language, and not only do their authors use a smaller number of adjectives, but they also avoid the use of tropes and rhetorical figures. In contrast to narrative *hypotheseis*, descriptive ones mainly use the present tense. Their authors shunned the depiction of any given version of the myth presented by the poet, focusing on the description of the performance itself. In this type of summary, readers can find the greatest number of comments on stage directions. Authors of learned (or scientific) summaries also refrained from focusing mainly on the description of the plot and provided more information on the circumstances of the initial staging of the play. They described and evaluated individual parts of the play, frequently giving information whether the mythical story had already been incorporated in other poets' work, or if the discussed dramatic text has been preserved.

Part II.

In the next part of the article, selected *hypotheseis* referring to a single mythical story will be presented in order to illustrate the manner in which scholars from various periods described dramatic texts, and what miscellaneous approaches they took to discuss the same literary genre of *hypothesis*. For the purposes of the article, the summaries describing the dramas on the fate of the House of Atreus have been selected, with Orestes as one of the main characters.

Prior to quoting the texts of the *hypotheseis*, it is worth to remind the most crucial (i.e. unchanged in any version of the myth) events in the history of the House of Atreus, on which the tragic poets based the plots of their dramas. The two main protagonists in the story of the House of Atreus are a married couple, Clytemestra and Agamemnon, and their children, Iphigenia, Electra and Orestes. Prior to sailing off to war against Troy, Agamemnon – to ensure good luck in his military enterprise – sacrificed his own daughter, Iphigenia. For this deed, upon his return to Argos, he is slain by his wife, Clytemestra, who is later murdered by her own son Orestes, avenging the death of his father. Having committed matricide, Orestes is pursued and tormented by the Erinyes, the deities of vengeance.

The Phoenissae (*The Phoenician Women*) was the archetype of Aeschylus' play, and discussing the differences between the two tragedies. Moreover, the *hypotheseis* contain standard information on the person enouncing the prologue, the composition of the chorus, the setting and the list of *dramatis personae*. Other information include the name of the winner in the dramatic competition, the winning tetralogy and the name of the *archon* in charge. (The texts of the *hypothesis* to *The Persians* by Aeschylus can be found in Dähnhardt 1894.)

The oldest preserved dramas related to the fate of the house of Atreus are the tragedies constituting the only extant trilogy *The Oresteia* (*Agamemnon, The Libation Bearers, The Eumenides*) by Aeschylus. The quotations below originate from the *hypotheseis* to two plays within the trilogy (*Agamemnon, The Eumenides*) and are credited to Demetrius Triclinius. The content of the summaries by Triclinius coincides, however, with the anonymous *hypotheseis* which are part of the *scholia vetera* to these tragedies, and – in the case of *The Eumenides* – with the version credited to Aristophanes of Byzantium.

> Heading for Ilion, Agamemnon promised Clytemestra that if he captures the city, he will, on the very same day, notify her by a signal fire. Therefore, Clytemestra paid the watchman to look for the agreed signal-flare. When he saw (the sign – K.Ch.), he told (her about it – K.Ch.), and she called for the elderly to inform (them – K.Ch.) about the sign. They (scilicet Elders) are the members of the chorus, who – while listening to the news – are also singing a paean. Shortly afterwards, this is followed by the arrival of Talthybius, who tells the story of the sea voyage. Soon, Agamemnon returns home on a ship, followed by another vessel carrying both the spoils of war and Cassandra. He (Agamemnon – K.Ch.) walks into the house with Clytemestra, and Cassandra, upon entering the king's palace, prophesies her own and Agamemnon's death. She also foretells that Orestes will slay his own mother. Then she dashes inside, breaking and throwing away the chaplets of white wool, since she (knows that – K.Ch.) will die. This part of the play is highly esteemed as it causes an emotional shock (ἔκπληξις) and evokes great compassion.
> Aeschylus' unique motif is that he shows Agamemnon's assassination (is heard – K.Ch.) on stage, while the killing of Cassandra (takes place – K.Ch.) in silence and (on stage – K.Ch.) the audience can only (later – K.Ch.) see her dead body.
> Aegisthus and Clytemestra justify the murder (of Agamemnon – K.Ch.) with one major argument: she (refers to – K.Ch.) the death of Iphigenia, and he – the harm done by Atreus to his father (Thyestes – K.Ch.).
> The play was staged under the archon called Philocleos in the second year of the 18th Olympiad. It (the competition – K.Ch.) was won by Aeschylus for (the following tetralogy – K.Ch.): *Agamemnon, The Libation Bearers, The Eumenides* and the satirical drama of *Proteus*. The choragus was Xenocles Aphidnaios.
> *Dramatis personae*: watchman, chorus, messenger, Clytemestra, Talthybius, herald, Agamemnon, Cassandra, Aegisthus. The Prologue is enounced by the watchman, Agamemnon's servant.

The author of the quoted *hypothesis* does not pay too much attention to the myth presented by Aeschylus and refers only to the events which were interesting due to their theatrical and dramatic potential. He mentions the spectacular signal fire heralding the return of Agamemnon, and two scenes that, in all probability, made the greatest impression on the audience. In the first one, Cassandra builds tension by prophesying her own death and the doom of Agamemnon. The second scene is the instance of their death behind the closed door of the *skene* and the presentation of their corpses. The author of the *hypothesis* draws our attention to the fact that Aeschylus let Agamemnon speak in the face of death, while Cassandra died in silence. The comments on staging the play are accompanied by a great amount of extra information on the history of theatre: the date of the first public performance, the results of the dramatic competition and the name of the choragus responsible. The author of the *hypothesis* also included information on who enounces the prologue. Another reason that makes this *hypothesis* so interesting is the fact that the information on the tragedy is at odds with the extant versions of the literary work. The greatest discrepancy seems to be Talthybius' presence[9] in the summary, since in the versions of the tragedy available today he is substituted by a nameless herald.

The *hypothesis* to the third part of Aeschylus' trilogy – *The Eumenides* – is quite different in its nature.

> Pursued and tormented by the Erinyes (Furies) in Delphi, Orestes follows Apollo's advice and visits the Temple of Athena, and when the Jury announces the verdict in his favour, he returns to Argos. The Erinyes turn to good and should be called by the genial name of 'Eumenides'. This story is not present in the texts by other (poets – K.Ch.).
> *Dramatis personae*: the Pythian priestess, Apollo, Orestes, the Ghost of Clytemestra, the Chorus of Furies, Attendants of Athena.[10]

The author of the *hypothesis* summarises the plot in just a few sentences, without giving any personal comments or information on the history of theatre. The only addition is the list of the *dramatis personae* and a remark informing the reader that none of the other poets used this structure of the story. It is generally assumed that Aeschylus unique contribution to the subject matter of the myth is implementing changes into the commonly known plot including – most likely – the renaming of the Erinyes to the Eumenides. The laconic format of the *hypothesis* does not confirm whether the author was convinced that Aeschylus was the only poet to rename the deities. If such was the author's intention, then he could not have been aware that the Eumenides appeared in other classical dramas. Among the extant

---

9   Talthybius was Agamemnon's herald and friend, who fought by the king's side in the Trojan War. Talthybius appears in Homer's *The Odyssey* and Euripides' *Hecuba* and *The Trojan Women*.

10 Ὀρέστης ἐν Δελφοῖς περιεχόμενος ὑπὸ τῶν Ἐριννύων βουλῆι Ἀπόλλωνος παραγίνεται εἰς Ἀθήνας εἰς τὸ ἱερὸν τῆς Ἀθηνᾶς· ἧς βουλῆι νικήσας κατῆλθεν εἰς Ἄργος. τὰς δὲ Ἐριννύας πραείας γινομένας κατ' εὐφημισμὸν προσηγόρευσεν Εὐμενίδας. παρ' οὐδετέρωι κεῖται ἡ μυθοποιία.
τὰ τοῦ δράματος πρόσωπα· προφῆτις τῆς Πυθίας, Ἀπόλλων, Ὀρέστης, Κλυταιμνήστρας εἴδωλον, χορὸς Εὐμενίδων, Ἀθηνᾶ, προπομποί.

texts, they can be traced in Sophocles' play entitled *Oedipus at Colonus* (lines 42 and 486) (Sophocles 1908).

The fate of Orestes was also described by the youngest of the great classical tragic poets: Euripides. In *Orestes*, he presents the protagonist in a seemingly no-win situation. Orestes has already committed matricide, having killed Clytemestra and her lover Aegisthus, and now he is pursued and tormented by the Erinyes. Together with his sister Electra, who is looking after him, he is sentenced to be stoned to death. The verdict is given by the assembly of Argive men. The siblings are assisted by Orestes' friend, Pylades, who helps them out of care and compassion.

The two *hypotheseis* to the play of *Orestes* quoted below have different origins. The first one comes from the oldest collection of scholia to this drama, while the second one is authored by the before-quoted Aristophanes of Byzantium.

> Avenging the death of his father, Orestes slayed Aegisthus and Clytemestra. His sudden madness was an immediate punishment for having dared to commit matricide. Tyndareus, Clytemestra's father, took the case to court, so that Argives could legally decide what punishment should be laid upon the culprit.
> When, by the will of fate, Menelaus was to return from his journey, he sent Helen by night and he himself came during the day. He was asked by Orestes for help, but he (Menelaus – K.Ch.) held Tyndareus' opinion in higher esteem and refused to do so (scilicet offer assistance to Orestes). In the public vote, the majority of attendants opted to sentence Orestes to death.
> [Orestes managed to defer the sentence by one day], by making an oath that he would take his own life. His friend Pylades advised him to commence with taking revenge on Menelaus by slaying Helen. Thus, they began to act, but (their – K.Ch.) plan was thwarted by the gods, who had kidnapped Helen. Next, Electra appeared, bringing them (scilicet Orestes and Pylades) Hermione, who they intended to murder. At that moment, Menelaus showed up and, having realised that he can lose both his wife and daughter, he made the decision to storm the palace. However, they forestalled him, threatening to burn down (the palace – K.Ch.). That was when Apollo arrived and declared that he had placed Helen among the stars, ordered Orestes to take Hermione to be his wife and to undergo a purifying ritual (necessary – K.Ch.) after committing a murder, and to take the reins in Argos.[11]

---

11 Ὀρέστης τον φόνον τοῦ πατρὸς μεταπορευόμενος ἀνεῖλεν Αἴγισθον καὶ Κλυταιμνήστραν· μητροκτονῆσαι δὲ τολμήσας παραχρῆμα τὴν δίκην ἔδωκεν ἐμμανὴς γενόμενος. Τυνδάρεω δὲ τοῦ πατρὸς τῆς ἀνηρημένης κατηγορήσαντος κατ' αὐτοῦ ἔμελλον κοινῇ Ἀργεῖοι ψῆφον ἐκφέρεσθαι περὶ τοῦ δεῖ παθεῖν τὸν ἀσεβήσαντα. κατὰ τύχην δὲ Μενέλαος ἐκ τῆς πλάνης ὑποστρέψας νυκτὸς μὲν Ἑλένην εἰσαπέστειλε, καθ' ἡμέραν δὲ αὐτὸς ἦλθε. καὶ παρακαλούμενος ὑπὸ Ὀρέστου βοηθῆσαι αὐτῷ ἀντιλέγοντα Τυνδάρεων μᾶλλον ηὐλαβήθη. λεχθέντων δὲ λόγων ἐν τοῖς ὄχλοις ἐπηνέχθη τὸ πλῆθος ἀποκτείνειν Ὀρέστην.

As can be seen from the quotation, the *hypothesis* originating from the collection of *scholia vetera* is similar in its form to a standard summary. The main purpose of its author was to present the mythical story which had been told in the drama. He ignored all the information on the play that were not related to the myth. It can be assumed that the researcher who wrote the *hypothesis* to *Orestes* in this form was guided by the specific nature of the drama, since Euripides showed there his very own, modified version of the myth, which was not commonly known.[12] Thus, it comes as no surprise that the (plausibly) Hellenistic researcher reckoned that what he should focus on is the myth modified by the poet. Another reason might have been the specific genre of Euripides' drama – the so-called new tragedy, also referred to as "melodrama" or, less often, "tragicomedy" – which, to a certain extent, also influenced the plot of the play. The most characteristic feature of such dramas is a happy ending, which is also present in *Orestes*.

An entirely different approach than making the reader familiar with the myth is taken in the *hypothesis* to *Orestes* which has been preserved in the manuscripts signed by Aristophanes of Byzantium.

> Petrified by the matricide and forced by the actions of the Erinyes and the death sentence voted by Argives, Orestes intended to kill Helen and Hermione (to lay his vengeance upon Menelaus, who could have helped him but refused to do so); he was, however, stopped by Apollo. This story is not present in any other poet's work.
> The plot is set in Argos, the chorus consists of Argive women and Electra's companions, who arrive to learn more about the tragedy of Orestes. The prologue is enounced by Electra. The play possesses a somewhat comical ending.
> The play is arranged in the following manner. Orestes is introduced in Agamemnon's palace, suffering from intense madness and confined to bed, with Electra sitting at his feet. It is peculiar that she is not sat closer to his head, which would make her show more care for her brother by sitting closer to him. Apparently, the poet arranged this for the

---

[παρῃτήσατο δὲ πρὸς μίαν ἡμέραν βιοῦν Ὀρέστης.] ἐπαγγειλάμενος αὐτὸν ἐκ τοῦ βίου προΐεσθαι. συνὼν δὲ τούτοις ὁ Πυλάδης ὁ φίλος αὐτοῦ, συνεβούλευσε πρῶτον Μενελάου τιμωρίαν λαβεῖν Ἑλένην ἀποκτείναντας. αὐτοὶ μὲν οὖν ἐπὶ τούτοις ἐλθόντες διεψεύσθησαν τῆς ἐλπίδος θεῶν τὴν Ἑλένην ἁρπασάντων· Ἠλέκτρα δὲ Ἑρμιόνην ἐπιφανεῖσαν ἔδωκε εἰς χεῖρας αὐτοῖς, οἱ δὲ ταύτην φονεύειν ἔμελλον. ἐπιφανεὶς δὲ Μενέλαος καὶ βλέπων ἑαυτὸν ἅμα γυναικὸς καὶ τέκνου στερούμενον ὑπ' αὐτῶν ἐπεβάλετο τὰ βασίλεια πορθεῖν. οἱ δὲ φθάσαντες ὑφάψειν ἠπείλησαν. ἐπιφανεὶς δὲ Ἀπόλλων Ἑλένην μὲν ἔφησεν εἰς θεοὺς διακομίζειν, Ὀρέστῃ δὲ ἐπέταξεν αὐτὸν μὲν Ἑρμιόνην λαβεῖν, Πυλάδῃ δὲ Ἠλέκτραν συνοικίσαι, καθαρθέντι δὲ τὸν φόνον Ἄργους δυναστεύειν·
(The texts of *hypotheseis* to Euripides' plays were quoted from: Euripides 1979)

12 More information on innovations within the plot of Euripides' plays can be found in Czerwińska 2013.

sake of the chorus. (Had Euripides opted for a different arrangement – K.Ch.) Orestes, who had just fallen asleep with difficulty, could have been woken up by the chorus of women standing close to him, which can be concluded from what Electra says to the chorus: "Hush, hush! let your footsteps fall lightly! not a sound!"[13] (line 140). It can thus be alleged that this was the reason behind arranging (the stage – K.Ch.) in such a way. The play may be one of the successful ones, but its dramatis personae are wicked. All but Pylades are bad characters.[14]

The author of the quoted *hypothesis* does not pay substantive attention to the plot of the play, describing it in a very synthetic manner, in just one opening sentence at the beginning of the summary. Thus, it can be alleged that the only reason to refer to the events of the drama is to inform the reader that the version of the myth proposed by Euripides had not appeared in the work of any other playwright. Further in the *hypothesis*, the author offers numerous pieces of information on various branches of knowledge. He stipulates the setting, points to the person enouncing the prologue and lists the members of the chorus. He also adds a comment on the genre to which the play belongs, drawing our attention to the fact that the Euripidean plot does not finish in a way that we could expect from a tragic poem.

What is of most interest, however, is the second part of the *hypothesis*, where the author focuses on the elements of staging the drama. He offers an analysis

---

13 The English translation of *Orestes* is quoted after Euripides 1938.
14 Ὀρέστης διὰ τὴν τῆς μητρὸς σφαγὴν ἅμα καὶ ὑπὸ τῶν Ἐρινύων δειματούμενος καὶ ὑπὸ τῶν Ἀργείων κατακριθεὶς θανάτῳ, μέλλων φονεύειν Ἑλένην καὶ Ἑρμιόνην ἀνθ᾽ ὧν Μενέλαος παρὼν οὐκ ἐβοήθησε, διεκωλύθη ὑπὸ Ἀπόλλωνος. παρ᾽ οὐδετέρῳ κεῖται ἡ μυθοποιία.
Ἡ μὲν σκηνὴ τοῦ δράματος ὑπόκειται ἐν Ἄργει· ὁ δὲ χορὸς συνέστηκεν ἐκ γυναικῶν Ἀργείων ἡλικιωτίδων Ἠλέκτρας, αἳ καὶ παραγίνονται ὑπὲρ τῆς τοῦ Ὀρέστου πυνθανόμεναι συμφορᾶς. προλογίζει δὲ Ἠλέκτρα. τὸ δρᾶμα κωμικωτέραν ἔχει τὴν καταστροφήν.
ἡ δὲ διασκευὴ τοῦ δράματός ἐστι τοιαύτη· πρὸς ιὰ ιοῦ Ἀγαμέμνονος βασίλεια ὑπόκειται· Ὀρέστης κάμνων ὑπὸ μανίας ἐπὶ κλινιδίου, ᾧ προσκαθέζεται πρὸς τοῖς ποσὶν Ἠλέκτρα. διαπορεῖται δὲ τί δήποτε οὐ πρὸς τῇ κεφαλῇ καθέζεται· οὕτως γὰρ <ἂν> μᾶλλον ἐδόκει τὸν ἀδελφὸν τημελεῖν, πλησιαίτερον προσκαθεζομένη. ἔοικεν οὖν διὰ τὸν χορὸν ὁ ποιητὴς οὕτω διασκευάσαι. διηγέρθη γὰρ ἂν Ὀρέστης, ἄρτι καὶ μόγις καταδαρθείς, πλησιαίτερον αὐτῷ τῶν κατὰ τὸν χορὸν γυναικῶν παρισταμένων. ἔστι δὲ ὑπονοῆσαι τοῦτο ἐξ ὧν φησιν Ἠλέκτρα τῷ χορῷ ['140]· σῖγα σῖγα, λεπτὸν ἴχνος ἀρβύλησ. πιθανὸν οὖν ταύτην εἶναι τὴν πρόφασιν τῆς τοιαύτης διαθέσεως.
τὸ δρᾶμα τῶν ἐπὶ σκηνῆς εὐδοκιμούντων, χείριστον δὲ τοῖς ἤθεσι. πλὴν γὰρ Πυλάδου πάντες φαῦλοι ἦσαν.

and interpretation of the scene in which Electra is watching over her sleeping brother. The Byzantine researcher strives to recreate the organisation of the scenic space and the positioning of the actors, as suggested by Euripides. The valuable thing is that the author quotes a fragment of the play to support his words, which provides the reader with the opportunity to take a critical attitude towards the presented ideas. In the closing sentences of his *hypotheseis*, the Byzantine scholar assesses the characters (ἤθη) of the Euripidean drama. He informs the reader that, despite being popular, almost all of its *dramatis personae* are negative characters, with whom, as can be presumed, the reader will find it quite difficult to identify.

The analysis of the aforementioned *hypotheseis* shows what different approaches to dramas were taken by scholars and how dissimilarly they treated the myth which is presented in the texts. Depending on the purpose of the *hypothesis*, its authors focused on various constituents of the scrutinised work. For some Hellenistic or Byzantine researchers, the myth told by the poet was of the utmost importance, whereas others used it only as a starting point to discuss the issues which were, to their mind, more significant. The content of the quoted *hypotheseis* to the works describing the myth of the House of Atreus shows that the substantive content of the summaries depended, above all, upon the scientific interests of the individual scholars. It is, however, a fact that *hypotheseis* had such a capacious and non-standardised form, far exceeding the framework of regular summaries that makes their reading so fascinating and informative.

Translated by Konrad Brzozowski

References:

Czerwińska, Jadwiga. 2013. *Innowacje mitologiczne i dramaturgiczne Eurypidesa. Tragedia, tragikomedia*. Lodz: Lodz University Press.

Dähnhardt, Oscarus (ed.). 1894. *Scholia in Aeschyli "Persas"*. Lipsiae: B. G. Teubner.

Dickey, Eleanor. 2007. *Ancient Greek Scholarship: A Guide to Finding, Reading, and Understanding Scholia, Commentaries, Lexica and Grammatical Treatises, from their Beginnings to the Byzantine Period*. New York: Oxford University Press.

Euripides. 1938. *The Complete Greek Drama*. Eds. by Whitney J. Oates and Eugene O'Neill Jr. Vol. II. Trans. by E. P. Coleridge. New York: Random House.

—.1979. *Tragödien*. Griechisch und Deutsch von Dietrich Ebener. Vol. IV. Berlin: Akademie-Verlag.

Moore, Clifford Herschell. 1901. "Notes on the Tragic Hipotheses". *Harvard Studies in Classical Philology* 12: 287–298.

Nünlist, René. 2009. *The Ancient Critic at Work: Terms and Concepts of Literary Criticism in Greek Scholia*. Cambridge: Cambridge University Press.

Rossum-Steenbeek, Monique van. 1998. *Greek Readers' Digests? Studies on a Selection of Subliterary Papyri*. Leiden – New York – Köln: Brill.

Sophocles, 1908. *Tragoediae*. Ed. by Guilelmi Dindorfii. Lipsiae: B.G. Teubneri.

Untersteiner, Marius (ed.). 1947. *Aeschyli fabulae quae exstant*. Vol. II. Milano: Instituto Editoriale Italiano.

West, Martin L. 1990. *Studies in Aeschylus*. Stuttgart: B.G. Teubner.

Françoise Lecocq[*]

The Palm Tree, the Phoenix and the Wild Boar: Scientific and Literary Reception of a Strange Trio in Pliny the Elder (*Natural History* 13, 42–43) and in *Satyricon* (40, 3–8)

Abstract: According to Pliny the Elder, an Egyptian palm tree bearing "big, hard, fibrous" *syagri* dates with a "taste of venison so characteristic of the wild boars" existed in his time, in synchrony with the phoenix bird (*NH* 13, 42–43). Greek and Latin poets usually use the homonymy of φοῖνιξ, meaning both "tree" and "bird", making the former one the abode of the latter, and having license to play with the word. Pliny adds another pun: *syagros* understood as σῦς ἄγριος, meaning "wild boar", in Latin *porcus singularis*, literally translated as "solitary pig" – meaning the same as φοῖνιξ, according to Isidore of Seville. What is real, what is invented, and why about the tree, the taste and the symbiosis with the bird? The trio – palm tree, phoenix and boar – also appears in *Satyricon*, as ingredients of an extravagant course served at the Feast of Trimalchio (40, 3–8): a roasted boar stuffed with live birds, served with Egyptian and Syrian (or Phoenician) dates. This course is comparable to other recipes consisting of boar and exotic birds, described by Apicius and other authors. Expressing criticism of luxury and gluttony, they also testify to the dream of eating the phoenix (substituted in literary descriptions and iconographic illustrations with flamingos), as expressed by the emperor Heliogabalus. The present article explores the two texts – together with the problem of their dating and their connection with contemporary events implicating the phoenix as an Egyptian marvel and an imperial omen.

Keywords: Pliny the Elder, *Satyricon*, palm tree, phoenix, boar, Egypt.

Some poets had long ago already used the homonymy of the Greek word φοῖνιξ signifying the miraculous, sacred to the Sun bird, and the palm tree (precisely the date palm)[1] – by making the tree the abode of the bird.[2] It is more surprising to find this homonymy in the work of the Latin scholar Pliny the Elder, who ac-

---

[*] University of Caen Normandy, France.
1 *Phoinix dactylifera* L.
2 The first to do so were probably Ezechiel the Dramatist, *Exagoge*, frag. 17, 253–269 and, for sure, Ovid, *Metamorphoses* 15, 392–409 (with a bilingual pun, because the homonymy does not exist in Latin: the word for "tree" is *palma*): see Lecocq 2016.

cepted it, and seemed to add to it another pun about a rare species of Egyptian palm trees, whose fruits were appreciated because of their "taste of wild boar": the palm tree *syagrus*[3] which, as Pliny asserts, had some kind of synchrony with the unique bird. The text is strange in many respects, and the alliance of words and things – some rare trees, a rare bird and a "solitary" animal – is curiously to be found again in the novel *Satyricon*, in the description of a dish comprising a wild boar stuffed with live birds and served with dates.

In the present work I am going to determine the meaning of Pliny's text by identifying the kind of tree he wrote about, since *syagrus* is a hapax in Latin. I am going to examine the Egyptian documentation on various species of palm trees and the nature of their fruits, as well as the animals linked to them. In fact, the couple boar – palm tree has more to do with philology than with botany: one has to think in a bilingual way to understand *syagrus* as σῦς ἄγριος – "wild boar" – corresponding to Latin *porcus singularis* – "single pig" – "single" in the sense of "solitary", as is also the bird phoenix, one of its kind, according to the legend, and even some Roman etymologists.

The dish served at the Feast of Trimalchio, after another famous plate – the zodiac dish – included boar, dates and birds and has been interpreted as an image of the phoenix reborn from the flames, showing the Roman luxury and culinary extravaganza. While the ingredients of the dish at the same time are typical for a lavish banquet, their combination and theatrical staging make them the culinary transposition of the passage of Pliny. To the various symbolic readings of this, I add the dream of eating the phoenix, which has been attested many times, from the comic poet Aristophanes to the Roman emperor Heliogabalus. To conclude, I will examine the topicality of the passage of Pliny in the 1st century, and the ways in which it appears in *Satyricon*, providing some information about its author and his times.

The Palm Tree, the Phoenix and the Wild Boar in Pliny the Elder

In his book on birds, Pliny did not mention the connection between phoenix and the homonymous tree.[4] In his book on trees, however, he made the hierarchical list of the fruits of Egyptian palm trees: the *margarides*, the *sandalides* and the *syagri*. Furthermore, he noted that a specimen of the *syagrus* species, of a life cycle

---

3   I use *syagrus* as the name of the tree for convenience: in fact, Pliny only used the plural *syagri* to refer to its fruits. Today, "syagrus" is a South American palm tree, producing edible seeds similar to coconut.
4   *Natural History* 10, 3–5.

more or less synchronous with the phoenix bird, was growing at his time south of Alexandria, or in Upper Egypt:

> At in meridiano orbe praecipuam optinent nobilitatem syagri proximamque margarides. Hae breues, candidae, rotundae, acinis quam balanis similiores, quare et nomen a margaritis accepere. Vna earum arbor in Chora esse traditur, una et syagrorum, mirumque de ea accepimus, cum phoenice aue, quae putatur ex huius palmae argumento nomen accepisse, intermori ac renasci ex se ipsa, eratque, cum proderem, fertilis. Pomum ipsum grande, durum, horridum et a ceteris generibus distans sapore quodam ferinae in apris euidentissimo, quae causa nominis. Quarta auctoritas sandalidum a similitudine appellatarum. Iam in Aethiopiae fine quinque harum, nec plures, arbores tradunt, non raritate magis quam suauitate mirabiles.

> In the southern parts of the world, the dates known as *syagri* hold the highest rank, and next after them those that are called *margarides*. These last are short, white, and round, and bear a stronger resemblance to grapes than to dates; for which reason it is that they have received their name, in consequence of their close resemblance to pearls [*margaritae*]. It is said that there is only one tree that bears them, and that in the region known as Chora.[5] The same is the case also with the tree that bears the *syagri*. We have heard a wonderful story too, relative to this last tree, to the effect that it dies and comes to life again in a similar manner to the phoenix, which, it is generally thought, has borrowed its name from the palm tree, in consequence of this peculiarity; at the moment that I am writing this, that tree is still bearing fruit. As for the fruit itself, it is large, hard, and of a rough appearance, and differing in taste from all other kinds, having a sort of wild flavour peculiar to itself, and not unlike that of the flesh of the wild boar; it is evidently this circumstance from which it has derived its name of *syagrus*. In the fourth rank are the dates called "sandalides," from their resemblance to a sandal in shape. It is stated, that on the confines of Æthiopia there are but five of these trees at the most, no less remarkable for the singular lusciousness of their fruit, than for their extreme rarity.[6]

Margarides were small dates, as white as pearls (in Greek *margarita*); Pliny wrote that they were the most prized,[7] but did not describe their taste. *Sandalides* had their name from their similarity to the shape of a sandal, a shoe often made of braided palm fibre; Pliny wrote about the dates' good taste and rarity. The Greek-origin word *syagrus*, which appears with this meaning only in this particular text, is a compound of σῦς ἄγριος, "boar" (literally "wild pig", a periphrasis for

---

5   Pliny defined *Chora* in *NH* 6, 39 as the lower parts of Egypt: the Nile Delta.
6   Pliny 1855 (*NH* 13, 42–43); Rackham, in Pliny 1942, translated *syagri* as "Maldive nut date", *horridum* as "prickly" and *sapor* as "smell". However, the Areca, or betel nut, is not prickly.
7   On the various colours of dates, see *NH* 13, 49.

κάπρος),[8] and this qualifier could be explained, according to Pliny, with the gamy taste of its fruit. The remark is strange.

What then could be this tree in Egyptian flora? Neither Theophrastus[9] nor Strabo[10] is here the source for Pliny: he must have had some local and recent information about native trees. It is known that the Egyptian gardens contained some trees which were unique to their kind: the garden of the scribe Ineni, for example, possessed, among other species, a unique specimen of palm tree, according to the list in his funeral chapel.[11] So, what Pliny wrote about the rarity of the tree is very likely to be true. But the description does not make sense: there is no other element of identification than the fruit described as *horridus*, literally meaning "with bristly hair". Does this refer to its fibrous outside look, stringy flesh or a bitter taste?[12] On twelve occurrences of that adjective in Pliny, eleven concern a bristly or unpleasant look; only one concerns the taste, in the utterance *saporem horridum* – "abominable taste" – which refers to some toxic liquid, and not fibre.[13]

In any case, the fruit clearly is more a nut than a date. What are then the possible hypotheses? *Syagrus* could be a place-name, since there was a cape Syagros in Yemen; however, what gave the name to that cape?[14] It could also be an extinct species of palm tree, because there is today a drastic reduction of the biodiversity exisiting in Antiquity: Pliny counted forty-nine species, but did not mention them

---

8   See Athenaeus, *Deipnosophists*, 9, 402a; in 7, 6, that author used the word *syagrides*, with the same suffix *-ides* as in *margarides* and *sandalides* (meaning in Greek "similar to"), for a fish (*capros aper* L., a perch).
9   The Greek botanist is mentioned as a source for the book 13 of Pliny, but in the *History of Plants* 2, 6, nothing is said about the *margarides*, the *sandalides* or the *syagri*. See Amigues 1995.
10 *Geography* 17, 2 (on the Egyptian palm trees); the Greek author said almost the contrary to Pliny: "Throughout the whole of Aegypt the palm tree is not of a good species; and in the region of the Delta and Alexandria it produces fruit that is not good to eat." (Strabo 1932).
11 See Baum 1998.
12 So are the interpretations of various translators. In French, the translation "âpre", erroneous according to me, is based on another pun: Varro wrote that the word *aper* comes from *asper*, "rough" (*On the Latin language* 5, 101).
13 *NH* 34, 33, about a metallic taste.
14 The *Syagros promunturium* (Pliny, *NH* 6, 100 and 153, for Σύαγρος ἄκρα in *Periplus of the Erythraean Sea*, 30) is Port Ras Fartak in Yemen. The word Fartak, meaning "boar" in Arabic, was possibly borrowed by the medieval geographers from the ancient Greeks.

all, and some have not been identified. However, by looking at the fruits known to us, one can think of three different kinds: the coconut, the nut of the doum palm, and the nut of the argun palm.

Today's scientists agree that the coconut palm of Indian origin (*Cocos nucifera* L.) did not exist in ancient Egypt, even though this hypothesis was proposed several times in the 19th century by editors of Pliny, travellers and Egyptologists. Although its life span is shorter than a century, the resemblance of the coconut to the coat and colour of the boar certainly would suit the text of Pliny well enough, assuming that *horridus* describes the look and not the taste of the fruit, as I believe. It is also well known that the three indentations on the coconut shell resemble the facial features – a nose and two eyes – of a monkey or a pig. But an essential indication would be missing: the liquid inside the nut. It is not necessarily a problem: in the texts by other authors who mentioned the fruit by an only bookish knowledge, that detail does not appear before the 6th century.[15]

The doum palm (*Hyphaene thebaica*) is a tree bearing fruits named *koukou* (both in the hieroglyphs and in Greek). Theophrastus called it κουκιοφόρον,[16] but he mentioned as its only peculiarities branched stems (the Egyptian name of the tree was *mama*, meaning "divided into two", "double") and big, yellowish fruit with a sweet flavour. A papyrus mentions "the water inside the fruit" of this palm tree in the prayer of a scribe to the god Thot.[17] Pliny named the doum palm *cucus*; he too described its fruit as apparently different from the *syagri*.

> At e diuerso cuci in magno honore, palmae similis, quando et eius foliis utuntur ad textilia. Differt quod in bracchia ramorum spargitur. Pomo magnitudo quae manum inpleat, colos fuluus, commendabili suco ex austero dulci. Lignum intus grande firmaeque duritiae, ex quo uelares detornant anulos. In eo nucleus dulcis, dum recens est; siccatus durescit ad infinitum, ut mandi non possit, nisi sit pluribus diebus maceratus. Materies crispioris elegantiae et ob id Persis gratissima.

> On the other hand, the wood of the cucus is held in very high esteem. It is similar in nature to the palm, as its leaves are similarly used for the purposes of texture: it differs from it, however, in spreading out its arms in large branches. The fruit, which is of a size large enough to fill the hand, is of a tawny color, and recommends itself by its juice, which is a

---

15 Cosmas Indicopleustes, *Christian Topography*, 11. The first name of that fruit was "nut of India" (in Greek κάρυον Ἰνδικόν), produced by the Argel tree (from Sanskrit *narikela*, "springing water"). It is certainly already mentioned by Philostratus as a marvel of India (*Life of Apollonius* 3, 5).
16 *HP* 2, 6, 9.
17 Papyrus Sallier I, 8, 2–6, see Loret 1946. This liquid becomes hardened in a mature fruit.

mixture of sweet and rough. The seed in the inside is large and of remarkable hardness, and turners use it for making curtain rings. The kernel is sweet, while fresh; but when dried it becomes hard to a most remarkable degree, so much so, that it can only be eaten after being soaked in water for several days. The wood is beautifully mottled with circling veins, for which reason it is particularly esteemed among the Persians.[18]

Modern botanists, however, call the tree, among other names, *hyphaene crinita*, because its fibres, being bristly when dried, look like a brush.[19] This variety still exists today and its fruit are eaten by people, but there is nothing that makes them particularly special, other than a light taste of gingerbread (hence the popular name of Gingerbread tree), and one can hardly understand what would make its fame to the eyes of Pliny. The tree's life span is also less than a century.

Fig. 1: Doum palm, or Gingerbread tree (Hyphaene thebaica)
Courtesy of the National Tropical Botanical Garden

---

18 Pliny the Elder 1855, *NH* 13, 62; the qualifier for the taste is *austerus* ("bitter"), not *horridus*.
19 See pictures on http://ntbg.org/plants/plant_details.php?rid=2975&plantid=12087.

Fig. 2: *Doum palm, or Gingerbread tree* (Hyphaene thebaica), *fruit showing fibre under pericarp*
Courtesy of the National Tropical Botanical Garden

The Argun palm (*Medemia argun*) is a relative of the doum. Its nuts were found by archaeologists in Pharaonic tombs, before botanists discovered some still living specimens in the 19th century. Today, there are less than fifty preserved trees of this endemic to Nubian Desert species left in Egypt.[20] It is possible that they could also be scarce in Antiquity, because it is the tree mentioned as unique in the list of Ineni, under its Egyptian name *mama n khanen* (or *xanin*), meaning "doum with a seed".[21] The description and the taste of the fruit could also correspond to the *syagri*,[22] with a fibrous and sweet mesocarp, even if it is not a delight either (fig. 1 and 2). Possibly, this nut was intended specifically for offering to gods, because it was found in some graves until the end of the Roman era, having a more religious than alimentary val-

---

20 See http://whc.unesco.org/fr/listesindicatives/6067/.
21 Theophrastus wrote that the fruit of the doum has no seed (*HP* 2, 6, 3), but this indication is missing in Pliny.
22 Its mesocarp is described by the specialists as "spongy", like the one of the Doum palm (Zahran and Willis 1992: 371–372). See pictures on http://meine.plantzone.net/community/viewtopic.php?f=77&t=2668.

ue.[23] Pliny himself wrote that some fruits were exclusively dedicated to the gods.[24] Due to its scarcity, the life span of the Argun palm is unknown.

To approach the question of the *syagri* from another angle, the only animal clearly connected to the Egyptian palm tree is not the boar, rarely present in the local economy and iconography.[25] The only thing that Pliny mentioned was that the inedible fruits of some palm trees were left for the pigs to eat,[26] as in other countries, and as still today: nowadays, there is a palm tree species going by the scientific name of *Hyophorbe* after the Greek words "swine food".[27] The only animal related to the Egyptian palm tree was the monkey: on some paintings showing scenes of the everyday life, we can see cercopithecus monkeys or baboons picking or stealing dates.[28] Monkeys are also associated with the cult of the god Thot, who is sometimes depicted with a palm branch as the symbol of time and eternity.[29]

After this botanical and animal study, let us examine the name of palm tree itself. The Greek word σύαγρος or its derivation συάγριος appears as a proper noun denoting a place-name,[30] or an anthroponym,[31] and as a common word for the boar, of course,[32] a species of fish,[33] and a variety of frankincense.[34] But why

23 See Ibrahim 2009: 10, 15 (height) and 17 (bristly), and Rzóska 2012: 57.
24 Pliny 1855, *NH* 13, 46: "Those of this sort which we consecrate to the worship of the gods".
25 See Manlius – Gautier 1999.
26 See Pliny, *NH* 13, 49.
27 Hyophorbe Gaertner 1791, native of the Mauritius Island.
28 An *ostrakon* from Deir el-Medina depicts a baboon picking dates (Paris: Louvre Museum); for other examples of monkeys, see Spanel 1989. The baboon was named κυνοκέφαλος, "dog-head". There was also a curious pig-monkey, the χοιροπίθηκος, (Aristotle, *History of Animals* 2, 11, 2), but almost nothing is known about it; it might be, however, another name for the baboon.
29 In ancient Egypt, the palm branch *renpit*, was the symbol of the year because the tree was supposed to produce one frond every month; it was featured stripped of the leaves, with one notch or more: { or {. See Santolini 1984 and Dunand 1991.
30 See n. 14.
31 See the examples given by Athenaeus, *Deipnosophists* 9, 61.
32 See Isidore 2005, *Etymologies* 12, 1, 27: "The wild boar is named after wilderness, *a feritate*, with the letter *f* removed and replaced by *p*., whence, also, among the Greeks it is called σύαγρος, it is wild pig".
33 See n. 8. Athenaeus, *Deipnosophists* 7, 6: fish not similar to the boar fish (*Deipnosophists* 7, 4), see Louyest 2009: 121. In Latin, there is an *apriculus piscis* (Ennius, *The Art of Dining* 1, 5 and Apuleius. *Apology* 34 and 39); Pliny used the name *caper* and explained it by its grunt (*NH* 11, 267).
34 Dioscorides, *The materials of Medicine* 1, 81: συάγριος.

The Palm Tree, the Phoenix and the Wild Boar 63

of the two remarkable palm trees producing the *syagri* and the *margarides*, it is the first one, rather than the latter, that is claimed to be synchronous with the phoenix bird? I believe that it is because of the Latin, and not Greek, name: it is a bilingual association of ideas[35] that seems to have occurred to Pliny, or was taken by him from an unspecified source. "Wild boar" is translated into Latin as *porcus singularis*, "solitary pig", designating an old male pig[36] and solitude is the main feature of the phoenix. In Greek there is the same word for "bird" and "tree" – *phoinix* – and the unique term *syagrus* reinforces their similarity.

The classic authors describing the phoenix generally used the utterance *auis unica*,[37] but we can find it described as *singularis*, "single", in Tertullian's Christian text on the apology of celibacy,[38] as well as in an apocryphal text.[39] Isidore even gives the word *phoinix* a possible Arabic etymology, with the meaning "single": "the phoenix is a bird from Arabia, so called because either it possesses a scarlet color, or it is singular and unique in the entire world, for the Arabs say *phoenix* for 'singular'".[40]

The pun made by Pliny in the *Natural History*, making sense only in Latin,[41] and the synchrony seemingly inferred from it, are possibly invented as an etymological

---

35 On the Graeco-Roman bilingualism, see Rochette 1998.
36 See Aelian, *On the Nature of Animals* 7, 47: "There is also a kind of pig said μόνιος, id est solitary" (my translation), or *Vulgate, Psalms* 79, 14, where *singularis ferus*, "solitary wild animal", is synonymous with *aper de silua*, "boar from the forest".
37 Ovid, *Amores* 2, 6, 23; Pomponius Mela, 3, 8; *Didascalia Apostolorum*, 40; Ambrose, *Hexameron* 5, 78; Lactantius, *Poem on the bird phoenix* 31–32; Claudian, *On Stilicho's Consulship* 2, 418; Isidore, *Etymologies* 12, 7, 22.
38 Tertulllian 1960, *On the Resurrection of the Flesh* 13, 2: "That bird (…) notable because there is only one of it at a time [*de singularitate famosum*]".
39 Epistle of Pseudo-Titus 1960, *On the State of Chastity*, 11: "The Lord made the divine phoenix and not given it a wife, but allowed it to remain in loneliness [*singularem permanere*]?"
40 *Etymologies* 12, 7, 22. About the palm tree, Isidore wrote that this long-living tree took its name from the long-living bird (17, 7, 1).
41 I think that there is a similar pun about an accomplice of Verres, Apronius, having his name derived from *aper* – "boar", in the famous passage where the orator played on the similarity of *sus* – "pig" – and *suus* – "his" – about Verres "the Breeding boar" (Cicero 1856, *Against Verres* 2, 3, 22, see Pocetti 2009: 17): "Apronius, (…) concerning whose extraordinary wickedness [*improbitate singulari*, = and/or "boarish" or "piggish wickedness"] you have heard the complaints (…). This Apronius is the man whom Verres – (…) though he had taken with him no small number of men like himself [*sui similes* = and/or "like a boar" or a "pig"] in worthlessness (…), still considered most like himself [*sui simillimum* = and/ or "like a boar" or "a pig"] of any man in the whole province". In French, the pun about

explanation apparently as simple and obvious as for the meaning of the words *margarides* and *sandalides*.[42] The text includes two other examples of this kind of etymological explanations: Pliny mentions that the dates *caryotae* have their name from Greek κάρη, "head", and ὑῳδία, "stupidity", because the wine made from the fruit goes to one's head, and for the dates *adelphides*, from Greek ἀδέλφια, "sister", that they are of a "sister quality" to the former ones. For me, it looks like due to the double bilingual pun – *phoinix*, meaning "palm tree" in Greek, and "bird phoenix" in Greek and Latin, and *syagrus*, meaning "wild boar" in Greek, translated in Latin as *singularis*, meaning "the singular one"[43] – Pliny considered that the tree, apparently unique in the area, had the life span of the phoenix, and he imagined that its fruit had the taste, rather than the bristly look, of the boar because the boar was a well-known delicacy on the Roman tables.[44]

A curious dish at the Feast of Trimalchio: the wild boar with dates, stuffed with living birds

The double pun in the name of the tree *syagrus* seems to appear also in *Satyricon*. At the feast of Trimalchio, among other elaborate recipes,[45] there is a dish consisting of an oven baked wild boar served with dates (the fruits of the palm tree), and living birds which escape from its innards, resembling the rebirth of the phoenix from the fire: the ingredients are the three verbal components of the palm tree *syagrus*, with the words *aper*, then *porcus siluaticus* for the boar, and *palmula*, diminutive of *palma*, "palm tree", for the material of the baskets with dates.

> Repositorium, in quo positus erat primae magnitudinis aper, et quidem pilleatus, e cuius dentibus sportellae dependebant duae palmulis textae, altera caryotis, altera thebaicis repleta. Circa autem minores porcelli ex coptoplacentis facti, quasi uberibus imminer-

---

improbitate singulari is easily translated as "une perversité sanglière", instead of "singulière". See Wolff 2001: 328–329 for puns on anthroponyms and 330–331 for bilingual puns.
42 *NH* 13, 44–45.
43 There is no occurrence of *singularis* meaning "boar" in Pliny.
44 For the idea that sheer puns can generate legends, see Deroy 1959 and Fruyt 1996. As for why the palm tree producing *margarides* and not the palm tree producing *sandalides* was also described as "solitary", I have no other explanation than the scarcity of the pearls and the commonness of the sandals. 19th century travellers have reported some "hard and dry" white dates (Dybowski 1889: 18). Perhaps the nuts were used to make beads for botanical jewelry, as it is done today with seeds of some palm trees in South America. So, maybe also for the *sandalides*, the explanation of the name could be the use of the nuts as well as their look.
45 See Fick 2004: 49–502, Amat 2007: 394–396, Badel 2012.

ent, scrofam esse positam significabant. Et hi quidem apophoreti fuerunt. (…) Latus apri uehementer percussit, ex cuius plaga turdi euolauerunt. Parati aucupes cum harundinibus fuerunt, et eos circa triclinium uolitantes momento exceperunt. Inde cum suum cuique iussisset referri, Trimalchio adiecit: "Etiam uidete, quam porcus ille siluaticus totam comederit glandem." Statim pueri ad sportellas accesserunt quae pendebant e dentibus, thebaicasque et caryatas ad numerum diuisere cenantibus.

A huge tray, on which lay a wild boar of the largest size, with a cap on its head, while from the tusks hung two little baskets of woven palm leaves, one full of Syrian dates, the other of Theban. Round it were little piglets of pastry dough, as if at suck, to show it was a sow we had before us; and these were gifts to be taken home with them by the guests. (…) [The servant] gashed open the boar's flank, from which there flew out a number of thrushes. Fowlers stood ready with their rods and immediately caught the birds as they fluttered about the table. Then Trimalchio directed each guest to be given his bird, and this done, added: "Look, this wildwood pig had eaten all the acorns." Instantly slaves ran to the baskets that were suspended from the animal's tusks and divided the two kinds of dates in equal proportions among the diners.[46]

Jean Hubaux and Maxime Leroy, in their book on the myth of the phoenix, were the first to make the link with Pliny, but they explained nothing about its nature, meaning or origin.[47] Florence Dupont studied the symbolic values of the recipe: in the dinner-show it has many interpretations,[48] and I will propose one more.

In the case of the first served dish, the zodiac dish,[49] its meaning, as well as the connection between the food items and the twelve signs of zodiac the is explained twice: first, by the narrator who describes the dish, and later, in the next chapter, by the character Trimalchio. The reader is therefore invited to look for a symbolic meaning in that plate too. The dish itself, in the culinary domain, is an actual dish, a variation on the recipe of the *porcus Troianus*, very much appreciated by the Romans, as one can see in various sources from Apicius[50] to Macrobius.[51] It is also a baroque recipe, according to the aesthetics of metamorphosis, combining various opposites: inside and outside (a meal, a hunt), cooked and raw (the boar, the birds), the dead and the living (again, the boar and the birds), venison and poultry, the salty and the sweet, and so on. In the artistic and literary domain, it is a theatrical performance, involving a

---

46 *Satyricon* 1930: 42–43.
47 Hubaux – Leroy 1939: 116.
48 Dupont 1977: 107–110. See also Martin 1988 and Rimell 2002.
49 *Sat.* 35–39.
50 Apicius has a recipe of cold gravy with dates for a boiled boar dish (*The Art of cooking* 334).
51 Macrobius, *Saturnalia* 3, 13, 13.

boar hunt, followed by a bird hunt. It is at the same time a parody of the literary genre of the philosopher's banquet; more particularly, it is also a mythological and literary reference to the prodigious white sow in the *Aeneid* of Virgil.[52] It is also a rebus-dish, containing a pun with a botanical reference to the palm tree *syagrus* – its only explicit indication being the word *palmula*.

The two kinds of dates on the plate are not those mentioned by Pliny,[53] but the ones certainly better known to the Romans, coming from the countries between which the phoenix migrates: Syria (formerly Phoenicia) and Egypt.[54] Soon after, in another bilingual pun, the dates are called *glandes*, a partial translation of φοινικοβάλανος – "acorn of the date palm"[55] (acorns were the usual pig fodder). With regard to the host, the dish is an allegory of the return to freedom: the Phrygian cap on the head of the animal is not only explicitly related to the fact that the dish is served for the second time (having been dismissed by other guests the day before),[56] but it is also implicitly related to the new status of the host, an emancipated former slave, reborn as free man like the phoenix is reborn to its new life. With regard to the author, the dish is a conventional critique of the *luxuria* ("luxury") and *gula* ("gluttony") of the rich Romans, as it is said afterwards in the same novel:[57] the boar was an expensive food item,[58] both appreciated and depreciated[59] as the main target of the critique of moralists from Cato the Censor.[60] The ancients liked game and its strong flavour,[61] especially as the product of their own hunt.[62] It is the first meat mentioned in the majority of the menus in literature, from the times of Horace to the end of Rome: from private tables

---

52 *Aeneid* 8, 43–45.
53 Although Pliny wrote about the *caryotes* just after the *sandalides* (*NH* 13, 44).
54 Syria (or Assyria) sometimes has replaced Arabia as the homeland of the phoenix since Ovid (*Met.* 15, 393), by a sheer pun (see Lecocq 2016).
55 Pliny used the word in the same chapter for the fruits of the palm trees: "In some parts of Phoenicia and Cilicia, they are commonly called '*balani*', a name which has been also borrowed by us"; he said further that "they are much used for fattening swine and other animals" (Pliny the Elder 1855, *NH* 13, 48–49).
56 As later explained by Trimalchio (*Sat.* 39).
57 *Sat.* 55: Trimalchio listed the various fowl served on the tables of the wealthy Romans, quoting a poem supposedly written by Publilius Syrus.
58 See Martial, *Epigrams* 13, 41.
59 See Martial, *Ep.* 12, 48 and Athenaeus, 9, 402a.
60 See Pliny, *NH* 8, 78: chapter on the wild boar.
61 Latter in the novel, Trimalchio ate a lot of bear meat because it resembled the meat of a wild boar with a smell so strong that it made his wife Scintilla vomit (*Sat.* 66).
62 See Martial, *Epigrams* 7, 27.

to the tables of the emperors, there was no feast without a boar.[63] This tendency, although early restrained by sumptuary laws and condemned by philosophers, continued to aggravate.[64] The wealthy Romans wanted for their tables the rarest, most expensive, most extraordinary food, trying to break records in its size or weigh, doing so, with an ulterior motive, to show their dominance over the world which had become a kitchen safe of Rome.[65] Another passage from *Satyricon* mentions a mortician who was used to feasting like a king, eating wild boars, cakes and fowl.[66] Providing examples of culinary debauchery, Seneca mentioned first the boar and the flamingo, *phoenicopteros*, both in Greek and Latin, which – in my opinion – is the substitute of the phoenix.

> You are doing no great thing if you can live without royal pomp, if you feel no craving for boars which weigh a thousand pounds, or for flamingo tongues, or for the other absurdities of a luxury that already wearies of game cooked whole, and chooses different bits from separate animals.[67]

Flamingo tongues became popular from the times of Apicius:[68] this bird has indeed a very fleshy tongue, but it was served for its exoticism, colour, relative rarity and high price, rather than for its taste, just like the pheasant, the peacock, and the ostrich. Pliny also denounced this fashion.[69] Martial talked about the breeding of this species of birds by the rich Bassus,[70] and he listed the flamingo in his enumeration of *xenia*, "food presents", including dates, boar and thrushes;[71] Juvenalis did not want to have a flamingo served alive on his table,[72] like the one featured still alive in its string shopping bag on the *triclinium* mosaic of Thysdrus

---

63 The whole theme of the *cena Trimalcionis* was already present in the *cena Nasidieni* of Horace: the first dish was a boar, followed by a crane and a goose (*Satires* 2, 8); see Hugoniot 2011. See also Martial, *Ep.* 9, 77. For other historical examples, see Cabouret 2008.
64 The Fannia law in 161 BC was already aiming at the exotic fowl, see Pliny, *NH* 10, 140 and Macrobius, *Saturnalia* 3, 13, 13 (Corbier 1989: 133; Garnsey 1999, 125; Coudry 2004: 170).
65 See Nadeau 2010, chap. 5.
66 *Sat.* 38, 16. See Wolff 2003a: 121–122.
67 Seneca 1920, *Letter to Lucilius* 110, 12. See Wolff 2003b.
68 None of the recipes of Apicius are concerned with the tongue only. The three flamingo recipes use the whole animal (*The Art of cooking* 220, 230 and 231).
69 *NH* 10, 68.
70 *Ep.* 3, 58, 14.
71 *Ep.* 13, 27: dates; 13, 41 and 93: boar; 13, 51 and 92: thrushes; 13, 71: flamingo.
72 Juvenal, *Satires* 11, 138–39 (boar and flamingo, among other food items).

(El Djem, Tunisia) – but intended to be cooked – among other numerous food items such as – again – baskets of fruits, boar and thrushes.[73] I believe that the same situation can be found in Heliodorus' novel, in which the lover has to buy a flamingo for his mistress: the flamingo is not to serve as a pet, but become dinner. Another character comments jokingly that the φοινικόπτερος was fortunately less rare to find than the phoenix.[74] In the dish of Trimalchio, the served fowl are thrushes, not very exotic, but very appreciated for their taste,[75] and other birds small enough to be held inside the belly of a boar; here, the fact that they come out alive of a cooked meal, approximates them to the phoenix reborn from fire. I even wonder if within this dish there is an allusion to the famous imperial recipe of *tetrapharmacum*,[76] because it comprises a boar, sow's udder (real or fake), valuable poultry, as well as dough.[77]

I finally think that this dish also testifies of the old, more or less serious dream of eating the phoenix, attested from the comedies of Aristophanes to the emperor Heliogabalus, and later sources, as we shall see. In Aristophanes, the Greek ambassadors, at the table of the Persian king, are served a whole ox roasted in the oven, and a φέναξ bird, in whom the Hellenists have long ago seen a parody of the phoenix and, at the same time, a pun with the verb φενακίζω, meaning "to deceive": the bird is named "hoax" and it is meant to "hoax" people.[78] The phoenix – here an Eastern animal and not the Egyptian *benu*[79] – belongs to the imaginary birds one wishes to eat, like the ῥυντάκης, little bird full of fat, allegedly served on the table of the Persian king Artaxerxes.[80] The emperor Caligula reserved the exotic birds for the food of the

---

73 Dating from the middle of the 2nd or 3rd c. CE, now in the Bardo National Museum; see Ennaïfer 1990: 24 and Blanchard-Lemée 1996: fig. 83, "Pink flamingo prepared for cooking".
74 *Aethiopica* 6, 3. The anecdote seems especially intended to make a pun between these two Egyptian birds. For a philosophical interpretation, see Dowden 2007.
75 See Pliny, *NH* 10, 30 and Oroz Reta 1977.
76 *Augustan History, Hadrian* 21, 4; *Aelius* 5, 4; *Alexander Severus* 30, 6.
77 The guests will leave the feast with the traditional presents (ἀποφόρητα or ξενία), consisting of the dough piglets, some dates and thrushes, that is the whole dish on a small scale and in separate parts.
78 *Acharnians*, 89–90. In French, another translation of the pun is "the bird Phinace" and the verb "finasser", "to use trickery" (Aristophanes 1822). These verses are quoted by Athenaeus, *Deipnosophists* 4, 3, 6 (130 f.). But no reference to the *Acharnians* neither in Hubaux – Leroy 1939, nor in Van den Broek 1972.
79 See Lecocq 2008.
80 Plutarch, *Artaxerxes*, 19, 4–5. Paradoxically, the meat is used for poisoning a princess. See Almagor 2012: 19 and n. 76.

gods,[81] but his successor Heliogabalus let them be served on his own table.[82] Some of the special dishes he ate had a prophylactic value,[83] for beyond being an ostentatious display of luxury and of a discerning taste, the exotic breeds of fowl were an object of superstition, as in the famous medicinal dish of the Antonine emperors, the *tetrapharmacum*, the exotic fowl were supposed to guarantee good health and maybe even immortality. Similarly, a late magico-medical treaty, the *Cyranides*, mentions another imaginary bird – the ἡλιοδρόμος, "runner of the sun",[84] in some ways similar to the phoenix[85] – the eating of which can bring health and wealth.[86] Heliogabalus had several things in common with the phoenix: he was a native of Syria, one of the homelands of the bird,[87] and he was a sun worshipper in his very name.

Another solar bird is the legendary Jewish bird Ziz, which similarly to other biblical monsters – Leviathan and Behemoth, masters of water and land, respectively – is the master of the sky.[88] Its name originated from an expression to be found in two *Psalms* – *ziz saday* – probably meaning "animals of the fields",

---

81 Suetonius, *Caligula* 22, 2 (flamingo is the first on a list of six exotic birds) and 57, 4. See Thévenaz 2001.
82 *Augustan History* 1921: 23, 6: "He also promised a phoenix to his table guests, it is said, or, in lieu of the bird, a thousand pounds of gold, to dismiss them imperially (*imperatorie*)". In some editions, one reads *in praetorio* instead of *imperatorie*: it is a nonsense.
83 *Augustan History* 1921: 20, 5.
84 The bird shares some common features with the phoenix, but is not the phoenix, although sometimes, willingly or not, it is mistaken for it by ancient authors (and modern researchers): the Greek *Apocalypse* of 3 Baruch portrays, under the name of "phoenix", a giant celestial bird protecting earth from the sun rays, i.e. an Eastern celestial rooster assuming the function of the runner of the sun (see Kulik 2010 and Lecocq 2018).
85 The Egyptian phoenix – the *benu* – carrying on its back the funeral egg of myrrh with the paternal corpse enclosed in it (according to Herodotus 2, 73), is also an image of a celestial bird transporting the sun.
86 *Cyranides* 3, 15. The fact that the animal served for the dinner of Trimalchio is called *aper*, i.e. a male, then *scrofa*, i.e. a female, does not mean that the phoenix was considered a hermaphrodite like, apparently, the progeny of the solar bird ἡλιοδρόμος of the *Cyranides* (according to Hubaux – Leroy 1939, 7); about the gender of the phoenix, see Lecocq 2013 and Lecocq 2018 for a new interpretation of the ἡλιοδρόμος.
87 From Ovid (*Met.* 15, 393) to Lactantius (*Poem on the bird phoenix*, 65). See n. 54.
88 See http://www.jewishencyclopedia.com/articles/9841-leviathan-and-behemoth. In the Bible of Joseph Ben Moses, from Ulm, featuring the three creatures together, the bird Ziz looks like a griffin (Milan, Bibliotheca Ambrosiana, Ms B 32, Inf, fol. 156r, dating from 1236–1238), above another picture displaying the eschatological banquet of the Righteous. In another miniature of a Hebrew manuscript, one can see under the name of Bar Yokni a kind of a big blue-and-red duck, sitting on a giant egg (Talmud,

opposite to "birds of the mountains" and the "wild boar of the forest".[89] This gigantic creature was similar to Eastern celestial birds, whether good or bad, like the Persian cock Parodarsh announcing the rising sun,[90] or the Mesopotamian griffin Anzu, depriving the earth from the solar beams with the shade of its wings, in its revolt against the creator.[91] What is interesting here is that the medieval rabbis explained the name *ziz* with the taste of the bird's flesh similar to "this" and "this" – in Hebrew, *zi* and *zi*.[92] Indeed, according to some exegetes, the bird will be eaten by the Children of Israel in a big feast at the end of time as a compensation for their abstinence from impure fowl during their terrestrial life.[93]

Surprisingly, the dream to eat the phoenix is still alive in the twenty-first century, as one can see in the book of Allan S. Weiss *Comment cuisiner un phénix? Essai sur l'imaginaire gastronomique*.[94] That book also recently inspired a French artist and a media-staged chef to present a dining performance entitled "The Feast of the Phoenix", held in Paris in 2014.[95] The bird was associated not with a boar, but with a bull, alluding to the bullfight, but also making sense in relation to ancient religions: the bull Apis and the bird *benu*-phoenix were both honoured in the Egyptian city of Heliopolis, and the Persian cult of Mithras, with an initiatory grade named *Heliodromus*, practiced the ritual of sacrificing bulls (tauroctony). Paradoxically, the food served at the performance was mostly vegetarian.[96]

Bekhorot, fol. 57 col. 2, British Library, Shelfmark: Add. MS 11639, circa 1280). See Gutmann 1968 and Frojmovic 2015: 20–22.
89 *Psalms* 50.11 and 80.14.
90 Parodarsh, the "foreseer", is the sacred bird of the Avesta, see Ahbabi 2013.
91 See Ginzberg 1925–1938: I, 11 and 20; Wazana 2009: 119–124.
92 Rabbi David Kimhi (12th c.) in a commentary to Psalm 50, 11. This popular etymology has no scientific base: the meaning is rather "winged" (Ginzberg 1925–1938: V, 47–48, n. 134) or "moving" (Wazana 2009: 116–119, Kulik 2010: 242–244).
93 See Elijah Levita (16th c.) in *Tishbi*, a dictionary explaining some words used in the *Talmud* and the *Midrash* (under the name Bar Yokni).
94 With three errors in one sentence, p. 64: no hunt, no Lydia, no two hundred coins in the *Augustan History* (see n. 83).
95 See http://www.lemonde.fr/arts/article/2014/10/21/yves-camdeborde-torero-d-une-performance-dinatoire_4509963_1655012.html, and http://www.telerama.fr/scenes/delphine-gigoux-martin-l-artiste-qui-mange-dans-une-carcasse-en-toute-delicatesse,120500.php.
96 As for *Satyricon*, it inspired a half artistic half culinary performance that took place at Villa Medici in Rome in 2009: the re-enactment of the Feast of Trimalchio. The menu, among other dishes, included a whole boar cut in front of the guests, filled up with alive thrushes. See http://www.villamedici.it/fr/programme-culturel/programme-culturel/2009/09/le-festin-de-trimalchion/.

To conclude the topic of Pliny, I believe that the word *syagri* refers to the look of the nuts, as it is in the case of the *margarides* and *sandalides*. The nuts, being bristly or spongy at some stage of their development, are probably the fruits of the *Hyphaene thebaica* or its close relative, the *Medemia argun*, mentioned by Pliny, but they are not clearly identified and described.[97] The reference to the taste, rather than to the look, might be explained with the gingerbread taste of these nuts, but, more surely, it is a more or less conscious bilingual pun: a Latin speaker will associate the term "boar nut" with the most prized meat served on the Roman tables, and the Latin name of the animal *(porcus) singularis*, evokes the single legendary bird having the same name as the tree – *phoenix* – the three sharing here the feature of being rare, or solitary.

I venture the hypothesis that the remark on the synchrony of the real tree and the mythological bird can be explained by the supposed topicality of a miracle, as for the previous rumours on the appearance of the bird under the emperors Tiberius and Claudius.[98] Some popular superstitions may have been encouraged: Egypt then had at its head a faithful supporter of the emperor-to-be – Vespasian – and it is to his son, Titus, that Pliny dedicated his book around 77. The alleged prodigy of the tree could be a discreet imperial omen of the advent of the new ruler, to be added to the others which occurred in the same country[99] under the rule of that same prefect, Tiberius Julius Alexander.[100] It was difficult to claim that the phoenix, appearing only every five hundred years, had already returned, but it was easy to transfer the miracle to the homonymous tree, especially since the palm tree frequently appeared in prodigies concerning gods, great men and important events, both in Roman history and Greek mythology.[101]

To conclude the discussion about *Satyricon*, I add to Florence Dupont's analysis of the extravagant dish comprising boar, dates, and birds, served at the *Cena*, a new symbolic meaning: the desire to eat the phoenix, as a royal Persian or an imperial Roman dish, and/or as a magical recipe, resulted from the belief in its special health-improving powers. Furthermore, a French researcher had recently proposed as the author of the book a Greek emancipated slave named Encolpius which is very close to the actual name of the hero of the novel, Encolpus. Encolpius

---

97 See Newton 2001.
98 Tiberius: Tacitus, *Annals* 6, 28; Claudius: Pliny, *NH* 10, 5.
99 According to Tacitus, *Histories* 4, 81 and Suetonius, *Life of Vespasian* 7. See Vigourt 2001, chap. 8–9. To compare with an Egyptian prodigy about his predecessors Galba, see Poulle 1999: 42 and Vitellius, see Carré 1999.
100 In charge from 66 to 69.
101 See Leppin 2013.

was the private secretary of Pliny the Younger being himself the nephew of Pliny the Elder.[102] Some passages of the novel are parodies of previous, mostly post-Neronian, literary works.[103] I would add that Pliny the Younger was a friend of the historian Tacitus, who wrote about the supposed appearance of the phoenix under the reign of Tiberius. Pliny the Younger was also a friend of the emperor Trajan, who was honoured by his successor Hadrian with the first coin ever showing the phoenix bird; Hadrian later struck another coin on which the bird was associated with the zodiac.[104] The association of the phoenix and the zodiac is to be seen in the two successive dishes served during the feast in *Satyricon*: they are participating, in their own manner, in the reflexions of Trimalchio on time, life, destiny, death and rebirth.[105] Thus, the association of birds, dates and boar in the dish of *Satyricon* would take a peculiar taste: Encolpius, the Greek secretary of Pliny the Younger, evoked, under a culinary form, a topic popular in his time at the Roman court and among intellectuals like Pliny the Elder, to whose work he undoubtedly had privileged access; he had probably found there the ingredients of this strange recipe, based on homonymic bilingual collisions of the words *phoenix* and *syagri*.[106]

References:

Ahbabi, Mahin. 2013. "The Holiness of 'Rooster' in Mithraism". *Journal of American Science* 9. 1: 40–44.

Almagor, Eran. 2012. "Ctesias and the importance of his writings revisited". *Electrum* 19: 9–40.

Amigues, Suzanne. 1995. "Les plantes d'Égypte vues par les naturalistes grecs". *Entre Égypte et Grèce*. Cahiers de la Villa Kérylos: 51–67.

Aristophanes. 1822. *Le théâtre des Grecs*, tome 12: *Aristophane, Les Acharniens*. Trans. by Pierre Brumoy. Paris: Cussac.

---

102 *Letters* 8, 1, 2: *Encolpius lector*. Hypothesis of Martin 2000a and 200b, followed by Ratti 2011.
103 See Flobert 2003, Martin 1975, 2000a, 2000b, 2006, 2009, Rimell 2007. For other textual coincidences between the *Satyricon* and the *Natural History*, see Soubiran 2007.
104 See Lecocq 2001: 45–46 and 2009: 84–87. The association between the phoenix and the zodiac can also be seen on a gnostic gem: the bird is featured inside an oval zodiac adorned with the twelve signs (Mastrocinque 2003: 225, fig. 134).
105 See Martin 2000b: 47–48.
106 See Nicolas 2007.

Badel, Christophe. 2012. "Alimentation et société dans la Rome classique: bilan historiographique (IIe s. av. J.-C. – IIe s. ap. J.-C.)". *Dialogues d'histoire ancienne,* Supplément 7.1: 133–157.

Baum, Nathalie. 1988. *Arbres et arbustes de l'Égypte ancienne. La liste de la tombe thébaine d'Ineni (n° 81).* Leuven: Peeters (Orientalia Lovaniensia Analecta, 31).

Blanchard-Lemée, Michèle, and Mongi Ennaïfer, Hedi Slim, Latifa Slim. 1996. *Mosaics of Roman Africa: Floor Mosaics from Tunisia.* London: British Museum Press.

Cabouret, Bernadette. 2008. "Rites d'hospitalité chez les élites de l'Antiquité tardive". In *Pratiques et discours alimentaires en Méditerranée de l'Antiquité à la Renaissance.* Ed. by Jean Leclant, André Vauchez, and Maurice Sartre. Paris: Académie des Inscriptions et Belles Lettres (Cahiers de la Villa Kérylos, 19). 187–222.

Carré, Renée. 1999. "Vitellius et les dieux". In *Pouvoir, divination, prédestination dans le monde antique.* Ed. by Elisabeth Smadja and Evelyne Geny. Besançon: Presses universitaires de Franche-Comté. 43–80.

Cicero. 1856. *Against Verres.* Trans. by Charles D. Yonge, London: Bohn.

Corbier, Mireille. 1989. "Le statut ambigu de la viande à Rome". *Dialogues d'Histoire Ancienne* 15: 107–158. English translation: "The ambiguous status of meat in ancient Rome". *Food and Foodways* 3.3: 223–264.

Coudry, Marianne. 2004. "Loi et société: la singularité des lois somptuaires de Rome". *Cahiers du Centre Gustave Glotz* 15.1: 135–171.

Deroy, Louis. 1959. "Jeux de mots, causes de légendes". *Aiôn* 1: 23–34.

Dowden, Ken. 2007. "Novel Ways of Being Philosophical, or: A Tale of Two Dogs and a Phoenix". In *Philosophical Presences in the Ancient Novel.* Ed. by John R. Morgan and Meriel Jones. Groningen: Barkhuis (Ancient Narrative, Supplementum 10). 137–149.

Dunand, Françoise. 1991. "Le babouin Thot et la palme. A propos d'une terre cuite d'Égypte". *Chronique d'Égypte* 66: 340–348.

Dupont, Florence. 1977. *Le plaisir et la loi, du Banquet de Platon au Satiricon.* Paris: Maspero. Reedited in 2002. Paris: La Découverte.

Dybowski, Jean-Thadée. 1889. "Le dattier et ses utilisations". *La nature. Revue des sciences et de leurs applications aux arts et aux industries* 863: 17–19.

Ennaïfer, Mongi. 1990. "Quelques mosaïques à *xenia* du Musée national du Bardo". In *Recherches franco-tunisiennes sur la mosaïque de l'Afrique antique I. Xenia.* Ed. by Catherine Balmelle et al. Rome: École française (Collection de École française de Rome, 125). 23–28.

Epistle of Pseudo-Titus. 1992. In *New Testament Apocrypha*. Ed. by Wilhelm Schneemelcher. Trans. by Robert McL. Wilson, London: J. Clarke & Company (1st ed. 1965). vol. 2.

Fick, Nicole. 2004. "La cuisine, média culturel ou le festin de Trimalchion redégusté (Pétrone, *Satyricon*, 29-79)". In *L'imaginaire de la table: convivialité, commensalité et communication*. Ed. by Jean-Jacques Boutaud. Paris: Éditions L'Harmattan. 47-62.

Flobert, Pierre. 2003. "Considérations intempestives sur l'auteur et la date du *Satyricon* sous Hadrien". In *Petroniana. Gedenkschrift für Hubert Petersmann*, edited by Józef Herman and Hannah Rosén. Heidelberg: Carl Winter. 109-122. Reprinted in 2014 in *Grammaire comparée et variétés du latin. Articles revus et mis à jour (1964-2012)*. Genève: Droz. 234-248.

Frojmovic, Eva. 2015. "A Sense of Order: Text and Image in some of the earliest illuminated Hebrew Manuscripts from Ashkenaz". In *Zu Bild und Text im jüdisch-christlichen Kontext im Mittelalter*. Ed. by Frank Bussert, Sarah Laubenstein, and Maria Stürzebecher. Jena: Quedlinburg (Erfurter Schriften zur jüdischen Geschichte, 3). 48-65.

Fruyt, Michèle. 1996. "Lexique et conscience linguistique: sens fonctionnel et sens parallèle". In *Structures lexicales du latin*. Ed. by Michèle Fruyt and Claude Moussy. Paris: Presses universitaires de Paris Sorbonne. 97-119.

Garnsey, Peter. 1999. *Food and Society in Classical Antiquity*. Cambridge: University Press.

Ginzberg, Louis. 1925-1938. *The Legends of the Jews*, vol. I: *From the Creation to Exodus*, and Vol. V: *Notes to volumes I and II*. Philadelphia: The Jewish Publication Society of America. Reedited Baltimore and London: Johns Hopkins University Press: 1998.

Gutmann, Joseph. 1968. "Leviathan, Behemoth and Ziz: Jewish Messianic Symbols in Art". *Hebrew Union College Annual* 39: 219-230.

Augustan History 1921. *Elagabalus*. Trans. by David Magie. The Loeb Classical Library, London: Heinemann.

Hubaux, Jean and Maxime Leroy. 1939. *Le mythe du phénix dans les littératures grecque et latine*. Liège-Paris: Droz.

Hugoniot, Christophe. 2011. "Les ombres de Mécène. A propos de la *cena Nasidieni* d'Horace (*S.*, II, 8)". *Food and History* 9, 2: 23-70.

Ibrahim, Haitham and William J. Baker. 2009. "*Medemia argun*. Past, Present and Future". *Palms* 53.1: 9-19 (on-line).

Isidore. 2005. *Etymologies*. Trans. by Priscilla Throop, on line edition.

Kulik, Alexander. 2010. *3 Baruch: Greek-Slavonic Apocalypse of Baruch*. Berlin: de Gruyter (Commentaries on Early Jewish Literature).

Lecocq, Françoise. 2001. "L'empereur romain et le phénix". In *Phénix: mythe(s) et signe(s)*. Ed. by Silvia Fabrizio-Costa. Peter Lang: Berne. 27–56.

—.2008. "Les sources égyptiennes du mythe du phénix". In *L'Égypte à Rome, Cahiers de la MRSH-Caen* 41. Ed. by Françoise Lecocq. Second edition augmented (first edition 2005). 211–266.

—.2013. " 'Le sexe incertain du phénix': de la zoologie à la théologie". In *Le phénix et son Autre. Poétique d'un mythe des origines au XVIe siècle*. Ed. by Laurence Gosserez. Rennes: Presses universitaires. 187–210.

—.2016. "Inventing the Phoenix. A Myth in the making through Words and Images". In *Animals in Greek and Roman Religion and Myth*. Ed. by Patricia Johnston, Attilio Mastrocinque, and Sofia Papaioannou. Cambridge: Cambridge Scholars Publishing. 449–478.

—.2018. "Deux oiseaux solaires en un: le coq, le phénix et l'héliodrome". In *Mélanges Catherine Jacquemard*, Caen: Presses universitaires. (Forthcoming).

Leppin, Hartmut. 2013. "Imperial Miracles and Elitist Discourses". In *Miracles Revisited: New Testament Miracle Stories and Their Concepts of Reality*. Ed. by Stefan Alkier and Annette Weissenrieder. Berlin: De Gruyter. 233–248.

Loret, Victor. 1946. "Une exhortation à la patience et au silence dans l'Égypte ancienne (Pap. Sall., l, VIII, 2–6)". *Comptes-rendus des séances de l'Académie des Inscriptions et Belles-Lettres*, 90.1: 9–15.

Louyest, Benoît. 2009. "Mots de poissons: *Le banquet des sophistes* livres 6 et 7". Villeneuve d'Ascq: Presses universitaires du Septentrion (coll. "Cahiers de philologie").

Manlius, Nicolas and Achilles Gautier. 1999. "Le sanglier en Égypte". *Comptes Rendus de l'Académie des Sciences*, Series III, Sciences de la Vie, vol. 332.7: 573–577.

Martin, René. 1975. "Quelques remarques concernant la date du *Satiricon*". *Revue des études latines* 53: 182–224.

—.1988. "La *Cena Trimalchionis*: les trois niveaux d'un festin". *Bulletin de l'Association Guillaume Budé* 1.3: 232–247.

—.2000a. "Qui a (peut-être) écrit le *Satyricon*?". *Revue des Études Latines* 78: 139–163.

—.2000b. "Le 'grand air' de Trimalchion (*Satyricon* 75–77)". *Vita Latina* 158.1: 42–50.

—.2006. "Le *Satyricon* peut-il être une œuvre du IIe siècle?". In *Aere perennius. Hommage à Hubert Zehnacker*. Ed. by Jacqueline Champeaux et Martine Chassignet. Paris: Presses de la Sorbonne.

—.2009. "Petronius Arbiter et le *Satyricon*: où en est la recherche?". *Bulletin de l'Association Guillaume Budé* 2009.1: 143–168.

Mastrocinque, Attilio. 2003. *Sylloge gemmarum gnosticarum*, I, *Bollettino di numismatica*. Roma: Istituto poligrafico e zecca dello Stato (Monografia 8.2).

Nadeau, Robin. 2010. *Les manières de table dans le monde gréco-romain*. Rennes: Presses Universitaires.

Newton, Claire. 2001. "Le Palmier Argoun Medemia argun (Mart.) Württemb. ex Wendl." In *Encyclopédie religieuse de l'univers végétal, II. Croyances phytoreligieuses de l'Égypte ancienne*. Ed. by Sydney Hervé Aufrère. Montpellier: Université Paul Valéry (Orientalia monspeliensia 11). 141–153.

Nicolas, Christian. 2007. "Collisions homonymiques bilingues dans les commentaires lexicologiques grecs et latins". In *L'homonymie dans les lexiques grec et latin*. Ed. by Alain Blanc and Alain Christol. Nancy: ADRA. 149–166.

Oroz Reta, Jose. 1977. "Nil melius turdo. Gastronomia clasica y moderna". *Helmantica* 28: 403–416.

Philostratus. 1912. *Life of Apollonius* 3, 5. Trans. by Frederick C. Conybeare. The Loeb Classical Library, London: Heinemann.

Pliny. 1855. *Pliny the Elder, Natural History. Book 13*. Trans. by John Bostock and Henry T. Riley, London: H. G. Bohn.

—.1942. *Pliny the Elder, Natural History. Books* 6 and 13. Trans. by Harris Rackham. The Loeb Classical Library, London: Heinemann.

Pocetti, Paolo. 2009. "Un animal au centre du monde. Le cochon dans l'Antiquité italique et romaine". *Schedae* (on line) 8.1: 125–142.

Poulle, Bruno. 1999. "Les présages de l'arrivée de Galba au pouvoir". In *Pouvoir, divination, prédestination dans le monde antique*. Ed. by Elisabeth Smadja and Evelyne Geny. Besançon: Presses universitaires de Franche-Comté. 33–42.

Ratti, Stéphane. 2011. "Le monde du *Satyricon* et la maison de Pline le Jeune". *Anabases* 13: 79–94.

Rimell, Victoria. 2002. *Petronius and the Anatomy of Fiction*. Cambridge: University Press.

Rimmel, Victoria. 2007. "Petronius' Lessons in Learning–The Hard Way." In *Ordering Knowledge in the Roman Empire*. Ed. by Jason König and Tim Whitmarsh. Cambridge: Cambridge University Press. 108–132.

Rochette, Bruno. 1998. "Le bilinguisme gréco-latin et la question des langues dans le monde gréco-romain". *Revue belge de philologie et d'histoire* 76.1: 177–196.

Rzóska, Julian. 2012. *The Nile, Biology of an Ancient River*. Junk: The Hague (Monographiae Biologicae, 29).

Satyricon. 1930. Translated by Alfred R. Allinson, New York: The Panurge Press.

Santolini, Gérard. 1984. "Thot, le babouin et le palmier doum". In *Mélanges Adolphe Gutbub*. Montpellier: Université Paul Valéry. 211–218.

Seneca. 1920. *Letters to Lucilius*. Trans. by Richard M. Gummere. The Loeb Classical Library, London: Heinemann.

Soubiran, Jean. 2007. "Pétrone, *Sat.* CXIX, 9-12: Note critique et exégétique". *Pallas* 75: 77-88.

Spanel, Donald B. 1989. "The Herakleopolitan Tombs of Kheti I, Jt(.j)jb(.j), and Kheti II at Asyut". *Orientalia* 58: 301-314.

Strabo. 1932. *Geography*. Trans. by Horace L. Jones. The Loeb Classical Library, London: Heinemann.

Tertullian. 1960. *On the Resurrection of the Flesh* 13, 2. Trans. by Ernest Evans, London: S.P.C.K.

Thévenaz, Olivier. 2001. "Spectacles et théâtralité dans la *Vie de Caligula* de Suétone". *Chronozones* (on line) 7: 4-13.

Van den Broek, Roelof. 1972. *The Myth of the Phoenix according to Classical and Early Christian Tradition*. Trans. by I. Seeger. Leiden: Brill (Études Préliminaires aux Religions Orientales dans l'empire romain, 24).

Vigourt, Annie. 2001. *Les présages impériaux d'Auguste à Domitien*. Paris: de Boccard.

Wazana, Nili. 2009. "Anzu and Ziz: Great Mythical Birds in Ancient Near Eastern, Biblical, and Rabbinic Traditions". *Journal of the Ancient Near Eastern Society* 31: 111-135.

Weiss, Allan S. 2004. *Comment cuisiner un phénix? Essai sur l'imaginaire gastronomique*. Paris: Mercure de France.

Wolff, Étienne. 2001. "Les jeux de langage dans l'Antiquité romaine". *Bulletin de l'Association Guillaume Budé* 1.3, 317-334.

—.2003a. "La mort symbolique d'un souverain dans le *Satyricon* de Pétrone". In *La mort du souverain*. Ed. by Brigitte Boissavit-Camus, François Chausson, and Hervé Inglebert. Paris: Picard. 121-125.

—.2003b. "La *Cena Trimalchionis*: au-delà des apparences". *Pallas* 61: Symposium. *Banquet et représentations en Grèce et à Rome*, 341-348.

Zahran, Mahmoud A. and Arthur J. Willis. 1992. *The Vegetation of Egypt*. London: Chapman and Hall.

Internet Resources:

http://ntbg.org/plants/plant_details.php?rid=2975&plantid=12087 (Accessed 5 September 2016).

http://whc.unesco.org/fr/listesindicatives/6067/ (Accessed 5 September 2016).

http://www.jewishencyclopedia.com/articles/9841-leviathan-and-behemoth (Accessed 5 September 2016).

http://www.lemonde.fr/arts/article/2014/10/21/yves-camdeborde-torero-d-une-performance-dinatoire_4509963_1655012.html (Accessed 5 September 2016).

http://www.telerama.fr/scenes/delphine-gigoux-martin-l-artiste-qui-mange-dans-une-carcasse-en-toute-delicatesse,120500.php (Accessed 5 September 2016).

Cíntia Martins Sanches[*]

Seneca's *Phoenissae*:
Anger and the Myth of Oedipus

Abstract: The myth of Oedipus for Seneca, as presented in his tragedy *Phoenissae*, concerns extreme passions and their consequences. The two excerpts making up the unfinished *Phoenissae* base on two distinct opposites – reason and emotion. In both parts of the text, the female is associated with reason and balance, and the male with extreme emotions and *furore*. Antigone, in the first part of *Phoenissae*, tries to convince Oedipus not to commit suicide using arguments about his innocence, the possibility of preventing the war to be declared by Eteocles and Polynices on Thebes, and suchlike. In the second part, it is Jocasta who holds the reason before the thoughtless fight for the throne between her children and tries to convince them to stop fighting. This subject matter is directly related to the philosophy of Seneca, since there is a close proximity between the behaviour of the individual possessed by anger – present in the philosophical works of Seneca himself and other Stoics – and the anger of tragic characters, e.g. Oedipus, Eteocles and Polynices appearing in the aforementioned drama. This reflection shows us how the myth of Oedipus was related to the Roman culture (by means of Stoicism) at the time that the work was written. The present study investigates how the theme of "reason *versus* emotion" was introduced to Seneca's tragedy and what was its relation to the Stoic philosophy. The word *manus*, which appears frequently in the text, has several meanings relevant to this theme, mainly because it refers alternatively to violence and restraint.

Keywords: Seneca, *Phoenissae*, anger, *manus*, Oedipus' myth.

The reception of Greek works in Roman literature has to do with imitation – and it is not different in the case of the Senecan tragedy. The *imitatio* is a concept first discussed by Aristotle in his *Poetics*, which subsequently appears in the works of several other authors up till the Renaissance. Aristotle defines art as imitation of human nature, and tragedy as imitation of actions and life. However, the concept of imitation we use here concerns the imitation of one author by another, i.e. of Greek works by Roman writers. Therefore, imitation would be an assimilative movement, a creative recreation of the chosen models. This is not a vision of art as something that must overcome the previously performed works. The imitation of classics by themselves was involved in an ethical thought and in the construction of affinities. This was a concept of art very different from the current one

---

[*] São Paulo State University (UNESP), Brazil.

(currently, art is innovation: in that time, it was imitation). It is important to note that imitation is not the restoration of the old, but its recreation, i.e. imitation says more about the one who imitates than about the one who is being imitated.

In some of his writings, Seneca moves away from the precepts of tragedy as dictated by Aristotle and Horace in their poetics – for example, he breaks the law of three units, and actions of his plays are set in different places at different times. However, he remains loyal to the tradition of writing tragedies on the basis of already established fables and is inspired by the larger existing tragedians (today, his name is also included among them).

Seneca's *Phoenissae* is an incomplete tragedy and has no chorus, which commonly appears in ancient tragedies (all other Senecan tragedies have choruses). The play has two parts which are directly related to the Greek tragedies *Oedipus at Colonus* (by Sophocles) and *Phoenissae* (by Euripides), respectively.

The first part of the text (lines 1–362) begins with the scene in which the tragedy's protagonist, Oedipus, who gouged out his eyes upon realising that he fulfilled the prophecy of committing parricide and incest given to him by the oracles, wanders in exile, guided by his daughter, Antigone. Oedipus is searching for death (the punishment he wishes to inflict upon himself for the murderer of Laius) and hopes to end his life on Cithaeron, where he was abandoned to die when he was a baby. Antigone, tries to convince him to give up on the idea of dying, and take him back to Thebes to try to prevent the fight for the throne between her brothers – and Oedipus' sons – Eteocles and Polynices, in which the two will eventually die. Oedipus wants his daughter to give up on him and return home; she, however, resolves to die with her father if he does not change his decision. The scene in which Antigone, using her arguments, made more effective by her innocence and sincere tears, almost manages to convince her father not to kill himself, becomes interrupted by an unexpected arrival of a messenger from Thebes arrives, asking Oedipus to return and save his children. The protagonist is then hidden among rocks near the Theban battlefield, to listen to what happens in the next scene. The same events are described by Sophocles in the second tragedy of his Theban Cycle trilogy, *Oedipus at Colonus*. The similarities between the two works regard their beginning, the point of view of the narrator, and the form of construction of the dialogues. The differences are related to style and to several events occurring during Oedipus and Antigone's trip (such as the appearance of Laius' ghost in Seneca's play).

In the second part of *Phoenissae* (lines 363–664), Antigone is back in town and encourages Jocasta to intervene and stop the fight between Eteocles and Polynices. Jocasta tries to make the brothers reconcile with each other. She physically places herself between them and convinces them to make peace, however, they continue to fight and their argument is interrupted by an abrupt break in the line 664, thus leaving the tragedy with no end. *Phoenissae* by Euripides describes the duel between Eteocles and Polynices, watched by Jocasta, who begs for the fight to stop. In the Greek play, however, the messenger only narrates the duel, whereas in the Senecan *Phoenissae* the dialogue between the throne heirs takes place in public. Both Euripides' and Seneca's versions have introduced and assigned the feminine figure in a context that at the time was seen as strictly masculine. By doing so, Seneca appreciated and assimilated the Euripidean model.

The dichotomy "reason *versus* emotion" is present in both parts of the work, always connecting the male characters (Oedipus, Eteocles and Polynices) to extreme passion and lack of reason, and making them act on impulse. The female characters (Antigone and Jocasta), however, are related to argumentation and logic, they attempt to restore peace among family members and solve problems in a better way. The reflection of this dichotomy can be seen, for instance, in the different ways in which the word *manus* (hand) is used in Seneca's tragedy.

Antigone holds her father's left hand and does not let him go to dangerous paths. Thus, Oedipus' right hand becomes for him the only means to punish himself for murdering his father and committing incest with his own mother. Hands appearing several times in parts of the text contribute to the portrait of the struggle between characters (a struggle to die, and a struggle to stay alive). For Marica Frank, "*manus* is a prominent word motif in Seneca's *Phoenissae* (…). The use of *manus* in *Phoenissae* (…) is closely related to the theme of "violence vs. restraint" which is central to the play (and conspicuous in Senecan drama in general)" (1995: 94–95).

The word *manus* appears fourteen times only in the first part of the play: twelve times in lines of Oedipus, two times in lines of Antigone. The hand serves as one of Oedipus' interlocutors, also symbolising parricide and incest. The hand acts as an independent character, it is like a third person moving between father and daughter in the course of the scene. Oedipus' hand is the only thing able to punish him for his crimes (by inflicting blindness, deafness, death). In contrast, by holding Oedipus' hand, Antigone prevents him from hurting himself during the dialogue. In the text, the hand symbolises perception, action, strength and power. The following example shows the task that Oedipus assigned to his right hand during the events:

> nil quaero: dextra noster et nuda solet/ bene animus uti. dextra, nunc toto impetu,/ toto dolore, viribus totis veni./ non destino unum vulneri nostro locum:/ totus nocens sum: qua voles mortem exige./ effringe corpus corque tot scelerum capax/ evelle, totos vis-

cerum nuda sinus;/ fractum incitatis ictibus guttur sonet/ laceraeve fixis unguibus venae fluant./ aut derige iras quo soles: haec vulnera/ rescissa multo sanguine ac tabe inriga;/ hac extrahe animam duram, inexpugnabilem. (Sen. *Phoen*.154–165)[1]

What seems important here is the synaesthesia marking the way in which the main character perceives the world: the blind Oedipus "sees" through his ears and his touch. Asking his hands to help him destroy his ears is yet another way he tries to cut himself off from the truth, which is the same thing he was trying to achieve by gauging out his eyes.

In the above extract (lines 154–165) we can first observe the negation *nil quaero*, followed by sundry requests. This contradiction mirrors Oedipus' deep desire for self-punishment and thus "I want nothing" or "I ask for nothing" would mean "I want nothing from life" or, more specifically, "I want to die". It would mean that he does not have a preference as to the way of dying – any type of death would be in accordance to the death sentence that is hanging over him. Afterwards, we can highlight the repetition of *toto, toto, totis* (lines 155–156), also followed by *totus* (line 158), *tot* (line 159) and *totos* (line 160). This repetition is connected to the recurrence of the consonants "t" and "d", particularly in the early lines of the excerpt. The alliteration in "t" and "d" highlights the "*todo* [all]" guilty, the "*todo* [all]" to be punished, which contrast with the expressions *unum locum* and *qua voles* indicating only one place to be chosen, and thus forms a chiasmus. From there, the character shows some alternatives clarifying this with the use of *aut*, in line 163. The sentence *totus nocens sum* (line 158) strengthens the use of the term *nocens*, so common throughout the text. Therefore, there is a materialisation of guilt, i.e. the guilt becomes something physical in the body, and not just an abstract concept anymore. Moreover, the meaning of "I am all guilty" eliminates any possibility of innocence and clarifies the character's total acceptance of his guilt, even if he has committed the crimes believing he was innocent, as he himself says in line 218: *et dira fugio scelera quae feci innocens* ("and I flee the terrible crimes I did in innocence"). Concerning the use of *sce-*

---

1 "I require nothing: my right hand, even unarmed, has been well used before by my spirit. Come now, my hand, with all your force, all your pain, all your strength. I do not fix on any one place for wounding; all of me is guilty, exact death where you will. Break open my body and tear out this heart, capable of so many crimes, lay bare all my coiling guts; smash my throat with forceful blows so it chokes, or implant your nails to tear my veins so they flood. Or else direct your anger as before; pull open these wounds, drench them with blood and gore, and by this route drag out this tough and impregnable life". All excerpts, both Latin and English, from Seneca's tragedies are based on the edition Seneca 2002 (ed. and trans. by John Fitch).

Ierum in the mentioned excerpt, we can look at the metonymy "heart capable of countless crimes", which together with other metonymies present in the text of this drama, shows that for Oedipus it is easier to accuse himself using the third person, since he always ran away from his fate and in fact never wanted to be the murderer of his own father and husband of his own mother. Commenting on lines 154–155, Frank (1995: 123) states that:

> The hyperbaton is effective. The position of *noster* causes stress to fall on *nuda* (already given prominence by the concessive *et*) as a result of the alliteration so achieved; *noster*, placed as it is before *et nuda*, with which it is linked in terms of position and sound (viz. the alliteration), though not of syntax, comes to have an association not only with its rightful substantive, *animus*, but also with *dextra*; the emphatic position of *bene* brings out Oedipus' twisted thinking: *bene* is not a word most people would use to describe an act as grotesque as Oedipus' self-blinding.

In the next passage, the hands of Oedipus are presented as his only hope to destroy his ears and keep the information that the world brings away from him, which would allow him to gradually destroy himself and die a bit more to the world: *utinam quidem rescindere has quirem vias,/ manibusque adactis omne qua voces meant/ aditusque verbis tramite angusto patet/ eruere possem!* ("If only I could cut off these pathways, drive in my hands and root out every avenue for voices, every narrow passageway open to words!") (Sen. *Phoen.* 226–229).

Antigone, by contrast, uses her hands with opposite intentions: *Vis nulla, genitor, a tuo nostram manum/ corpore resolvet, nemo me comitem tibi/ eripiet umquam* ("Father, no force shall loosen my hold on your body, no one shall ever tear me from your side") (Sen. *Phoen.* 51–53); and next: *non si revulso Iuppiter mundo tonet/ mediumque nostros fulmen in nexus cadat,/ manum hanc remittam* ("not even if Jove should thunder, rending the heavens, and the bolt should fall right between our close bodies, would I release this hand") (Sen. *Phoen.* 59–61). These two excerpts illustrate one of the paradoxes within Oedipus: he is a cruel criminal who hurts his own family and the whole city, but he is not able to use his own strength to get rid of a girl holding his hand. This proves the parental love and admiration he has for Antigone: rather than using violence to free himself, he prefers to beg her to leave him alone and return to the city. Beyond that, however, the presented passages also reflect the great psychological strength of Antigone, who is willing to die with her father if he does not give up the idea of punishing himself. It is a superhuman strength – there is no physical strength that exceeds the power of a force as strong as that, and not even the most powerful god would be able to get through it. For Frank, "assertions involving defiance of Zeus' power are as old as Homer and are topical in Greek and Latin literature" (1995: 96).

In the second part of *Phoenissae*, the sign *manus* appears eleven times. The brothers use their hands to hold weapons ready to attack, while Jocasta's hands part the fighters. Jocasta, like Antigone in the first part of the tragedy, says that she is willing to be the first to die if a peaceful solution is not found. As soon as the mother meets her children and places herself between them, the guard describes the reaction of Polynices and Eteocles, as well as other soldiers:

> victa materna prece/ haesere bella, iamque in alternam necem/ illinc et hinc miscere cupientes manus/ librata dextra tela suspensa tenent./ paci favetur, omnium ferrum latet/ cessatque tectum – vibrat in fratrum manu. (Sen. *Phoen.* 434–439)[2]

In the above excerpt, *manus* appears twice; *dextra*, appears once. While the other soldiers seem to want the war to end, the brothers still have the irrational will to fight. In this passage, the presence of weapons in brothers' hands symbolises hatred which exists only between the two brothers – all other fighters have put their weapons away. This allows us to observe the following contradictory pairs built in the form of "x", resulting in a chiasmus: 1) *haesere bella* and *vibrat in fratrum manu*; 2) *alternam necem* and *paci faventur*. The interchange of words denoting peace and war clearly delineates the environment of the second part of *Phoenissae*: Jocasta's struggle for peace is opposed to her children's unwillingness to make peace (the first part of the tragedy shows this very opposition as well) – it is clear that the form of these lines resonates with the greater meaning of the entire tragedy. This chiasmus is alternated between *manus* and *dextra*, and appears in another fragment in which the hands, in a metonymical manner, signify their owners. In the excerpt, the hands hold weapons and are willing to kill, as if it were impossible for the brothers themselves to want to kill one another; hence, a third party becomes guilty – their hands. According to Frank, in lines 438–439, "the staccato effect achieved by the asyndeton in the ascending tricolon contributes to the atmosphere of suspense, as does *vibrat* with its implication of barely controlled violence" (1995: 195).

Lines 454 and 455 demonstrate very well that the disagreement between the brothers can only be solved by themselves: *in vestra manu est,/ utrum uelitis* ("Your choice is in your hands") (Sen. *Phoen.* 454–455). In a towering anger, both brothers long for the death of each other and do not listen to Jocasta's arguments. Polynices wants to do justice and compel his brother to honour what he promised, giving him the throne; Eteocles, believing he is the only one prepared

---

2 "Conquered by a mother's prayer, the warfare has halted. Now, though keen to join battle from each side in mutual slaughter, they hold their weapons suspended, their right hands poised."

to rule, wants to remain in power. Thus, Jocasta resorts to family ties and asks the children to drop the weapons from their hands and hold her hands instead. Even so, she allows them to stay armed so that either can show trust and love for the family:

> ego utrumque peperi: ponitis ferrum ocius?/ an dico et ex quo? dexteras matri date,/ date dum piae sunt. (Sen. Phoen. 449-451)[3]
> Redde iam capulo manum,/ astringe galeam, laeva se clipeo inserat:/ dum frater exarmatur, armatus mane. (Sen. Phoen. 480-482)[4]

Polynices realises a part of his mother's wish and drops the weapon, but does not hold her hand afraid of being betrayed. He mistrusts his brother and his own mother. Eteocles does not agree to any of the requests and adds: *qui vult amari, languida regnat manu* ("One who wants to be loved rules with a feeble hand") (Sen. Phoen. 659). This is how the use of the word "hand" contributes to the development of the theme of "reason *versus* emotion".

Seneca uses the myths he found in Greek tragedy (before tragedy, these myths existed in Greek literature in general) with a didactic purpose and connects them with his philosophical ideas. The treatment of the theme of "reason *versus* emotion" in tragedies may be related to *De ira* ("On Anger") – the philosophical work of Seneca, as the *furor* in tragedies matches the concept of *ira*. This comparison is based on the fact that the feeling of *furor* of the tragic hero and the behaviour of an individual filled with anger, as described by Seneca, are very close. This is the link between his tragedies and philosophical works. To complement and define the Stoic ideas he discussed, Seneca wrote didactic plays employing aesthetic means, natural to the work of art, and highlighted those ideas.

The Stoic philosophy brings to Senecan tragedy the theme of the consequences of the actions of people who lost reason. According to Norman Pratt Jr., "stoicism contributed largely to make Senecan drama a drama of character, full of strong emotions and violence, and marked by intensity of tone: a landmark, in fact, in the development of psychological drama" (1948: 11). Pratt also adds that:

> Stoicism shaped the nature of this drama both in superficial and in fundamental ways. The influence of philosophy is much deeper than any simple correspondence between the themes of the two genres. Stoic dogma concerning evil and the conflict between reason and passion lies beneath the plays in various aspects including choral passages, concept

---

3 "I bore you both: will you lay aside your swords at once? Or must I also say from what father? Give your mother your right hands, give them while they are loyal."
4 "Then return your hand to the sword hilt, fasten on your helmet, thrust your left arm into the shield. While your brother disarms, remain under arms."

of character, introspection, and tone, to a degree which amounts to a distinctive concept of the tragic. (*ibid.* 10–11).

As stated by Zélia A. Cardoso, "for Seneca, passion makes go out of control; *furor*, triggers catastrophe" (2005: 130). And for Dupont, "ce furor se construit à partir de l'ira" (1995: 87).[5] In *De ira*, Seneca writes about anger (addressing *Novatus*, his interlocutor):

> [...] you've rightly come to fear this passion, especially and above all, as foul and frenzied. All the other passions have something calm and quiet about them; this one consists entirely in aroused assault. Raging with an inhuman desire to inflict pain in combat and shed blood in punishment, it cares nothing for itself upon the very weapons raised against it, hungry for a vengeance that will bring down the avenger too. (Sen. *De ira* I, 1, 2010: 14).[6]

In *Phoenissae*, Oedipus says he is full of anger using the following words: *tumet animus ira, fervet immensum dolor,/ maiusque quam quod casus et iuvenum furor/ conatur aliquid cupio* ("My spirit is swelling with anger, my pain is burning beyond measure, and I want some outcome greater than the random efforts of young men's madness") (Sen. *Phoen.* 352–354). The similarity between the description of anger in the philosophical work and the feeling of the tragic character characterises certain intratextual intention.[7]

Seneca uses many terms to name a person or a character possessed by anger. "*Furor*" is one of them. The word "madness" is used to describe such a feeling as well since, according to the author, "anger is a brief madness" (Sen. *De ira*, I, 1, 2010: 14). In *De ira*, Seneca shows several ways to describe anger:

> All the other categories that distinguish different kinds of anger with a differentiated terminology in Greek lack their own labels in Latin, and so I'll pass them by – though it's true that we use the terms *amarus* [bitter] and *acerbus* [harsh], as also *stomachosus* [testy] and *rabiosus* [frenzied] and *clamosus* [ranting] and *difficilis* [difficult] and *asper* [prickly], which are all different forms of anger; you can also include among these *morosus* [peevish], a hypersensitive sort of wrathfulness. Indeed, there are certain forms of anger that simmer down short of shouting, some that are both frequent and difficult to shake, some that are savagely physical and not very verbal, some that are let loose in a torrent of bitter abuse and curses; some forms don't go beyond complaining and sulking, some are deep and weighty and inward-turning. There are thousand other varieties of this polymorphous evil. (Sen. *De ira* I, 4, 2010: 18).

---

5   "This furor is built from anger".
6   The passages from *De ira* herein are all translated by Robert A. Kaster and Martha C. Nussbaum (2010).
7   It means intertextuality among works of a same author.

Seneca describes the various faces of anger in the text of *Phoenissae* using the following terms: *crudelis, cruente, dirus, execrabilis, ferox, fervidus, furens, furo, furor, incestificus, infandus, impius, invisus, ira, iratus, monstrum, nefas, nefandus, odium, pestifer, saevus, scelestus, scelus, semifer*. In addition to this, there are also contexts built through telling the myth, which suggest the feeling of furore, hatred and anger. These terms are keywords, and for Rosenmeyer "they are fused in a spirit of precipitancy; one metamorphoses into another in an irresistible rush of malign enlargement, with dire social consequences and an eventual infection of the cosmos" (1989: 74). Characters like these in *Phoenissae*, e.g. Oedipus and his sons Eteocles and Polynices, give in to atrocious attitudes which make them act thoughtlessly, against human reason. Seneca, in his philosophical work, tries to reflect on how to end anger and whether this momentary madness can be controlled, e.g. just as a doctor does when he is trying to do away with a disease (Sen. *De ira* I, 6). In Herrera's words: "los *exempla mythologica* se insertan en las tragedias senecanas para reforzar el contenido de las mismas a través de sus diferentes funciones y, todo ello, sin renunciar a su evidente valor estético" (1997: 221).[8] As a literary procedure, *exempla mythologica* "se insertan en las obras senecanas con un objeto, con una serie de funciones no excluyentes entre sí, que hemos denominado: corroborativa, contrastiva, alusiva, idealizadora y persuasiva" (Herrera 1997: 218).[9] These functions complement each other when characterising the use of mythological examples, increasing the expression of universal feelings and wishes expressed in the characters of Oedipus, Eteocles and Polynices from *Phoenissae*.

In conclusion, it might be added that in this entire context, the myth of Oedipus is related to Roman culture, as it exposes the creation of literature and the emergence of philosophical ideas during the course of the production of the work. Roman society has always lived in contact with Greek culture. In addition, the reception of Greek literature in Latin language context is more than a simple reception: we are talking about Greco-Roman literature which shared similar cultural topics. This is why for Romans it is common to use myths as illustrations of social attitudes – the imitation of Greeks is an intrinsic part of Latin literature. Seneca is a philosopher and the mythological characters in his tragedies are perfect models

---

8   "the *exempla mythologica* are inserted into the Senecan tragedies to reinforce their content through their different functions and all this without giving up their obvious aesthetic value" (translation C.M.S.).
9   "are inserted in Seneca works with an object, with several non-exclusive functions together which we have called: corroborative, contrastive, allusive, idealised and persuasive" (translation C.M.S.).

to illustrate his Stoic ideas. Anger, present in the Senecan tragedy and philosophy, is just one of many research possibilities within this vast subject.

References:

Cardoso, Zélia de Almeida. 2005. *Estudos sobre as tragédias de Sêneca*. São Paulo: Alameda.

Dupont, Florence. 1995. *Les montres de Séneque*. Paris: Berlin.

Frank, Marica. 1995. *Seneca's Phoenissae: introduction & commentary*. New York: E.J. Brill.

Herrera, Gregorio Rodríguez. 1997. "Exempla mythologica en las tragedias de Séneca". In: *Séneca dos mil años después*: Actas del Congreso Internacional Conmemorativo del bimilenario de su nacimiento. Ed. by Miguel Rodrigues Pantoja. Cordoba: Universidad de Cordoba y Cajasur.

Pratt Junior, Norman Twombly. 1948. "The Stoic Base of Senecan Drama". In *Transactions and Proceedings of the American Philological Association*, Vol. 79: 1–11. The Johns Hopkins University Press.

Rosenmeyer, Thomas Gustav. 1989. *Senecan Drama and Stoic Cosmology*. Berkeley: University of California Press.

Seneca, Lucius Annaeus. 2010. *De ira*. Trans. by Robert A. Kaster and Martha C. Nussbaum. Chicago: The University of Chicago Press.

Seneca's Tragedies. 2002. Edited with introduction and translation by John G. Fitch. London, Cambridge MA: The Loeb Classical Library.

Damian Pierzak*

Is Pelias a Mistake for Aeson? Towards a New Interpretation of Cicero's *De senectute* 23, 83

Abstract: In Cicero's philosophical dialogue *De senectute* 23, 83, the author, at first sight, seems to mistake Pelias for Aeson, attributing the miraculous rejuvenation to the former. The scholars are divided as to how this confusion should be understood. Some of them believe it is an actual error made by Cicero, others – which is even more surprising – argue for the existence of another version of the myth. Both parties pertain somehow to a passage from Plautus' play *Pseudolus*, where the same sort of alleged misrepresentation occurs. Unlike in the case of the play, so far none of the various attempts at explaining the puzzling snippet of Cicero's text have turned out convincing. No one, however, has yet paid enough attention to the internal evidence: the *persona* of Cato the Elder from *De senectute* possibly making a direct reference to the exchange of replies between Ballio and the cook from *Pseudolus*. The present article, therefore, aims above all at highlighting the role of the *decorum* in shaping the characters of participants in Cicero's dialogue.

Keywords: Cicero, myth, *De senectute*, Pelias, mistake.

Our knowledge of Greek mythology differs from that of the ancients, among other things, in that although we have access to much less material, we tend to put together all we collect from the often fragmentary or second-hand sources into handbooks and lexica, so that every piece of information can be easily checked,[1] whereas in the past one had to look through many "volumes" in order to grasp but the rudiments of the tradition. At the same time, a great deal of what is now lost still existed until the late Antiquity. Given the numerous and often vague references of Cicero to authors whose works both did and did not survive to our

---

* Independent scholar.
1 It should suffice to mention here Roscher's *Ausführliches Lexikon des griechischen und römischen Mythologie* (in six volumes, Leipzig 1884–1937), Rose's *A Handbook of Greek Mythology* (numerous editions), Gantz's *Early Greek Myth* (in two volumes = Gantz 1996) and the monumental *Lexicon iconographicum mythologiae classicae*, edited by Ackermann and Gisler in Zurich (1981–1999), with the participation of specialists from all around the globe. See in general Gantz 1996: xixf, liii, n. 1.

times,[2] as well as his reputation as an erudite among fellow citizens (cf. Aleksandrowicz 2002: 27; Wisse 2002), it is tempting to unconditionally attribute to him an acquaintance with all that we now know about the fates and deeds of mythical characters (obviously, not in the same scientific way in which they are understood in modern times). There are, however, some indications pointing to Cicero's possible mistakes in this respect, which the scholars approached with various results. In what follows, I will briefly analyse one of such potential errors in *De senectute* in a puzzling allusion to the myth of Medea, Pelias and his daughters; I will outline and assess its explanations proposed so far, and then present my own view on the problem.

Towards the end of his dialogue *On Old Age* (23 [83]), Cicero, in a sense recapitulating the previous arguments, has Cato the Elder dwell on the past and appraise his own career. It makes him wonder what he would have done if he had been given a chance to live his life anew. Although well aware of the imminence of death, Cato persists in asserting that he would not have changed a thing about his life, not to mention starting it over. He accounts for this by expressing his eagerness to be reunited with the fathers of Scipio and Laelius, his inquisitive interlocutors, and to have the opportunity of meeting other famous men of the past. He then reinforces his statement by uttering the following sentence: "Quo quidem me proficiscentem haud sane quis facile retraxerit nec tamquam Peliam recoxerit". One of the commentators of the late 19th century, Huxley (1966: 40), confined himself to explain *ad locum*: "Pelias is a mistake for Aeson", and this mythological detail, as handled by Cicero, seems to have troubled modern classicists ever since.[3] The present paper aims at addressing the question of whether Cicero actually made a mistake or maybe "confused" the two mythical characters

---

2 See e.g. *Att.* 13.38.2, 13.41.2 = Pind. fr. 213 S-M = 254 Turyn; Cic. *Mur.* 29 [60]; *Flacc.* 29 (72); *N.D.* 1.14 (36) = *SVF* 1.167 = Hes. T 119 Most, 3.19 (48); *Tusc.* 1.44 (105), 2.25 (60 f.), 3.18 (39), etc.
3 Similarly D'Agostino 1967: 150: "Si noti l'errore di Cicerone, il quale dice di Pelia quel che doveva dire di Esone". Cf. Wuilleumier 1969: 133, von Wyss 1889: 14: "[…] haben manche Erklärer […] einen mythologischen Irrthum des Plautus annehmen wollen, den auch Cicero (de senect. 23, 83) begangen habe. *Bei Cicero würde ich das eher für möglich halten* als bei Plautus […]" (emphasis added). I have been misled by Cato's words myself when I wrote (Pierzak 2015: 59, n. 3): „The story was probably recorded from memory both by Plautus and later by Cicero (Sen. 23 [83]), for both of them confuse 'the facts' in that it was Aeson 'actually' who got miraculously rejuvenated, and not Pelias". Second thoughts on the subject have instigated me to investigate these passages more thoroughly.

Is Pelias a Mistake for Aeson? 91

on purpose. In the course of this examination, as already declared, I will take a survey of past insights of scholars into this matter in order to show that no satisfactory interpretation thereof has yet been arrived at.

Apart from some other perplexities involved, the fact that Cicero would confuse two quite rudimentary characters from Greek mythology, as it were, appears unconvincing in principle. The only instance of such a mistake on his part[4] is to be found in another philosophical dialogue, namely *On Glory*, when translating a few lines from Homer (*Il.* 7.89 ff.), Cicero wrongly ascribes, as seems at first sight, the words of Hector to Ajax. This might have been just a memory lapse, for in fact two of the three verses in question are put by the Trojan prince into the mouth of a hypothetical Greek, thus perhaps making it more difficult to recall who the actual speaker was. It is rather surprising, however, as noted by Aulus Gellius, who recorded this passage of *De gloria*, that neither Cicero himself nor his freedman Tiro had later corrected this *error manifestus*.[5] A closer look at the original and Cicero's rendition allows for considering yet another possibility: as Marciniak argues, it might have been more convenient for Cicero, to swap the roles of the two men, so that instead of the victorious winner, it is the defeated one – Ajax – that speaks (Marciniak 2008: 106. Cf. Chinnici 2000: 73). "To *kill* for one's country" matched therefore his policy considerably less than "to *die* for one's country". Thus, such an understanding of the *Glor.* 2, fr. 9 Müller = *poet.* 61 Traglia (25 Blänsdorf), provides us with a general sense of how unadvised it would be to base judgement on this particular passage from the *Attic Nights* and to infer therefrom that Cicero did not know his Homer that well.

At the same time, the considered passage calls for an examination on two grounds in particular. Firstly – the playwright Plautus in *Pseudolus* seems, at first sight (again), to have committed the same mistake as Cicero. The part of the

---

4 Which does not mean, of course, that Cicero was otherwise infallible. In the year 56 BC (*Sest.* 27 [58]), for instance, he apparently mistook king Attalus II (reign: 158–138) for Eumenes II of Pergamum (reign: 197–158), for which see Kaster 2006: 249. Some ten years later, preparing his *Orator*, he realised at the last moment (*Att.* 12.6a.1) that what he would attribute to the comic poet Eupolis belonged in fact to Aristophanes (now *Orat.* 9 [29]). On the letter to Atticus, cf. Schmidt 1987: 265.
5 See Gell. 15.6.2, 4: "Quamobrem *non tam* id *mirabamur errase in ea re M. Tullium, quam non esse animadversum* hoc postea *correctumque* vel ab ipso vel a Tirone, liberto eius, diligentissimo homine et librorum patroni sui studiosissimo. [...] Huius autem sententiae versus, quos Cicero in linguam Latinam vertit, non Aiax apud Homerum dicit, [...] sed Hector dicit [...]" (Emphasis added). On Tiro's role in the editorial revision of Cicero's works see Zetzel 1973: 231–233, 241 f.; Gurd 2007: 53. Cf. Reynolds and Wilson 1991: 30 f.

text of where it occurs, however, has, in my opinion, already been satisfactorily explained (see next paragraph). Secondly – much less attention, in comparison with the corresponding portion of Plautus' comedy, has been paid to the motif of rejuvenation in *De senectute*. Thus, answering the question whether one of the most educated figures of his time was likely to confound some basic facts regarding a myth would enrich our knowledge about the reception of Greek myths in the late republican Rome in general.

The best point of departure is Plautus' comedy, for it will soon become clear that the two alleged errors should not be looked at separately. The allusion in the form which we came across in Cicero's work can be traced back to the fragment in Plautus' *Pseudolus*, where we encounter the cook boasting in front of Ballio that with his broth he can make him young again, just as Medea had rejuvenated Pelias (Pl. *Ps.* 868–872, emphasis added):

{Coc.} Quia sorbitione faciam ego hodie te mea, | *item ut Medea Peliam concoxit senem*, | quem medicamento et suis venenis dicitur | fecisse rursus ex sene adulescentulum, | item ego te faciam.

The ways of solving this crux suggested by scholars base on two conflicting lines of reasoning. First – the poet simply committed a mistake; second – and more controversial – there had been some other version of the myth, which is no longer available to us. Lorenz (cf. Forehand 1972: 293) made a suggestion that Plautus may have intentionally made one of his characters confuse the mythological tradition.[6] This idea was rejected by Fraenkel (2007: 308, n. 56) in his classical work *Plautinisches im Plautus*, although he did not feel obliged to put forward any counterarguments. An alternative explanation, however, was taken up by Forehand, who made an attempt to examine the passage basing on evidence from within the dramatic structure of the play. What he believes Platus intended to convey is part of a sarcastic exchange of replies between the *leno* and the cook and, moreover, that both characters understood each other's clever retorts. As Forehand (1972: 297) notes:

He defends himself against Ballio's slanders by saying that he will rejuvenate the *leno* as Medea did Pelias. But Medea had Pelias cut into pieces and boiled to death, and that is just the point: the cook's implication forms a clever rebuttal to his employer's charges against him and his profession.

---

6 Lorenz's edition of Plautus appeared in 1876. Somewhat later the ironical tone was detected, probably independently, by von Wyss (1889: 14) to whom Otto replied (1962: 271, n. 2): "Nach v. Wyss, […] liegt bei Plautus vielmehr Ironie zu Grunde, was ich bezweifle […]".

The solution is helpful not only because it provides a key to the reading of the *Pseudolus* segment in question, but mainly because it excludes Ciceronian *De senectute* from sort of a circular argumentation, which can be briefly summarised in the following way: for the most part, the statement of Cato the Elder has been used *a priori* to prove either that Plautus could have made an error since a learned man like Cicero did or, conversely, that there must have been another version of the myth, the only preserved references to which can be found, apart from the comedy, in the dialogue *On Old Age*. As a matter of fact, it seems odd that the scholars have more often used *Sen.* 23 (83) while trying to explain *Ps.* 868–872 and not the other way around.

There is no strong enough evidence based on the preserved body of Greek literature to support the view that there might have been a parallel story in which Medea acted benevolently towards Pelias, as is noticed by a recent commentator – Powell (1988: 263) – who, however, seems to have misrepresented the hypothesis of Dugas. The French scholar indeed admitted a possibility of the existence of an alternative version of the myth, but in making such a stand he relied on the text of the *Pseudolus* alone: "Aucun autre texte, à ma connaissance, ne fait allusion à un rejeunissement *réussi* de Pélias, et peut-être y a-t-il erreur, confusion de Plaute ou de l'auteur grec qu'il a suivi [original emphasis]". His ideas were effectively confronted by Meyer and, moreover, it has already been shown that there is another sound explanation open for Plautus' passage.[7] More impeding for the present considerations would be a fragment of *Menippean Satire* of Cicero's contemporary, Varro (*Men.* fr. 285 Bücheler), where it reads that Pelias insisted on Medea to make him young at any price: "Pelian Medeae permisisse, ut se vel vivum deglueret, dum modo redderet puellum". Be that as it may, neither this nor the relevant section of *De senectute*, basing on the context and the wording, points to anything more than just an attempt at rejuvenation, not necessarily an efficient one.[8]

Some scholars were inclined to think (e.g. Ostermayer 1884: 44, as referred to by Fraenkel 2007: 308, n. 55) that Cicero mistook the two characters *because* he

---

7   As illustrated above. For an alternative version, see Dugas 1944: 8 (cf. n. 4 and Forhand 1972: 295) and Meyer 1980: 113 ("Die Unhaltbarkeit der Thesen von Dugas ist mit wenig Mühe nachzuweisen"). For the mythological tradition regarding Medea and Pelias, cf. Gantz 1993: 365–368 and Meyer 1980.
8   Nevertheless, cf. V. Fl. 6.443 ff.: "mutat agros fluviumque vias [*scil.* Medea], †suus † alligat ignis, | †cuncta sopor† *recolit fessos aetate parentes* | datque alias sine lege colus [...]" (emphasis added). *Fessos parentes*, however, may be read as a poetical plural as well.

had read Plautus. To Fraenkel, who was the most prominent adherent of the "mistake" line of reasoning, the idea of a direct influence seemed out of the question. In the case of Cicero, he would postulate that "imprecise recollection or carelessness are the cause of the confusion [as translated by Drevikovsky and Muecke]" (Fraenkel 2007: 61; similarly D'Agostino 1967: 150). As a result, some of those who do not believe that such an author would let himself commit this kind of error take it as evidence for the existence of an alternative version of the myth. "And the vicious circle completes" – one cannot help noticing. Another possibility was tentatively offered by Forehand (1972: 295 following Dugas 1944: 8, n. 4). In his brilliant study of the *Pseudolus* passage, to which I have already referred earlier, he argues that Cicero might have only meant an *attempt* at rejuvenation and, undoubtedly, this was the actual case in mythological tradition, regardless of its outcome. Apart from such understanding, which was already hinted at above, there have been two more different lines of interpretation, which I shall now briefly outline.

One of the interpretations goes back to the old German school of philology, which pointed out more than once that what we are dealing with may have some proverbial connotations. The most recognizable, proponent of this view is Otto, the author of a useful collection of Latin *Sprichwörter*. Referring to both sentences, he claims (1962: 271; cf. von Wyss 1889: loc. cit.; D'Agostino 1967: 150; Meyer 1980: 115, n. 63) that their authors were probably relying on a Greek *paroemia* preserved by Zenobius, i.e. λούσαιο τὸν Πελίαν (Zen. 4.92), which may be literally rendered as "may you have a bath like Pelias"[9], meaning "may you get cut into pieces and boiled to death" or, in other words, "I wish something very bad which you did not see coming happens to you". Had the old Cato, as presented by Cicero, have this particular proverb in mind, however, he would have probably expressed himself differently. Moreover, this interpretation does not help to solve the actual problem, namely the motif of rejuvenation. The above-quoted fragment of Varro, ignored (or overlooked) by both Otto and Dugas, would provide far better evidence to support the hypothesis of a proverbial origin of Pelias' words. At least one parallel for the present context can be drawn on the basis of other philosophical writings known to us. In his works *On the Ends of Good and Evil* and *Tusculan Disputations*, Cicero avails himself of the myth of Endymion in a way betraying an influence of a proverb derived from Greek literary tradition

---

9 On the meaning cf. Zen. 4.92 = [Plut.] *De proverbiis Alexandrinorum*, fr. 13 Crusius: αὕτη ἡ παροιμία προήχθη ἐκ τῶν συμβεβηκότων τῷ Πελίᾳ· [...] ἐλούσαντο δὲ καὶ ἄλλοι πολλοὶ κακῶς; Apostol. 10.77; Diogenian. 6.6. The translation and the paraphrases are my own.

which later must have become a "popular saying" (*locutio trita*) in Latin.[10] And since we know that one of the *Menippean Satires* ascribed to Varro was entitled *Endymiones* (fr. 101–108 Bücheler), and that a common feature of this genre was to parody Greek myths (Styka 1994: 75), we can assume the existence of a certain proverb relating to the story of Pelias and Medea to which both authors of the late republican Rome had alluded. This would be only a partial explanation though, allowing for a good deal of imagination and supposition.

The last interpretation of which I am aware of was put forward by Meyer, the author of a comprehensive study of the myth of Medea and the daughters of Pelias. Taking into account Varro's fragment, to which I have called attention above, he assumes (1980: 116–119) that the scene of Pelias passionately begging Medea to make him younger could have been a part of the plot of some no longer existing comedy or satyr play. If that is the case, then, according to his view, both Plautus and Cicero would have alluded to this literary work. Cato of the *De senectute*, however, would not only not ask for the same, whatever in fact befell the "dramatic Pelias", but he would also strongly refuse had such an offer been made to him. The second sentence of the passage under discussion, i.e. "et si quis deus mihi largiatur ut ex hac aetate repuerascam et in cunis vagiam, valde recusem nec vero velim quasi decurso spatio ad carceres a calce revocari", is then invoked as additional support. Meyer's solution seems by far the most acceptable one, for it neither requires to charge Cicero with committing such an embarrassing mistake nor demands to excuse him by searching for an alternative version of the myth for the existence of which there is no evidence at all.[11] This solution, however, can be disputed on two grounds. For one thing, the response given by the cook to Ballio in the *Pseudolus* is better explained by its ironical tone, and secondly – it still requires making an assumption about a hypothetical play, which did not stand the test of time. In fact, the only "significant" evidence of its existence is based on a sentence from a *Satire*, which is itself completely devoid of any context, and it

---

10 See Cic. *Fin.* 5.20 (55) *ad fin.* and *Tusc.* 1.38 (92). For a detailed discussion of that myth, cf. Pierzak 2016. For the Greek proverbs on mythological themes in Rome, see e.g. Otto 1962: xxvii and passim.
11 Constant efforts are being made to prove the contrary. Apart from the article of Dugas (1944) listed in the bibliography below, who bases *his* evidence on the archeological records, cf. also the following statement, which I cannot help myself from quoting (von Wyss 1889: 14, n. 2): "Wie mir Herr Prof. Hitzig mittheilt, *hat Herr Prof. Sauppe einmal in einer Vorlesung die Vermuthung geäussert*, der Widerspruch erkläre sich wohl daraus, dass es im Alterthum zwei verschiedene Traditionen betreffend diese Sage gegeben habe" (emphasis added).

would perhaps be more likely that its author simply made reference to a proverbial expression. Meyer himself (1980: 120 f.) admits that his answer to the problem is only "a possibility": "Zum mindesten *die Möglichkeit* sollte als erwiesen gelten, daß ein solches Stück [*scil.* some comedy or satyr play on the subject – D.P.] einmal existiert hat und daß Plautus, Varro und Cicero darauf Bezug nehmen [emphasis added]".

Finally, since the question remains unsolved, I will share my own view of where this alleged error in the dialogue *On Old Age* may have come from. All the scholarly discussions which I previously reviewed are mainly focused either on other texts or on the myth itself, thus approaching the matter somewhat incidentally. My intention is to lay more stress on the philosophical work itself, its author, and its protagonist.

The dramatic action of *De senectute* is set in the year 150 BC (Cic. *Sen.* 5 [14]; Philippson 1939: 1163; Wuilleumier 1969: 12, 91). Young Scipio Aemilianus and Caius Laelius, aged thirty-five and thirty-eight respectively, inquire the eighty-four year old main protagonist, M. Porcius Cato, of his impressions about growing old and senility. Cicero made every effort to accommodate his *persona* both to his age and to his character. This would involve, among other things, an attempt to archaise the language of the dialogue as well as the way in which the main character expresses himself.[12] Such was a common practice of the great orator, who was fully aware of the requirements imposed on him within the standards of the *ethopoiia* or *sermocinatio*, i.e. to adjust the speech of a person whose role one is currently playing to its characteristics (Alfonsi 1955 = 1971: 209, 227 f.; Styka 1997: 33, 48. On the *senilis declamatio*, cf. Douglas 2002: 198). It would apply equally to the orations and the philosophical or rhetorical treatises. An example can be drawn from the dialogue *On Duties* where readers are reminded that not every utterance befits every person. "Let them hate, so but they fear [tr. Gardner]" ("oderint, dum metuant"), for instance, is not what one would expect to hear from Aeacus or Minos, but it would be appropriate to say for Atreus (Cic. *Off.* 1.28 [97]): "ut si Aeacus aut Minos diceret 'oderint dum metuant' […] indecorum videretur, quod eos fuisse iustos accepimus; at Atreo dicente plausus excitantur, *est enim digna persona oratio*" (emphasis added). Though these words relate in the most part to poetic *decorum*, it can safely be conjectured that Cicero

---

12 Among the most conspicuous examples of archaisms are the superlative forms with short 'u' instead of short 'i' (e.g. *optumam, maxumum,* etc.) or *gerundiva* where 'e' is replaced with 'u' (e.g. *a rebus gerundis…*), as in the fossilised names of the pontifical colleges, e.g. *quindecimviri sacris faciundis*. See Wuilleumier 1969: 56 f. with references, and on grammar cf. now Wolanin 2015: 84.

himself was particular about depicting precisely the characters of the interlocutors engaged in philosophical discourse in his writings. In the year 45 BC he wrote to his friend Atticus reporting on his progress in the work on *Academica*. He had transferred the parts previously intended for Catulus, Lucullus and Hortensius to Varro, Brutus and Cato (the Younger), for it seemed to him that the former would not be suited to such a conversation (*Att.* 13.16.1):

> Illam ᾿Ακαδεμικὴν σύνταξιν totam ad Varronem traduximus. Primo fuit Catuli, Luculli, Hortensi. Deinde, quia παρὰ τὸ πρέπον videbatur, quod erat hominibus nota non illa quidem ἀπαιδευσία sed in iis rebus ἀτριψία, simul ac veni ad villam, eosdem illos sermones ad Catonem Brutumque transtuli.[13]

This was, by the way, still an intermediate form. Later on, the roles of Brutus and Cato were taken over by Cicero himself and Atticus. Seen, therefore, in this perspective, even if we detect an error concerning any "factual" detail, it does not necessarily have to be due to a misrepresentation: It could be a part of Cicero impersonating somebody else.

It is now known that *Pseudolus* was first presented to the public on the occasion of the dedication of the Temple of Magna Mater in the year 191 BC, and it is implied in *De senectute* itself,[14] that Cato the Elder attended the accompanying games (Manuwald 2011: 57; cf. Liapis et al. 2013: 21 with references).[15] Cicero, for his part, had been a friend of Roscius, the greatest performer of comedy in the times of the Republic, who had in his vast repertoire of performed roles, among

---

13 See on this passage esp. Gurd 2007: 71–74, who discusses also similar threads of Cicero's correspondence. Cf. Dyck 1996: 255 f.; Tyrrell and Purser 1915: 127; Schmidt 1987: 318, 367. In the dialogue *On the Orator*, on the other hand, Cicero asks future readers in advance not to expect from his Crassus as much as they could have expected from the real person (3.4 [15]): "[...] nos postulamus [...] a ceteris, qui haec in manus sument, maius ut quiddam de L. Crasso, quam quantum a nobis exprimetur, suspicentur."
14 Cic. *Sen.* 14 (50): "Quid in levioribus studiis, sed tamen acutis? *quam gaudebat* Bello suo Punico Naevius! Quam Truculento *Plautus*, quam *Pseudolo*! Vidi etiam senem Livium, qui, cum sex annis ante quam ego natus sum fabulam docuisset Centone Tuditanoque consulibus, usque ad adulescentiam meam processit aetate" (emphases added).
15 The information concerning the date of the production of the *Pseudolus* we owe to the stage directions (*didascalia*), probably Varro's *de actis scaenicis* (or *de scaenicis actionibus*), preserved in some of the manuscripts of Plautus' plays. There are scholars who believe that Cic. *Sen.* 14 (50) is based on such material still available to Cicero. See esp. Deufert 2002: 88, who quotes Powell 1988 *ad loc*. Cf. Leo 1895: 70 f., Segal 1987: 123, 262, n. 41 with references.

many others, the role of Ballio (cf. Duckworth 1994: 70). At the same time, from the speech *In Defense of Quintus Roscius the Comedian* we learn that the orator had anything but superficial knowledge of *Pseudolus* (cf. Beacham 1999: 5, 256, n. 8). And even if the historical Cato did not watch the performance live, it would have no bearing on the text of the dialogue whatsoever. Because between the actual *ludi Megalenses* and the discussion held by M. Porcius there is an interval of over forty years, the author, perhaps on purpose, gives his readers a clue as to how the words of Cato spoken towards the end should be perceived. This would mean that he expected his audience to be familiar with Plautus' play and to be aware that his protagonist was familiar with it too. This being so, anyone who understood both the ironical tone of the comedy and the allusion to the games could at the same time imagine Cato the Elder loosely referring to the cook's lines, as would be appropriate of a witty old man addressing his younger fellows with a kind of avuncular sense of humour. Moreover, in *De oratore*, there is a passage in which Cicero has Crassus recall his father-in-law's anecdote about Scipio's and Laelius' leisure in the countryside (2.6 [22]): "Saepe ex socero meo audivi, cum is diceret socerum suum Laelium semper fere cum Scipione solitum rusticari *eosque incredibiliter repuerascere esse solitos*, cum rus ex urbe tamquam e vinculis evolavissent" (emphasis added). What draws attention is the wording used to describe how much the relaxation from the problems one is exposed to in a big city would make them feel like boys once again (*incredibiliter repuerascere*). Perhaps, it is not a mere coincidence, especially since these are the only two occurrences of that word in what survived of his writings (cf. Merguet 1997: 627 s.v. and *OLD*, s.v.).

As for Cato, even if he was not the author of the *Apophthegmata*, Cicero would attribute the collection to him, thereby recognizing the man as witty, facetious and urbane (Cic. *Off.* 1.29 [104]; cf. Styka 1990: 281, 285). It would follow then that what Cato says in the discussed section to some extent corresponds to how the author of the dialogue pictured both the protagonist and his interlocutors. As for Cicero, every time he referred to the myth of Medea, he had some Latin drama in mind.[16] This was probably so because it would best suit the tastes of his addressees, and because it was the way he himself preferred. Why then allude to some obscure version of the myth which, if ever existed, did

---

16 Most often it was the prologue of Ennius' *Medea* (based on Euripides' version): *Inv.* 1.91, *Cael.* 8 (18), *N.D.* 3.30 (75), *Top.* 61 (see also § 35), on which cf. e.g. Jocelyn 1967: 114 f. In the *Tusculan Disputations* Medea is adduced as an example of misery (3.26 [63] – Ennius) and passionate love (4.32 [69] – same playwright). In *Man.* 9 (22) there is an indirect reference to a tragedy (*trag. inc.* 165–171 R.³ = Cic. *N.D.* 3.26 [67]).

not even survive, and not to a play known to an average Roman, perhaps seen by the protagonist of Cicero's dialogue, and performed by the famous actor who Cicero was friends with?

At this point I would like to sum up the main issues which have been touched upon herein, so that my conclusions become sufficiently explicit. I have demonstrated that the author of the *De senectute* was certainly not omniscient, but, at the same time, that he sometimes intentionally distorted the facts in order to manipulate his recipients. It is not necessarily the case when it comes to the myth of Pelias and his daughters. During the past one hundred years of scholarship, both the theory of an alternative version of the myth and the theory of Cicero committing a mistake have been efficiently rejected. Some other explanations of the puzzling passage of the dialogue *On Old Age* have been suggested, but each of them, to a bigger or smaller extent, depended on suppositions. It would be tempting just to dismiss the problem by saying that what the author wished to convey was only an unsuccessful attempt at rejuvenation (Forehand 1972: 295), but the possibility of another interpretation has emerged. It requires bringing together a few facts: First, Cato the Elder may have seen the stage performance of *Pseudolus* in 191 BC, and if he had not, the play was probably well-known to him regardless; second, following the rules of the literary *decorum* should be listed among the most significant principles of Cicero's literary arsenal; third, the scene of Scipio and Laelius "miraculously getting younger" which Cicero had devised some ten years earlier may have reminded him somehow of the Plautus' passage. Given all this, interpreting "Cato's" allusion as a direct reference to the play seems to best solve the considered problem. It does not require assuming the existence of an alternative version of the myth, a misrepresentation on Cicero's part, or the existence of some hypothetical comedy or satyr play. There is something more though: the suggested interpretation complies with Cicero's observing of the rules of appropriateness. And, of course, it does not mean, like Ostermayer had it, that Cicero made an error because he had read the playwright's work; on the contrary, neither of them was mistaken. We must remember that in both cases it was not the author himself speaking *ex persona propria*. What Cicero did was taking up the irony of *Pseudolus* in order to render his Cato more genuine, thus conforming to the rules of the broadly conceived *decorum*.

Cf. 3.28 [71]), made either by Ennius (*Medea exul*) or Accius (*Medea sive Argonautae*), perhaps reflected as well in *N.D.* 3.19 (48). See also *Fam.* 7.6 (a letter addressed to Trebatius).

References:

Aleksandrowicz, Tadeusz. 2002. *Kultura intelektualna rzymskich konsulów w schyłkowym okresie republiki*. Katowice: Wydawnictwo Uniwersytetu Śląskiego.

Alfonsi, Luigi. 1955. "Il pensiero ciceroniano nel De senectute". In: Studi Litterari in onore di Giulio Sentini, Palermo: U. Manfredi. 1–16. Reproduced as Idem. 1971. "Das ciceronische Denken in ›De senectute‹". In: Das neue Cicerobild, ed. by K. Büchner. Darmstadt: Wissenschaftliche Buchgesellschaft. 208–228.

Beacham, Richard C. 1999. *Spectacle Entertainments of Early Imperial Rome*. New Haven–London: Yale University Press.

Chinnici, Valentina. 2000. *Cicerone interprete di Omero. Un capitolo di storia della traduzione artistica*. Napoli: Loffredo.

D'Agostino, Vittorio. 1967. *M. Tullio Cicerone. Cato maior de senectute*. Torino: Società Editrice Internazionale.

Deufert, Marcus. 2002. *Textgeschichte und Rezeption der plautinischen Komödien im Altertum*. Berlin – New York: Walter de Gruyter.

Douglas, Alan E. 2002. "Form and Content in the *Tusculan Disputations*". In *Cicero the Philosopher. Twelve Papers*, edited by Jonathan G. F. Powell. Oxford–New York: OUP. 197–218.

Duckworth, George E. 1994. *The Nature of Roman Comedy. A Study in Popular Entertainment*. Norman: University of Oklahoma Press (first published in Princeton: PUP 1952).

Dugas, Charles. 1944. "Le premier crime de Médée". *Revue des Études Anciennes* 46: 5–11.

Dyck, Andrew R. 1996. *A Commentary on Cicero, De Officiis*. Ann Arbor: The University of Michigan Press.

Forehand, Walter E. 1972. "*Pseudolus* 868–872: Ut Medea Peliam Concoxit". *Classical Journal* 67: 293–298.

Fraenkel, Eduard. 2007. *Plautine Elements in Plautus*. Trans. by Tomas Drevikovsky and Frances Muecke, Oxford–New York: OUP. Originally published as *Plautinisches im Plautus*. Berlin: Weidmann 1922 (Italian version: *Elementi Plautini in Plauto*. Tr. F. Munari, Firenze: La Nuova Italia 1960).

Gantz, Timothy. 1993. *Early Greek Myth. A Guide to Literary and Artistic Sources*. Vol. I, Baltimore–London: The Johns Hopkins University Press.

Gurd, Sean. 2007. "Cicero and Editorial Revision". In *Classical Antiquity* 26: 49–80.

Huxley, Leonard. 1966. *Cicero. Cato maior de senectute*. Oxford: OUP (repr. of the 1887 edition).

Jocelyn, Henry D. 1967. *The Tragedies of Ennius*. Cambridge: CUP.

Kaster, Robert A. 2006. *Marcus Tullius Cicero. Speech on Behalf of Publius Sestius*. Oxford: OUP.

Leo, Friedrich. 1895. *Plautinische Forschungen. Zur Kritik und Geschichte der Komödie*. Berlin: Weidmannsche Buchhandlung.

Liapis, Vayos et al. 2013. "Introduction: Making Sense of Ancient Performance". In *Performance in Greek and Roman Theatre*, edited by Vayos Liapis, George W. M. Harrison. Leiden–Boston: Brill. 1–42.

Manuwald, Gesine. 2011. *Roman Republican Theatre*. Cambridge: CUP.

Marciniak, Katarzyna. 2008. *Cicero vortit barbare. Przekłady mówcy jako narzędzie manipulacji ideologicznej*. Gdańsk: słowo/obraz terytoria.

Merguet, Hugo. 1997. *Handlexikon zu Cicero*. Hildesheim–Zürich–New York: Georg Olms (reprint of the Leipzig 1905–1906 edition).

Meyer, Hugo. 1980. *Medeia und die Peliaden. Eine attische Novelle und ihre Entstehung. Ein Versuch zur Sagenforschung auf archäologischer Grundlage*. Roma: Giorgio Bretschneider.

Ostermayer, Friedrich. 1884. *De historia fabulari in comoediis Plautinis*. Diss. Greifswald (Greifswald: Pohle).

Otto, August 1962 *Die Sprichwörter und sprichwörtlichen Redensarten der Römer*. Hildesheim: Georg Olms (repr. of the Leipzig 1890 edition).

Philippson, Robert. 1939. "M. Tullius Cicero: Philosophische Schriften". In: *RE* 7A1, coll. 1104–1192. Stuttgart: Alfred Druckenmüller.

Pierzak, Damian. 2015. "A Reading of Greek Myth in Cicero's Speeches. The Case of Medea". In: Ancient Myths in the Making of Culture, ed. by M. Budzowska, J. Czerwińska. Frankfurt a. M.: Peter Lang. 57–66.

—.2016. "Metaforyzacja mitu w literaturze Rzymu późnorepublikańskiego. Na przykładzie Endymiona". *Symbolae Philologorum Posnaniensium Graecae et Latinae* 26.1: 77–92.

Powell, Jonathan G. F. 1988. *Cicero. Cato maior de senectute*. Cambridge–New York–Port Chester–Melbourne–Sydney: CUP.

Reynolds, Leighton D., Wilson, Nigel G. ⁵1991. *Scribes and Scholars. A Guide to the Transmission of Greek and Latin Literature*. Oxford: OUP.

Schmidt, Otto E. 1987. *Der Briefwechsel des M. Tullius Cicero von seinem Prokonsulat in Cilicien bis zu Caesars Ermordung*. Hildesheim–Zürich–New York: Georg Olms (repr. of the Leipzig: B. G. Teubner 1893 edition).

Segal, Erich. 1987. *Roman Laughter. The Comedy of Plautus*. New York–Oxford: OUP.

Styka, Jerzy. 1990. "Estetyka komedii rzymskiej w pismach Cycerona". *Meander* 10–12: 279–292.

—.1994. *Studia nad literaturą rzymską epoki republikańskiej. Estetyka satyry republikańskiej; estetyka neoteryków*. Kraków: Wydawnictwo Uniwersytetu Jagiellońskiego.

—.1997. *Estetyka stosowności* (decorum) *w literaturze rzymskiej*. Kraków: PAU.

Tyrrell, Robert Y. and Purser, Louis C. 1915. *The Correspondence of M. Tullius Cicero*. Vol. V, Dublin: Hodges, Figgis–London: Longmans, Green.

von Wyss, Wilhelm. 1889. *Die Sprichwörter bei den römischen Komikern*. Zürich: Friedrich Schulthess.

Wisse, Jakob. 2002. "The Intellectual Background of Cicero's Rhetorical Works". In: *Brill's Companion to Cicero. Oratory and Rhetoric*. Ed. by James M. May, 331–374. Leiden–Boston–Köln: Brill.

Wolanin, Hubert. 2015. *Gramatyka opisowa klasycznej łaciny w ujęciu strukturalnym*. Kraków: Księgarnia Akademicka.

Wuilleumier, Pierre. 1969. *Cicéron. Caton L'Ancien (de la vieillesse)*. Paris: Les Belles Lettres.

Zetzel, James E. G. 1973. "*Emendavi ad Tironem*: Some Notes on Scholarship in the Second Century A. D.". *Harvard Studies in Classical Philology* 77: 225–243.

Hanna Zalewska-Jura[*]
Mythical Motifs in Early Byzantine Epigrams

Abstract: In the Early Byzantine writings from the 6th and 7th century, during which Christian thought permeated and influenced literature, the epigram seems to have appeared as a literary relic of the past. Moreover, the *Cycle* of Agathias Scholasticus elicited a certain revival of the epigram in its classical form and content (as "classical" the author refers to the epigrams composed in the Hellenistic period as well as the time of the Roman Empire, i.e. during the acme of the genre), in which the Greek poet collected the works of his own, but also of other, contemporary poets. A striking characteristic of the traditionalism of these poets, also comprising the followers of the new religion, is their use of references to the world of pagan myths. A few examples will allow us to recognize the purpose of revoking the motifs of past legends and beliefs, as well as the messages they conveyed.

Keywords: mythical motifs, Greek epigram, Early Byzantine literature.

Nearly all Early Byzantine writings[1] are permeated by the spirit of Christianity. This also refers to poetry, especially the so-called secular poetry, which reflected the quotidian social life along with its religious aspects (Jurewicz 1984: 81). In this regard, the epigram appears as a unique literary form. The genre exceeded the iconic themes of literature of that time and returned to the contents and artistic form it had achieved in its heyday, i.e. the Hellenistic and Roman periods. Noticeably, this was due to the poets-erudites such as Agathias Scholasticus. It is to him that we owe the collection and composition of an anthology containing his own works, as well as those of his contemporaries, entitled the *Cycle*, which he based on the *Garlands* of Meleager of Gadara and Philippus of Thessalonica. At the end of the 10th century, this work became a significant structural element of the collection known today as the *Palatine Anthology*.

Although the times of Christianity's aggressive expansion and destruction of all pagan manifestations were a thing of the past (Bowra 1970: 253–256), the fact that the ideas which only recently had been zealously exterminated by fanatic believers of Christ became revived in the epigram, can be considered as the triumph of humanism over pertinacious forms of fideism. The biographies of other poets surrounding Agathias, such as Paulus Silentarius, Macedonius Consul, Julian

---

[*] University of Lodz, Poland.
[1] As "Early Byzantine" I understand the period between 527–610, according to the periodisation proposed by Jurewicz 1984: 23–30.

of Egypt, Eratosthenes Scholasticus, Isidorus Scholasticus, Julianus Antikensor and many others, are not known to us. Nevertheless, it is difficult to ascribe to them pagan views, since they accompanied the royal court of the emperor of Constantinople, Justinian the Great. It was these poets, who having been taught in schools of rhetoric to respect the intellectual and artistic achievements of Antiquity, recognized this literary genre as a suitable means of expressing their own poetic passions and made many efforts to achieve a degree of sophistication in the language, metrical form,[2] content and artistic devices, which would make their poetry worthy of the works from the Hellenistic and Roman periods.

Among the *topoi* of the classical epigram are references to the world of myths (Kobus-Zalewska 1998). Interestingly enough, Byzantine poets did not avoid using mythical motifs as well. The adduced examples discussed below will allow us to evaluate the degree of their originality (or epigonism) in relation to past literary canons.

The device of imitation belonged to the tradition of declamatory epigrams. For instance, the relation model → imitation appears between epigram VI 1 ascribed to Plato, and three of its variants by Julian of Egypt (VI 18, 19, 20). In Plato's dedicatory poem, the famous courtesan Lais[3] offers her mirror to Aphrodite saying: "I wish not to look on myself as I am, and cannot look on myself as I once was".[4] Julian, however, juxtaposes the passing beauty of a young woman with the eternal beauty of Cypris (VI 18) who, *nota bene*, is also presented as the giver of female charm (VI 18, 19). In the imitation epigrams, despite their seemingly trivial topic (an aging courtesan, who gives back her mirror, a witness of her past looks, to the divine creator of beauty), we may notice elements of Plato's concept of Ideas and their reflection in the mutable and imperfect reality (Stumpo 1926: 188). It is well known that Plato's concept, transformed in Neoplatonism, did not become out-of-date in the Christianised Byzantine philosophy of the 6th century. Such an interpretation of Julian's works allows us to recognize the role of the mythical element (Aphrodite being the embodiment of ideal beauty) in new philosophical-theological contexts.

---

2   At the time, the language underwent alterations to such a degree that classical Greek became a "book language", comprehensible only to the intellectual elite. As a result, the phonetic transformations made the old metrical systems obsolete, cf. Wellesz 2006: 96.
3   In highest probability this is Lais of Corinth, who is mentioned by Diogenes Laertius in connection with Aristippus of Cyrene (II 74–75).
4   In this paper, the passages of epigrams are cited from the edited texts and English translation by Paton 1916–1918.

A similar sequence of imitations opens the exemplary work of the 1st century BC poet, Philippus of Thessalonica, in which a certain Callimenes, after having his sight veiled by old age, gives back his writing tools to the Muses (VI 62). We may also find the same name of the given offering, as well as the same recipient of the gifts offered, in the poem of Paulus Silentarius (VI 66). Curiously, in the other versions written by Byzantine poets (Damocharis VI 63, Paulus Silentatius VI 64, 65, Julian of Egypt VI 67, 68), Hermes becomes the recipient of the dedications of the poets – "emeriti" (Ławińska-Tyszkowska 1997: 61). Beniamino Stumpo explains such a large number of declamatory epigrams composed by scribes with the significance of their profession at the time: "Gli epigrammi ci dimonstrano quale importanza si desse in quell'epoca, ai copisti, che sin dal tempo dell'imperatore Valente erano assunti al grado di funzionari stipendiati e rispettati" (1926: 191–192).

Although dedicating the tools of a writer to the Muses may seem understandable, for instance, due to their association with certain traditional writing attributes (Calliope – wax tablet, stylus; Clio – scroll) as well as their relation to literature, having Hermes as the main recipient of similar dedications is not so evident. Certainly, the source of associating Hermes with writing may be found in the Late Hellenistic syncretic combination of the Greek god with the Egyptian Thoth, due to which Hermes received the name Trismegistus and was also worshipped as Hermes Logios, the patron of speech, writing, science and occult wisdom (Eliade 1988: 193–194). In this respect, we may notice that the references made by the Byzantine poets to this less popular function of the god followed, on the one hand, the manner typical for the Hellenistic period, which strived for originality. On the other, however, they appeared as a specific *signum temporis*, which reflected the growing significance of scribes in Byzantine society.

An example of abandoning the mythical stereotype can be found in an epigram of Macedonius, in which old Daphnis gives back to Pan his shepherd's stick, as he retires from his profession (VI 73). The poet relinquishes the version of the story containing the premature death of the legendary herdsman, as presented in the works of Stesichorus and Theocritus,[5] and also shatters the bucolic symbolism of a young, beautiful and talented shepherd which was popularised by Vergil (e.g. *Ecl.* II 25–28). The image of an old Daphnis, holding a cane in his hand, trying to play on the syrinx in a skilful manner, as he used to in his youth, takes a more realistic tone, albeit maintaining the bucolic *entourage*.

---

5   In a lost poem of Stesichorus, young Daphnis is punished with death for his infidelity to the nymph Nomia, whereas Theocritus (*Id.* I) presents him as a victim of Cypris.

In the examples adduced above, we may distinguish the motif of senility: an aging courtesan, the "emeriti" scribes, an old Daphnis. Isidorus Scholasticus gracefully applies this motif in a love context in his melancholic dedicatory epigram (VI 58):

> Thy friend Endymion, O Moon, dedicates to thee, ashamed, his bed that survives in vain and its futile cover; for grey hair reigns over his whole head and no trace of his former beauty is left.

According to the legend, the eternal slumber of Endymion, a gift from the enamoured Selene, was supposed to preserve his youth and beauty. Yet, in the rational approach of Isidorus, it is not about Endymion's eternal slumber, but about his love to the goddess remaining unrequited due to a long wait for his beloved, and the passing of time which brought the greying of hair and all the other shortcomings of old age.

Love, in particular, belongs to the category of themes which facilitate our search for parallels with mythical motifs. In an amatory epigram by Paulus Silentarius, the situation he describes reflects the story of the death of Glauce (V 288). The lyrical I of the poem speaks of his being affected with internal fire after a girl has placed a garland on his head during a banquet. Hence, he supposes that the same "fiery" garland must have scorched the body of Glauce. According to the well-known version popularised by Euripides, Glauce burned to her death from adorning a robe she received from the envious Medea. The poet, however, made a minor modification of the motif in order to depict the relation between the myth and the situational model.

A similar alteration of a mythical motif may be found in the witty poem of Agathias Scholasticus (V 289). The lyrical I is in love with a young girl who is watched over by a very old and stern woman. The desperate lover addresses Persephone: "If it be true, Persephone, that thou didst love Adonis, pity the pain of our mutual passion and grant us both one favour. Deliver the girl from the old woman before she meets with some mischance". Due to the fact that the old chaperon, "thrice as old as the oldest crow (…) has often (…) got a new lease of life", obstructs the young couple's happiness, the lyrical I prays to goddess Persephone who is not only capable of sending death, but also familiar with having one's feelings harmed by a third party. Here, the revoked theme is Persephone's love to Adonis, obstructed by Aphrodite. Accordingly, the goddess of love was taken by the beauty of the baby Adonis and entrusted him to Persephone. The latter, however, also fell for the beautiful child and refused to give it back to Aphrodite. In his poem, Agathias adapted the story – love of two people being endangered by a third party – to the style of the epigram. To a similar theme of an overprotective carer whose sharp sight hinders the flirtation with a girl, Paulus Silentarius uses as parallel the theme of Io, who was watched by Argus, the hundred-eyed monster sent by Hera (V 262).

A whole collection of mythological analogies is found in a poem of Agathias (V 222). The lyrical I compliments the beauty and talent of a citharist named Ariadne. She is described as someone who with her mastery in playing the instrument could compete with Terpsychora, in humming a tragic song was as good as Melpomene, and in a beauty contest could defeat even Aphrodite herself. A survey of the girls' features is closed with a punch line: "But hush! let us keep it to our own selves, lest Bacchus overhear and long for the embraces of this Ariadne too". The same names of the lovely citharist and the popular mythical heroin allowed Agathias to make a reference to the story of the relationship between Ariadne and Dionysus, who affected by the girl's beauty, decided to marry her and take her to Olympus.

In an epigram by Macedonius (V 225), an unhappily-in-love hero compares his beauty to that of Telephus, and asks a girl: "be thou faithful Achilles and staunch with thy beauty the desire wherewith thy beauty smote me". Noticeably, the figure of Telephus is connected to the less popular myth of the first military expedition against Troy. When the Greeks mistakenly landed on the island of Mysia, Telephus fought them heroically until he was wounded by Achilles. According to the oracle at Delphi, Telephus' wound, which was festering for years, could only be healed by the one who had inflicted it.[6] In the epigram, the revoked Trojan theme is used in an erotic context, which allows the hero to make a subtle, sexual innuendo to the beautiful young girl.

On the basis of the example of the earlier adduced epigram of Agathias Scholasticus about the old chaperon who prevents any access to a young girl (V 289), it becomes clear that Byzantine poets did not lack wit, and even allowed themselves to express a dose of sarcasm. Another instance of it can be found in the poem of Julianus Antikensor, composed in the tone of the satirical epigrams of Lucilius (e.g. XI 131, 212, 214, 253, 254), in which the narrator derides the appearance of a certain fellow whose face resembles that of an ostrich (XI 367): "You have a face just like an ostrich. Did Circe give you a potion to drink and change your nature into that of a bird?" Here, the author had to modify the revoked theme due to the physiognomy of the target of ridicule, since it is well known that Circe changed her victims into pigs, alternatively into mountain wolves or lions (*Od.* X 212). Nonetheless, the reference remains clear, and only adds to the power of the joke.

---

6   The same motif has been already used by Paulus Silentiarius in V 291.

Between parenesis and wit lies a poem by Macedonius Consul, included by the Late Byzantine editors in the book X of the *Palatine Anthology*, comprising of *epigramata protreptika*, i.e. admonitory epigrams (X 71):

> I smile when I look on the picture of Pandora's jar, and do not find it was the woman's fault, but is due to the Goods having wings. For as they flutter to Olympus after visiting every region of the world, they ought to fall on the earth too. The woman after taking off the lid grew pale-faced, and has lost the splendour of her former charm. Our present life has suffered two losses; woman is grown old and the jar has nothing in it.

Here, the Hesiodian myth of Pandora's mistake (Komornicka 1990: 63–77) has been completely reinterpreted; the only parallel we may find is Pandora's name and her act of opening the box, whereas other allusions became reversed. In the epigram, the contents of the box are Goods (*Agatha*), instead of the evils of the world. These winged Goods fly straight to the gods' abode, whereas the evils, listed by Hesiod in his *Works and Days*, remain on earth in order to bring suffering to mortals. The assumption that female charm and beauty belonged to these Goods makes a witty punch line: since all Goods flew up to Olympus, none regarding female attractiveness are left on earth. This is the first loss that mankind has suffered; the second loss is an empty jar – *pithos*. In contrast to Hesiod's admonitory version of the myth, in the epigram, the mention of an empty *pithos* may be understood literally: the jar is empty, because it does not contain that which it was made for, i.e. wine. Thus, according to Macedonius, the effects of Pandora's act are ugly women and lack of alcohol.

The discussed survey of epigrams belonging to the *Cycle* of Agathias Scholasticus shows that their authors did not follow the example of one of the Church Fathers, Gregory of Nazianzus, an excellent poet himself, who in the 4th century transformed the epigram into a medium for transmitting Christian ideas and filled it with profoundly religious content (Łanowski 1994: 81–90). Clearly, such an artistic decision must have been the result of the poets' admiration and fascination with the artistry of the ancient poets of the past. Moreover, Early Byzantine epigrams were not a revival of a classical literary genre, but a duplication of the form and content formed by ancient tradition, which proves of the distance the epigrammatists kept from trends dominating in the writings of their times. This also reflects the role the epigram played for them, i.e. a token of the eruditeness and intellect of an author, as well as a source of aesthetic experiences for the elite group of its listeners. The poets pursuing the genological *topos* determined their revoking of mythical motifs, whereas their will to manifest their broad intellectual horizons and artistic finesse provoked them to search for less known themes, place them in surprising contexts, and add unexpected meanings and metaphorical values. The chosen examples show that the efforts of the Byzantine poets were successful to such a degree that sometimes only their names speak of the period in which the small epigrammatic gems were composed. Against common expectation, epigonism is not an easy art, especially when its aim is to present an original view and bring forth traces of the artist's individuality. In this respect, it is obvious that the Early Byzantine scholar epigrammatists achieved complete mastery. Although the classical epigram of the 6th century served only a narrow group of intellectuals as a literary curiosity of the past, it is beyond any doubt that today it remains a precious cultural and intellectual artefact of that specific period of time.

References:

Bowra, Maurice. 1970. "Palladas and Christianity". In *On Greek Margins*. London: Clarendon. 253–266.

Eliade, Mircea. 1988. *Historia wierzeń i idei religijnych*, Trans. by Stanisław Tokarski, vol. I. Warszawa: Instytut Wydawniczy PAX.

Jurewicz, Oktawiusz. 1984. *Historia literatury bizantyńskiej*. Wrocław: Ossolineum.

Kobus-Zalewska, Hanna. 1998. *Wątki i elementy mityczne w epigramach „Antologii Palatyńskiej"*. Wrocław: Ossolineum.

Komornicka, Anna M. 1990. „L'Elpis Hesiodique dans la jarre de Pandore". *Eos* LXXVIII: 63–77.

Łanowski, Jerzy.1994. „Nad księgą epigramów Świętego Grzegorza z Nazjanzu". *Roczniki Humanistyczne* 1994, f. 3: 81–90.

Ławińska-Tyszkowska, Janina. 1997. „Wota 'emerytów': Leonidas i inni". In *Epigram grecki i łaciński w kulturze Europy*. Ed. by Krystyna Bartol, Jerzy Danielewicz. Poznań: Wydawnictwo Naukowe UAM. 57–64.

Paton, William R. 1916 *The Greek Anthology*, vol. I. London – New York: Loeb.

—.1918. *The Greek Anthology*, vol. IV, London – New York: Loeb.

Stumpo, Beniamino. 1926. *L'epigramma a Constantinopoli nel secolo VI dopo Christo*. Palermo: Loescher.

Wellesz, Egon. 2006. *Historia muzyki i hymnografii bizantyjskiej*. Trans. by Maciej Kaziński. Kraków: Domini.

Part II
Modern and Postmodern *Work on Myth*

Olympia Tachopoulou[*]
Ancient Tragedy in Seferis' Poetry: From Existential Historicism to Philosophical Existentialism[1]

Abstract: The aim of this paper is to explore the reception of Greek tragedy in George Seferis' poetry by considering his different responses to the Aeschylean and Euripidean tragedy. Building upon T.S. Eliot's dramatic conception of poetry, Seferis based an important part of his work on a modernist reactivation of Attic tragedy. His dialogue with Greek tragedy, as can be detected in his works from *Mythistorima* (1935) to *Thrush* (1946), is dominated by Aeschylus' work and especially by the ideas of natural order and the balance of justice. Seferis, as an existential historicist, intuitively perceives the past as a living part of the present. In *Logbook III* (1955), his interest shifts to Euripidean tragedy, particularly as a way to comment on the political present. Drawing upon Euripides' *Helen*, Seferis deals with the subjects of illusion and deception, and for the first time brings into question the heroic state of the myth. The existential quest in "Helen" of *Logbook III* echoes the existential philosophy of Albert Camus emphasizing the absurdity of a world that lacks divine justice. In other words, the move from Aeschylus to Euripides provides the grounds for considering his move from existential historicism to philosophical existentialism.

Key words: classical reception, existentialism, modernism, modern Greek poetry, existential historicism

Greek tragedy offered George Seferis a space of self- and cultural knowledge, interiorised to become part of his modernist aesthetics. Building upon T.S. Eliot's dramatic manner of poetry,[2] Seferis based an important part of his work on a modernist reactivation of Attic tragedy. His dialogue with Greek tragedy, as can be

---

[*] Open University of Cyprus, Cyprus.
[1] An earlier form of this paper was presented at the Open University of Cyprus (Dec. 2014) in the context of the research project "*Our Heroic Debate with the Eumenides: Greek Tragedy and the Poetics and Politics of Identity in Modern Greek Poetry and Theatre*". My thanks are due to the audience and to the anonymous reader of the manuscript for the insightful and constructive remarks. Obviously, responsibility for the views expressed in this article is the author's.
[2] Eliot conceptualised this relationship of poetry to drama in 1928 in the "Dialogue on Dramatic Poetry" where he argues that "there is no 'relation' between poetry and drama. All poetry tends towards drama, and all drama towards poetry" (Eliot 1999: 52). Seferis perceives this dramatic conception of poetry through reading Eliot's poetry.

detected from *Mythistorima* (1935) to *Thrush* (1946), is dominated by Aeschylus' work, particularly by *Oresteia*. In *Logbook III* (1955) his interest shifted to Euripidean tragedy, particularly as a way of commenting on the political present. Placing Euripides at the forefront provided a more political interpretative model, reaching the peak of its development in the poem "Helen" of *Logbook III*. This article aims to explore the reception of Greek tragedy in Seferis' poetry by considering his different responses to Aeschylean and Euripidean tragedy, as well as his move from existential historicism to philosophical existentialism, and its political implications. It has been argued by Dimitris Tziovas that existential historicism is latent in many of Seferis' poems and that it concerns the living and intuitive presence of the past to the present (2005: 230–231). Philosophical existentialism as an aspect of Seferis' poetry has been mentioned by some critics such as Nasos Vayenas (1991: 283),[3] Edmund Keeley (1996: 90)[4] and Carmen Capri-Karka (1985: 220),[5] but it has neither been thoroughly examined nor discussed in a specific theoretical context. Moreover, the existential quest of the poem "Helen" has received no attention, and it is on this aspect that I will focus in this essay, putting Seferis' poem in a comparative perspective with Euripides' *Helen*.

Let us begin by considering how Seferis became acquainted with Eliot's poetry. At Christmas of 1931, when visiting a bookshop on Oxford Street, Seferis came across a collection of Eliot's poems. What aroused his interest at that time was the "dramatic manner of expression", as he was to indicate much later in the "Letter to a Foreign Friend" (1948), where he wrote:

After the outburst of Dadaism and the experiments of Surrealism which I had witnessed in France, after these tremendous excavations and explosions of the ego which had brought into the atmosphere at that time [...] the renewal of the dramatic tradition

---

3   While discussing the genealogy of *Thrush,* Vayenas supports the relevance of Seferis' poetry to the philosophy of existentialism (1991: 283): «Η κοσμοθεωρία του Σεφέρη, αν θέλαμε να τη δούμε μέσα από το φως του φιλοσοφικού κλίματος της εποχής μας, θα λέγαμε πως βρίσκεται κοντά στον υπαρξισμό» ["If we were to examine Seferis' worldview in the light of the contemporaneous philosophical climate, we would say that it is close to existentialism".]
4   Commenting on Seferis' *Thrush*, Keeley (1996: 89–90) discusses the existential perspective that George Thaniel (cf. "George Seferis's '*Thrush*': a Modern Descent"), Vayenas (*Ο ποιητής και ο χορευτής*) and Beaton (*Seferis*) have found in it. However, Keeley suggests – at least for *Thrush* – a more transcendent worldview (89–90, 95). See further Keeley (1996: 89–91, 95–96), whence the references.
5   In the conclusion of her book, Capri-Karka mentions that "Like the French existentialist thinkers Sartre and Camus, Seferis believed that it is man's responsibility to create justice and order in the world" (1985: 220).

which I found in Eliot brought me back to a more temperature zone. [...] To put it in simpler words (...) the poetry of Eliot offered me something much deeper, something which was inevitably moving to a Greek: the elements of tragedy. (Seferis 1964: 51–52)

In 1936 in the "Introduction to Eliot" Seferis further elaborated this association of modern poetry with ancient drama. As he noted, Eliot's poetry "is not lyrical poetry [...] It is, essentially, dramatic poetry" and in Eliot's poems "we feel as though we have in front of us an excerpt from a drama [...] We have a stage before us" (Seferis 2009: 156). Seferis espoused this idea and made it work in his almost entire poetry. We can detect this relationship of poetry to drama in the first poem of his first modernist collection *Mythistorima* (1935):[6]

1.
The angel–
three years we waited intently for him
closely watching
the pines the shore and the stars.
One with the plough's blade or keel of the ship,
we were searching to rediscover the first seed
so that the ancient drama could begin again.

(Seferis 1981a: 3)

Reading these verses we can assume that "we have a stage before us", as Seferis affirmed for Eliot's poetry. The angel is the messenger of ancient tragedy who will give the sign for the drama to begin again in the present.[7] What is at issue here is how the past with its ancient mythical content will be activated in the present historical moment, but not as a dead past – on the contrary, as that "what is still living, present, contemporary" (Seferis 2009: 144). Seferis achieves this fusion creating "a continuous parallel between contemporaneity and antiquity", as Eliot has suggested in reference to *Ulysses* by Joyce (1923).[8] He creates an interplay

---

6   The colloquial meaning of the word is "novel", but Seferis chose the word for its two components: myth and history. See more in Seferis' notes to his poems (1981: 537). All translations of Seferis' poems are from Edmund Keeley and Philip Sherrard, 1981. Translations of Seferis' prose are my own, unless otherwise indicated.
7   Vitti 1978: 62–63. According to Vitti, the reference to the "ancient drama" alludes to the "eternal return" as a notion developed by anthropology, and life is considered as a drama repeated ritually in every man. See also Capri-Karka 1982: 231, who gives two meanings in the "immemorial drama": "one is the vegetation myth ... and the other myth is that of *Agamemnon* or the ancient drama in general, which often starts with a messenger arriving and announcing some important news" (231).
8   Eliot 1975: 175–178.

between Antiquity and the present using the *Odyssey* and Greek tragedies as his source texts.

In *Mythistorima*, we find clear allusions to Greek tragedies such as *Agamemnon* and *The Libation Bearers*, *Electra* by Sophocles and *Medea* by Euripides. But the tragedy that dominates in Seferis' poetry is Aeschylus' *Agamemnon*, as can be seen in verses from *Mythistorima* to *Three Secret Poems*.[9] Key topics of Aeschylean tragedy that are constantly propagated include reflections on human fate, acts of disrespect and hubris. Drawing systematically from Aeschylus' *Agamemnon*, as well as the whole trilogy (*Oresteia*), Seferis creates a poetic world that is trying to get rid of the vicious cycle of violence, but constantly takes on the nature of justice, human and divine. The cycle of violence is declared through repetition of verses uttered by Clytemnestra (*Agamemnon* 958–962):

> Κλυταιμνήστρα
> Ἔστιν θάλασσα— τίς δέ νιν κατασβέσει; —
> Τρέφουσα πολλῆς πορφύρας ἰσάργυρον
> κηκῖδα παγκαίνιστον, εἱμάτων βαφάς.
>
> There is a sea – who will ever dry it up? – which breeds an ever-renewed ooze of abundant purple, worth its weight in silver, to dye clothing with. (trans. by Sommerstein 2008: 113)

Seferis repeats the first verse with an insistence bordering on obsession.[10] These verses are taken from the point at which Agamemnon has been persuaded to step on the red purple carpet that Clytemnestra had laid down for him, and which would lead him to his death. This is the most central Aeschylian voice that runs through a big part of Seferis' poetry.[11]

One of the poems that allude directly and in a stimulating way to the Aeschylean cycle of violence is "Wednesday" (1934), from the *Book of Exercises* (1940). This conceptualization of the cyclical flow of life runs through Seferis' poetry up to the 1950s. Let us look at some verses from this poem:

---

9 For the perception of Aeschylus in Seferis' poetry, see Liapis 2014a: 74–76, 81, 85, 88. For references to *Agamemnon*, see pages 75, 85. Cf. Mastrodimitris 1964: 14–16.

10 We find direct allusions to this verse or this part of *Agamemnon* in *Mythistorima* 20 (p. 51), "Mycenae" (p. 69), "Monday" (p. 153), "Wednesday" (p. 161), «Last dance» (1934) from *Book of Exercises II* (Seferis 1976: 60) and a broader allusion to Clytemnestra in the poem "On Stage" from *Three Secret Poems* (p. 405–7).

11 Cf. Seferis 1981b: 290: «Αισθάνομαι πως ο Αισχύλος βλέπει καθαρά μπροστά του αυτήν την ατέλειωτη συνέχεια από το φονικό στο φονικό, αυτή την ανεξάντλητη πορφύρα». ["I feel that Aeschylus clearly sees in front of him this endless continuity from murder to murder, this inexhaustible purple".]

– Why doesn't it get dark?
– Have a look if you want to, the new moon must have
  come out somewhere.
– Everybody looks at what we're going to do
and you look at the crowds looking at you;
the glances inscribe a tight circle
that can't be broken.
If someone is born the circle will widen
If someone dies the circle will shrink
[...].
If we were to love, the circle would break,
we'd close our eyelashes for a second.
But we can't love.
[...]
The gramophone started up again.
Our bats now inscribe
circles that shrink as they fly
from one man to another man and on to
  another
no one escapes
and life is rich because we're many
and all of us the same
  [...]
  ....Look at
us!
We look at you. We too. We too. We too.
There is nothing beyond.
–   But the sea:
I don't know that they've drained it dry.

(Seferis 1981a: 159-161)

This view of the world as a continuous cycle or recurrent violence, drawing heavily on Aeschylus' *Oresteia*,[12] is not just a moment from the past, but also a moment of the present, as it is stressed in the following verses. "Look at us! We look at you. We too. We too." This suffering caused by the imposed violence in both Aeschylus and Seferis can be considered as "a step to wisdom" (Easterling-Knox 2003: 324).[13]

---

12 For the cycle of violence in *Oresteia* and its end in *Eumenides*, see Gregory 2005: 10–11.
13 See *Agamemnon* 176–178 ("Zeus who set mortals on the road/ to understanding, who made/ 'learning by suffering' into an effective law", trans. by Sommerstein 2008: 21). Cf. Easterling-Knox 2003: 289.

Seferis' view regarding a "living", "contemporary past" (2009: 144) bears a strong resemblance with the reenactment of the cultural past described by Jameson as part of existential historicism. Tziovas (2005) in his article entitled «Ο υπαρξιακός ιστορισμός του Σεφέρη» ("Seferis and Existential Historicism"), describes this contact between the past and the present in Seferis' poetry, and suggests that Seferis has deeply embraced existential historicism with his faith in an unchanging and timeless historical past (2005, p. 233: «κατά βάθος ασπάζεται έναν υπαρξιακό ιστορισμό με την πίστη του σε ένα αναλλοίωτο και άχρονο υπόστρωμα»). Existential historicism is a term coined by Fredric Jameson[14] to contrast "the sheer mechanical and meaningless succession of facts of empiricist historiography" (1988: 157). As Jameson explains, in existential historicism "the historicist act revives the dead and reenacts the essential mystery of the cultural past, which, like Tiresias drinking the blood, is momentarily returned to life and warmth and allowed once more to speak its mortal speech" (1988: 158). Therefore, the conception of the cycle of violence, which Seferis' drew from Aeschylus, also suggests a stance towards the past which is not characterised by a linear historical process,[15] but instead is manifested by "the contact between the poet's mind in the present and a given synchronic cultural complex from the past" (*ibid.*: 157). The cyclical pattern of life in Seferis does not allude to a dead past but to a manifestation of a timeless substrate of the past, "something like a transhistorical event" (*ibid.*: 157 and Tziovas 2005: 231). Thus, for Seferis, history (and consequently, the past) is a living part of the present that cannot be destroyed.

---

14 For the content of the term existential historicism, see Jameson 1988: 157: existential historicism does not involve the construction of this or that linear or evolutionary or genetic history, but rather designates something like a transhistorical event: the experience, rather, by which *historicity* as such is manifested, by means of the contact between the historian's mind in the present and a given synchronic cultural complex from the past. This is to say that the methodological spirit of existential historicism may be described as a historical and cultural aestheticism".

15 For the way Ezra Pound "substitutes linear history with a circular or cyclical history", see Beasley 2007: 68. Moreover Rebecca Beasley argues that "The *Waste Land* and *The Cantos* ... reject linear and chronological narratives in favor of organizing their material by juxtaposition". This approach to history is developed by Beasley as an example of existential historicism. However according to Tziovas (2005: 230) and James Longenbach (1987: 168), "For the existential historian, history is not conceived on the model of a linear or cyclical pattern of events, but a palimpsest in which the present is actually made up of remnants of the entire past".

This view of history takes Seferis closer to the matrix of modernism[16] and, in particular, to Eliot and Ezra Pound for whom the present is nothing more than "the sum of the entire past – a palimpsest, a complex tissue of historical remnants", as Longenbach (1987: 11) argued in his book about modernist poetics of history in Eliot and Pound.[17] Moreover, Seferis defines the existential and historicist framework of his poetry by the exemplary use of Aeschylean tragedy. Aeschylus' dramas help him to approach the idea of eternity[18] and transcend the sense of the ephemeral: "'Even if you feel that you yourself are ephemeral, you know that this is not ephemeral, you know that what part of yourself lies in there is not ephemeral'."[19] This perception of past and present through inner experience and self-questioning has more of a transcendental and less of an empirical character, at least at this stage of his poetics. Furthermore, Seferis was deeply interested in the idea that is principal in the Aeschylean world, namely this battle for freedom in the teeth of fate. It is an existential quest defined by the determinism of the cycle, but at the same time it lies within the sense of order, security and justice that Aeschylean world implies for the Seferian worldview:

> Αισθήματα που βρίσκω στον Αισχύλο που με αναπαύουν: η ασφάλεια και η ισορροπία της δικαιοσύνης χωρίς αισθηματολογία, χωρίς ηθικολογία, χωρίς ψυχολογία. Σαν ένας νόμος του σύμπαντος, καθαρός, χωρίς σκουριές. Και η αυθεντία αυτής της φωνής, το κύρος της. Η μεγαλύτερη τάξη που ξέρω. (3 Αυγούστου 1939) (Seferis 1984: 125–126)
>
> ["Feelings that I find in Aeschylus, that reassure me: the security and the balance of justice, without sentimentality, without psychology. Like a law of the universe, clear, uncorroded. And the authenticity of that voice, its authority. The greatest order (*taxis*) that I know" (entry for 3 August 1939). Translation by Beaton (2003: 172)]

In the above extract, the relationship with the past is identified with "an existential experience, a galvanic and electrifying event", to borrow once again Jameson's statement on existential historicism (1988: 175). Thus, the exchange of forces between past and present in Seferis' poetry is not controversial: there is no radi-

---

16 See Schwartz 1985: 139: "Like Dilthey, Pound sought to bridge the gap between past and present by recovering the lived experience of the author".
17 Longenbach (1987: 13) has argued that Eliot and Pound espoused existential historicism joining such philosophers as Dilthey, Croce and Collinwood. Longenbach draws the content of the term from Jameson's elaboration in "Marxism and Historicism".
18 See Seferis (1981b: 123–124) where it is written that "τα έργα αυτά που με βοηθάνε να πλησιάσω μια ιδέα της αιωνιότητας" [these plays that help me to reach the idea of eternity"].
19 Seferis 1977: 33. Translation by Liapis 2014a: 75.

cal questioning of truth or value of the past, but only of our efforts to reanimate its overall meaning.

After the 1950s, as Seferis' interest shifts from the Aeschylean to the Euripidean tragedy, his poetry undergoes a notable change in the use of myth and, consequently, in the reactivation of the past in the present. As many critics have emphasised, it is a progression from myth to history (Maronitis 1987: 159, 169) and from the Aeschylean world of justice to the Euripidean world that moves "between doubt and denial" (Nikolaou 1992: 162). As I will try to show on the following pages, this turn to Euripides can be associated and interpreted in the context of the new intellectual tendency, prominent in the existential philosophy of Jean-Paul Sartre and Albert Camus, which views the "human being as an isolated existence in a universe possessing no inherent truth, or value" (Abrams 1999: 1).

The significant change in Seferis' poetics occurred in 1953 when he visited Cyprus and wrote the collection ...*Cyprus Where it Was Ordained For Me*... (the quotation is from Euripides' *Helen* 148) (Beaton 2003: 293, 470). All the poems of this collection are directly linked to the political and social reality of ancient and contemporary Cyprus. In this poetry collection we have three poems drawing from Euripides' "Pentheus", "Euripides the Athenian" and "Helen", in which we can detect a shift from the "balance of justice" of the Aeschylean worldview to the Euripidean intellectual perspective and what it entails, namely the question of divine justice and the "haunted vision of the irrational forces … in the universe" (Easterling-Knox 2008: 325).

Let us look at "Helen" and the verses pervaded by the existential philosophy of the era. The poem was written in 1954 and was published in 1955, at the beginning of the armed struggle of EOKA (National Organization of Cypriot Fighters) that fought against the British rule in Cyprus. The poem departs from Stesichorus' *Palinode* and Euripides' *Helen,* and puts forward the myth in which the phantom of Helen was sent to Troy, while her real counterpart was transported by Hermes to Egypt, causing the Greeks and Trojans to fight over an eidolon.[20]

Euripides' *Helen* was first produced in 412 BC, one year after the destruction of the Athenians in Sicily. The Athenians felt despair during this period, and Euripides in his work expresses this feeling of defeat and futility of war. This

---

20 The so-called *Palinode* of Stesichorus concerns a brief fragment preserved in Plato's *Phaedrus* 243a, according to which a phantom of Helen was taken to Troy, while the real Helen was transported by Hermes to the palace of Proteus, king of Egypt. After writing the verses of his *Palinode*, Stesichorus regained his sight which he lost after he blamed Helen. For this radical example of myth's revision, see Allan 2008: 19–20.

is one of the reasons why Seferis selected this drama as a parallel of his own poem – in a way, both works criticise the historical and political reality of their times.[21] But as I will try to show, subsequently, there is also an inner connection that defines both works at the philosophical level, as Euripides was heavily influenced by the ideas of the sophists that prevailed at that time, and Seferis' poem was influenced by the ideas of existential philosophy that was becoming known in France, but also in Greece, from the 1940s onwards.

Helen is one of the most controversial works of Euripides and it has been interpreted as both comedy and tragedy, a dramatic exercise in philosophy and a romance. Bernard Knox considered *Helen* together with *Ion* and *Iphigenia in Tauris* to be plays of romantic intrigue (Easterling-Knox 2008: 318) that constitute a departure from tragedy. However, Charles Segal (1971: 555–6) considers the "tragedy-or-comedy" dilemma as not important, and instead emphasises the philosophical side of the work, which lies in its antithesis between appearance and reality. The play sets some questions: What is the "real" nature of the world? What is "word" (*onoma*) and what is "fact" or "deed" (*pragma*)?[22] Helen, with her double existence, lives in a world of both appearance and reality. Men, deceived by the false image of Helen, have fought a long and cruel war to possess her (*ibid.*: 559). These questions about the nature of reality are closely linked to the concerns of the late 5th century philosophical thought of Gorgias, Protagoras and Antiphon the Sophist, who asked: "Is there a stable reality? And if there is, can we know it?" (*ibid.*: 560). In particular, Gorgias' *The Encomium of Helen* has been considered as a parallel text to Euripides' *Helen*, as both works "deal in a similar way with the same philosophical theme" (Wright 2005: 276). In this work, Gorgias is concerned "not so much with how things are (or are not) as with the power of various types of illusions, including visual appearances". He attempts to discharge Helen "not by claiming that she was innocent of misdeed, but by arguing that she succumbed to the irresistible power of illusion" (*ibid.*: 273).

---

21 For the way Euripides comments on the political reality of the period, see Drew 1930: 187: "Athens was in a humble mood when Euripides' *Helena* came upon the public stage. Euripides, I think, gives expression to that mood in the *Helena*. He interprets that new attitude toward the war which failure and despondency were causing his countrymen to adopt."
22 Cf. Pippin 1960: 152: "The language, the plot, and the very form of the Helen all have been made to express this tension between what is and what only seems to be. Every character suffers from some misapprehension of the truth-all, that is, except the prophetess Theonoe, who has been granted a special understanding."

Seferis' "Helen"

But let us go to George Seferis' "Helen" which, as has been argued by Charles Segal (*ibid.*: 559), maintains the mysterious nature of reality that exists also in Euripides' *Helen*. The poem starts with a quote from *Helen* by Euripides that serves as a motto, or rather, as a guiding instruction to the reading of Seferis' poem.[23]

> **TEUCER:** .... *in sea-girt Cyprus, where it was decreed by Apollo that I should live, giving the city the name of Salamis in memory of my island home.*
> ....
> **HELEN:** *I never went to Troy; it was a phantom.*
> ....
> **SERVANT:** *What? You mean it was only for a cloud that we struggled so much?*
>
> Eur. Hel. 148–150, 582, 706–707[24]
> (Seferis 1981a: 355)

The quote from Euripides sets the main frame of the poem, which has to do with a progression from ignorance to knowledge. In Seferis, Teucer is the main persona of the poem. The poem takes the form of a dramatic monologue of Teucer who learns that the Greeks fought on a cloud, while in Euripides, Teucer departs without realizing he has met the real Helen. Therefore, Helen is a presence revoked and reactivated through Teucer's memory. It is through Helen and her dual nature that the Seferian Teucer will reach his own self-awareness.

In both texts, we have an idol made by the gods to fool the people. We face two worlds – the real one, and the one we think is real. This question of what is real is strongly expressed in Seferis' poem.

Euripides' *Helen* begins by placing us in an exotic setting in far-off Egypt. The place in Seferis' poem is set with certainty from the first verse by a voice which can be attributed to something like a chorus in the poem (Krikos-Davis 1994: 45):[25] "The nightingales won't let you sleep in Platres" (Seferis 1981a: 355). This verse is repeated, dividing the poem into three sections (Krikos-Davis 1994: 45). In the second section, the verse is followed by a question posed by Teucer the narrator: "Platres: where is Platres? And this island: who knows it?" (Seferis 1981a: 355). The verse is challenging the existence or non-existence of

---

23 Cf. Mastrodimitris 1964: 20.
24 It is quoted in English translation by Keeley and Sherrard; see Seferis 1981a: 355.
25 Cf. Georgis 1991: 103.

Platres,[26] but also of Cyprus. It subverts the certainty with which the poem began. A lack of awareness is now stated in the second part of the poem creating anxiety: What is real? How can we know the reality? Who knows this island?

The feeling of uncertainty is then reinforced through the sense of paradox and absurdity:

> I've lived my life hearing names I've never heard before:
> new countries, new idiocies of men
> or of the gods;
>
> (Seferis 1981a: 355–6)

The reference to "the idiocies of men or gods" adds an irrational angle to the behaviour of people – and of the gods. The divine is being challenged, and here god ceases to be a god, if he acts without prudence without logic.

This aspect of unknowability of the human being and his inability to perceive reality takes on a more philosophical dimension in the next question: "Truth, where's the truth?" (Seferis 1981a: 357). This question, as it is set out before the reference to the doubleness of Helen, displays a consciousness that is struggling to restore its true relationship with the world, so it turns to itself:

> I too was an archer in the war;
> my fate: that of a man who missed his target.
>
> (Seferis 1981a: 357)

The hero thus cannot define his fate, the world seems incomprehensible to him, and as a result a detachment from the certainties of real life is created. All existential philosophies focus on the common goal of associating reality with truth. According to existentialism, a human being cannot know truth but only a small number of truths (Wahl 1970: 227).

The concept of truth is central to the poem, as Helen cries: "It isn't true, it isn't true" (Seferis 1981a: 357). Also at the end of the poem, the phrase "if it's true" is repeated three times, indicating the desperate confrontation of humans with agonizing existential issues. Moreover, the discovery of the two Helens creates a distance in the conception of the Being, the real corporeal Helen that Teucer touched and spoke to, and the empty, non-existent Helen who is just a cloud, a hole in the Being, a nothing:

---

26 For Platres, see the notes in Seferis (1981a: 543): "Platres is a summer resort on the slopes of Mt Troödos in Cyprus".

> And at Troy?
> At Troy, nothing: just a phantom image.
>
> (Seferis 1981a: 359)

One of the ideas that have been developed in existential philosophy is that "being" and nothingness are closely related. This emptiness of Helen nullifies the reason for which the war was carried out and makes it absurd. Teucer must now confront the irrational aspect of reality.

The horrors of war described in the poem ("so many bodies thrown/into the jaws of the sea, the jaws of the earth" (*ibid*.: 359) make the reasoning of the war even more absurd and lead Teucer to question divine order and divine law:

> What is a god? What is not a god? And what is there in-
> between them?
>
> (Seferis 1981a: 359)

Man is alone now, alienated, he has pierced the net of the gods, and must redefine his relationship with reality.[27] This verse is at odds with the Aeschylean worldview and shows the extent to which Seferis moved away from the concept of divine justice, security and natural order, earning a spiritual awareness to be determined towards the sensible and the hypersensible.

This search for truth, the concept of the absurd, the relationship of the being with nothingness, allude to existential philosophy, especially to Albert Camus and his worldview. According to Camus, in *The Myth of Sisyphus* (1975: 20–22), the world is "dense", and "that denseness and that strangeness of the world is the absurd" (20), so "the mind's first step is to distinguish what is true from what is false", (22) "as soon as thought reflects itself, what it first discovers is a contradiction" (22). But we must, as Camus suggests in *The Rebel*, break the mirror "with its fixed stare … Once the mirror is broken, nothing remains which can help us answer the questions of our time […]. I proclaim that I believe in nothing and that everything is absurd, but I cannot doubt the validity of my proclamation and I must at least believe in my protest. The first and only evidence that is supplied me, within the terms of the absurdist experience, is rebellion." (1991: 10)

In Seferis' "Helen", at the end of the poem, we can find this sense of rebellion described by Camus. Teucer, has accepted the irrational aspect in the existence of Helen and despite the unknowability, which reflects the repeated phrase "if

---

27 Cf. Nikolaou 1992: 180. According to Nikolaou, the verse "What is a god? What is not a god?" alludes to Parmenides' dialectic.

it is true", he achieves a form of rebellion that pushes the person (unknown or anonymous person) to come out of his solitude and realise his existence:

> on sea-kissed Cyprus
> consecrated to remind me of my country,
> I moored alone with this fable,
> If it's true that it is a fable,
> If it's true that mortals will not again take up
> the old deceit of the gods;
>   If it's true
> that in future years some other Teucer,
> or some Ajax or Priam or Hecuba,
> or someone unknown and nameless who nevertheless saw
> a Scamander overflow with corpses,
> isn't fated to hear
> messengers coming to tell him
> that so much suffering, so much life,
> went into the abyss
> all for an empty tunic, all for a Helen.
>
> (Seferis 1981a: 359–361)

What Seferis accomplishes in these verses is to overcome the notion of the absurd by expressing a revolutionary mood and targeting his verses against the crime, the disaster, the repetition of war. It is a revolt against the war, against the abyss that he feels will come after the armed conflict – which actually began before these poems were published. And this time, for Seferis, the rebellion takes on not just a poetic nuance, but a real, historical direction. He is now engaged in the real world of political realities, assuming a transcendental narrowing of his worldview, which is now re-grounded in a more empirical vision. The poems of this collection were criticised and shocked many critics at the time, mainly because of their political character.[28] As Edmund Keeley (1987: 150) notes, some critics celebrated the political character of the poems, and others criticised the poet for writing "propaganda in verse". According to Keeley (1987: 151), "Helen" and "Salamis of Cyprus", possess the most prominent political and historical tone in the collection. For the latter, Katsimbalis expressed his astonishment after reading it, and Seferis replied as follows:

> As you see it's a cry addressed to my friends-my friends from Britain, a cry of love. I'd have burst if I'd kept it bottled up inside me...In Cyprus...there's a cold, subterranean

---

28 See Savvidis 1992: 44; Beaton 2003: 315–6; Drakopoulos 2002: 202–213; Pavlou S. 2000: 207–226.

mechanism that operates undisturbed and bastardises everything. I felt it as a person, I'm not talking politics […].[29]

For Seferis' state of mind and his conscious non-involvement in politics, the above is a form of revolt through poetry. It is probably no coincidence that the critics of the left welcomed the new poems of *Logbook III*. Lambridis in *Επιθεώρηση Τέχνης* [*Review of Art*] argued that the poetry of Seferis is a "cry of protest, a supreme rebellion" which "arouses indignation and rebellion for a particular form of life" (Drakopoulos 2002: 209).

But we have one more eloquent incident showing Seferis' disposition towards the Cypriot struggle. On 29 September 1955, during Seferis stay in Cyprus, in the centre of Famagusta a demonstration took place, during which the authorities used tear gas against the protesters who came out on the streets. Seferis described the atmosphere to Savvides as follows: "Great atmosphere: Momentum of youth, faith, and this strange breath of a people who suddenly knows itself".[30] The moment Seferis expresses his praises is the moment of revolt.

Based on the above, Teucer in Seferis' poem is a refugee, but also a warrior, torn between hope and doubt; he is a contradictory man who, although wounded, is aware of human and historical ambiguity. These, Camus argues, are the tragic circumstances in which modern tragedy can be regenerated. Teucer is a man who claims the revolt, but is also aware of the limits of this revolt, he is conscious and aware of the absurd, and this is the essence of his tragic existence (Camus 1968: 306–307).[31]

Thereafter, Seferis maintained a more political stance demonstrating, in a more evident way, his sense of social and political responsibility. In this spirit, during the Junta,[32] Seferis made a public statement that would have been unthinkable before the 1950s. On March 1969, he made a "statement against the Greek Colonels' junta" on BBC radio.[33] In this statement, he evoked Greek tragedy in order to give shape to his protest, reaching back to Aeschylus, whose influence, it seems,

---

29 Quotation from Beaton 2003: 315.
30 Seferis 1991: 85, quotation from Beaton 2003: 327. Cf. Pavlou S. 2000: 164; Seferis 2008: 181 ("strike-tear gases").
31 Camus in 1955 gave a lecture in Athens about the "Future of tragedy", and discussed with Greek intellectuals the future of Greek civilization, for which see Camus 2004.
32 It is to do with the Dictatorship of 1967–74 that ruled Greece after the military coup of 1967. The regime is known as "The Colonels" or "The Junta".
33 Seferis 1992: 261–262. Beaton 2003: 398. For a more detailed discussion of the circumstances under which Seferis took the decision to make the declaration and for the broader implications of the statement, see Keeley 1987: 162–166.

followed him to the end: "Everyone has now learned and knows that in dictatorships the beginning may seem easy, but tragedy awaits, ineluctably, at the end. The drama of this end tortures us, consciously or unconsciously, as in the age-old choruses of Aeschylus. As long as the anomaly lasts, evil will advance further and further."[34] Then followed a period in which Seferis achieved a high public profile evidenced by huge crowds that attended his funeral (Keeley 1987: 172–175).

Seferis and the Existentialists

The central question that now arises is connected to the real existential underpinnings of George Seferis' viewpoint. Seferis made explicit references to existentialist philosophers such as Albert Camus and Jean-Paul Sartre in his writings during the 1960s. These references provide evidence of his acquaintance with their work even at that late period.[35] The reference to Camus simply indicates his agreement with a view of Camus on the immortality of the soul: «καθώς έβλεπα τελευταία να παρατηρεί και ο Albert Camus, προτιμά το γυρισμό στην Ιθάκη από την αθανασία που του προσφέρει η Καλυψώ» (Seferis 1974: 240, 366) ["as I recently read Albert Camus commenting also, he prefers the return to Ithaca over the immortality of the soul offered by Calypso"]. The reference to Sartre and his play *Huis Clos* implies an ironic and subversive tone. Seferis (1974: 278, 372) calls Sartre a "Doctor of our times", and reverses the famous line "Hell is other people" from Sartre's *Huis Clos*, suggesting that "Paradise is other people" as well.

Undoubtedly, even if we accept Teucer as a real existential hero, we could hardly interpret his existential stance in a Sartrian pessimistic mould. In this respect, we could not attribute to Seferis' Teucer the "acceptance and even glorification of the ultimate meaninglessness of the world", as has been argued for Ritsos' *Orestes* (Liapis 2014: 121). On the contrary, what we can claim is that Seferis' "Helen" and, to some extent, *Logbook III* appear to echo existentialism as a movement that developed "a social conscience and, with it, a conviction that the fine arts, literature at least, should be socially and politically committed" (Flynn 2006: 14). Certainly, Seferis would not embrace the Sartrian idea of

---

34 Translation by Liapis 2014: 76. This statement along with the poems "On Aspalathoi…" and "The Cats of Saint Nicolas" constitute Seferis' anti-junta writings (Krikos-Davis 1984: 234).
35 We can assume that Seferis was acquainted with French existentialism, since Sartre's plays had been performed in Greece from 1948, and publications on existential philosophy could be found from 1946–7. See more in Liapis 2014b: 121–158; Pavlou M. 2013: 146.

"'taking action' or 'making political choices', at any cost" (Hughes 2007: 21), but he followed the political events in Cyprus closely.[36]

What further distinguishes Seferis' "Helen" is its preoccupation with certain philosophical issues seen through the lens of existentialism – more particularly, Camus' existential thinking and his conceptualization of absurdity. Camus describes "a world in which God is no longer present" and man struggles with absurdity (Hughes 2007: 18). As Camus argues in the *Myth of Sisyphus*, the feeling of absurdity "can strike any man in the face" (1975: 17) the moment that "a *why* arises" (1975: 19). Seferis found this specific moment of absurdity in Euripides' *Helen* as well, and this is probably the reason why he chose this tragedy in order to create his own poem.

Conclusion

In conclusion, what has been suggested in this article is that George Seferis found in Aeschylus the principles of justice and moral truth, and developed a transcendental vision of the past reanimated in the present. Like T. S. Eliot and Ezra Pound, Seferis conceived the past through a process of imaginative reactivation. This intuitive sense of the past has been examined in the context of existential historicism.

As Seferis turned to Euripides in the 1950s, his interest shifted to the irrational aspect of the myth and to the challenging of divine justice. The poem "Helen" reveals this questioning of the past and the new relationship with the present which is now set on a more historical substrate. Scepticism now replaces the assurance of the Aeschylean universe. The inability of the human being to perceive reality or the essence of truth, as expressed in "Helen", in addition to Seferis' interest in contemporary politics, support a latent dialogue with philosophical existentialism and, in particular, with the ideas of absurdity and rebellion as expressed by Camus. Taking into account Camus' description of absurdity as the "incalculable feeling that deprives the mind of sleep" (Camus 1975: 13), we could read Seferis' voice in "Helen" under the light of existential anguish of a man who is deprived of sleep: "The nightingales won't let you sleep in Platres". In brief, Seferis' move from Aeschylus to Euripides provided the grounds in this essay for considering his move from existential historicism to philosophical existentialism.

---

36 See Beaton 2003: 330–332.

References:

Allan, William. (ed.). 2008. *Euripides' Helen*. Cambridge: Cambridge University Press.

Beaton, Roderick. 2003. *George Seferis: Waiting for the Angel. A Biography*. New Haven, CT and London: Yale University Press.

Beasley, Rebecca. 2007. *Theorists of Modernist Poetry: T.S. Eliot, T.E. Hulme and Ezra Pound*. London and New York: Routledge.

Camus, Albert. 1968. *Lyrical and Critical Essays*. New York: Knopf.

—.1975. *The Myth of Sisyphus*. Trans. by Justin O' Brien. London: Penguin Books.

—.1991. *The Rebel. An Essay on Man in Revolt*. Trans. by Anthony Bower. New York: Vintage.

—.2004. *Το μέλλον του ευρωπαϊκού πολιτισμού. Μια συζήτηση με τον Albert Camus στην Αθήνα*. Trans. by Tatiana Tsaliki-Milioni. Athens: Alexandreia.

Capri-Karka, Carmen. 1982. *Love and the Symbolic Journey in the Poetry of Cavafy, Eliot and Seferis: An Interpretation with Detailed Poem-by-Poem Analysis*. New York: Pella Publishing.

—.1985. *War in the Poetry of George Seferis. A Poem- by- Poem Analysis*. New York: Pella Publishing.

Drew, D. L. 1930. "The Political Purpose in Euripides' Helena." *Classical Philology* 25/ 2: 187–189.

Eliot, Thomas Stearns. 1975. "'Ulysses', Order and Myth". In *Selected Prose of T.S. Eliot*. London: Faber and Faber. 175–178.

—.1999. "A Dialogue on Dramatic Poetry". In *Selected Essays*. London: Faber & Faber. 43–58.

Easterling, P. Elizabeth and Bernard M. W. Knox (eds.). 2008. *The Cambridge History of Classical Literature*. v. 1. Cambridge: Cambridge University Press.

Flynn, Thomas. 2006. *Existentialism. A Very Short Introduction*. Oxford: Oxford University Press.

Georgis, George. 1991. *Ο Σεφέρης περί των κατά την χώραν Κύπρον σκαιών*. Athens: Smili.

Gregory, Justina 2005. *A Companion to Greek Tragedy*. Oxford: Blackwell.

Hughes, Edward J. 2007. *The Cambridge Companion to Camus*. Cambridge: Cambridge University Press.

Jameson, Fredric. 1988. *The Ideologies of Theory Essays 1971–1986, vol. 2, The Syntax of History*. Minneapolis: University of Minnesota Press.

Keeley, Edmund. 1987. *Μύθος και φωνή στη σύγχρονη ελληνική ποίηση*. Trans. by Spiros Tsaknias. Athens: Stigmi.

—.1996. "*Nostos* and the Poet's Vision in Seferis and Ritsos". In *Ancient Greek Myth in Modern Greek Poetry*. Ed. by Peter Mackridge. London: Frank Cass & Co.ltd.

Krikos-Davis, Katerina. 1984. "Cats, Snakes and Poetry: A Study of Seferis' 'The Cats of Saint Nicholas'". *Journal of Modern Greek Studies* 2/2: 225–240.

—.1994. *Kolokes. a study of George Seferis' Logbook III (1953–1955)*. Amsterdam: Hakkert.

Liapis, Vayos. 2014a. "'The Painful Memory of Woe': Greek tragedy and the Greek Civil War in the work of George Seferis". *Classical Receptions Journal* 6/1: 74–103.

—.2014b. "Orestes and Nothingness: Yiannis Ritsos' 'Orestes', Greek Tragedy and Existentialism". *International Journal of the Classical Tradition* 21: 121–158.

Longenbach, James. 1987. *Modernist Poetics of History. Pound, Eliot, and the Sense of the Past*. Princeton: Princeton University Press.

Maronitis, Dimitris. 1987. "Μύθος και ιστορία στο *Ημερολόγιο Καταστρώματος Γ'*". In *Ο Σεφέρης στην πύλη της Αμμοχώστου*. Athens: National Bank of Greece Cultural Foundation. 153–169.

Mastrodimitris, P. 1964. "Η αρχαία παράδοσις εις την ποίησιν του Σεφέρη". *Parnassos* 4. offprint. 1–23.

Nikolaou, Nikos. 1992. *Μυθολογία Γ. Σεφέρη. Από τον Οδυσσέα στον Τεύκρο*. Athens: Zacharopoulos.

Pavlou, Maria. 2013. "Στοιχεία υπαρξισμού στον 'Αίαντα' του Γιάννη Ρίτσου". *Logeion. A Journal of Ancient Theatre* 3: 145–177.

Pavlou, Savvas. 2000. *Σεφέρης και Κύπρος*. Nicosia: Ministry of Education and Culture, Cultural Services.

Pippin, Anne N. 1960. "Euripides' 'Helen': A Comedy of Ideas". *Classical Philology* 55/3: 151–163.

Savvidis, George. 1992. *Οι αρχαιολογικές περιδιαβάσεις του ποιητή Γιώργου Σεφέρη*. Nicosia: Bank of Cyprus Cultural Foundation.

Seferis, George. 1964. "Letter to a Foreign Friend". Trans. N. Valaorites and E. Keeley, *Poetry Magazine* (October) 51–52. 105/1: 50–59.

—.1974. *Δοκιμές. Δεύτερος τόμος (1948–1971)*. Athens: Ikaros.

—.1976. *Τετράδιο Γυμνασμάτων, Β'*. Ed. by Giorgos P. Savvidis. Athens: Ikaros.

—.1977. *Μέρες Δ':1 Γενάρη 1941–31 Δεκέμβρη 1944*, Athens: Ikaros.

—.1981a. *Collected Poems, 1924–1955. Bilingual edition*. Trans. Edmund Keeley and Philip Sherrard, Princeton: Princeton University Press.

—.1981b. *Δοκιμές. Πρώτος τόμος (1936–1947)*. Athens: Ikaros.

—.1984. *Μέρες Γ': 16 Απριλίου 1934–14 Δεκέμβρη 1940*. Athens: Ikaros.

—.1991. *Κυπριακές επιστολές του Σεφέρη 1954-1962. Από την αλληλογραφία του με τον Σαββίδη*. Ed. by K. Kostiou. Nicosia: Bank of Cyprus Cultural Foundation.

—.1992. *Δοκιμές. Τρίτος τόμος (1932-1971)*. Athens: Ikaros.

—.2008. *Μέρες ΣΤ΄: 20 Απρίλη 1951-4 Αυγούστου 1956*. Athens: Ikaros.

—.2009. "Introduction to T. S. Eliot". Trans. Susan Matthias, *Modernism/ modernity* 16/1: 146-160.

Schwartz, Sanford. 1985. *The Matrix of Modernism. Pound, Eliot and Early Twentieth-Century Thought*. Princeton: Princeton University Press.

Segal, Charles. 1971. "The Two Worlds of Euripides' Helen". *Transactions and Proceedings of the American Philological Association* 102: 553-614.

Sommerstein, Alan H. (ed.). 2008. *Aeschylus Oresteia: Agamemnon, Libation-Bearers, Eumenides* (Loeb Classical Library 146). Cambridge, MA: Harvard University Press.

Tziovas, Dimitris. 2005. "Ο υπαρξιακός ιστορισμός του Σεφέρη". In *Από τον λυρισμό στον μοντερνισμό: πρόσληψη, ρητορική και ιστορία στη νεοελληνική ποίηση*. Athens: Nefeli. 223-233.

Vayenas, Nasos. 1991. *Ο ποιητής και ο χορευτής: μια εξέταση της ποιητικής και της ποίησης του Σεφέρη*. Athens: Kedros.

Vitti, Mario. 1978. *Φθορά και Λόγος: Εισαγωγή στην ποίηση του Σεφέρη*. Athens: Estia.

Wahl, Jean André. 1970. *Εισαγωγή στις φιλοσοφίες του υπαρξισμού*. Athens: Dodoni.

Wright, Matthew. 2005. *Euripides' Escape-Tragedies. A Study of Helen, Andromeda and Iphigenia among the Taurians*. Oxford: Oxford University Press.

Tomasz Kaczmarek[*]
Yvan Goll and Ancient Legacy in His Work

Abstract: Ivan Goll (1891–1950) represents the generation of expressionist writers who attempted to discover new forms of artistic expression. His unique works can be regarded as part of various avant-garde artistic trends seeking by any means to reject previous creative achievements. In order to implement the concept of renovation of the theatre, the author of *The Panama Canal* makes use of distant ancient legacy, in the same way as Antonin Artaud or Witkacy. In this manner, Goll – paradoxically and consequently – contributes to the crisis of drama and theatre and lays down the basis for postdramatic theatre. In this context, it seems interesting to quote Goll's *Le Surdrame (Das Überdram)*, where he specifies his new scenic visions, and to study his most important drama *Mathusalem ou l'Éternel Bourgeois (Methusalem oder Der ewige Bürger)* which is an attempt to implement these concepts in practice.

Keywords: Yvan Goll, ancient legacy, avant-garde, crisis of drama, postdramatic theatre

Literary legacy

[…] The art of the theatre is not a universal possession, available to all men as part of their cultural birthright. And even where a dramatic tradition exists, as in the ancient Near Eastern ritual performances, that tradition is not automatically identified with what Europe and America have come to regard as their theatre. European drama, Georg Lukács and others have shown, is almost entirely descended from Greek tragedy and comedy. Some, including Lukács himself, think that the twentieth-century innovations have succeeded in weakening the ancient hold. But it can also be argued that Strindberg, Wedekind, Beckett, and Pinter have, each in his way, forsaken the naturalist impasse of the nineteenth century and returned to forms and insights anticipated on the ancient stage. In spite of the manifestos of Artaud and Gordon Craig, and the directorial effects of Piscator and Vilar, modern playwriting continues in a vein that has more in common with the Greeks that with Japanese No drama or ancient Egyptian coronation texts. (Rosenmeyer 1981: 120)

It is hard nowadays to disagree with the above-quoted opinion, especially bearing in mind the fact that particularly in the first half of the 20th century, in France and elsewhere, there was a revival of interest in ancient theatre. Many French writers – the best-known being André Gide, who was considered the leader of this movement in France – referred to the ancient tradition in their neo-Hellenic dramas. It

---

[*] University of Lodz, Poland.

is the first half of the 20th century that marks the revival of ancient Greek theatre in France. Numerous playwrights made reference to ancient motifs and tried to breathe new life into tragedy (comedy was not forgotten, though) in the way that it was done by the author of *Corydon*: "they have all adopted many of his attitudes to myth, transforming and sometimes distorting the legends in the same way as he does; and they share something of his basic spiritual outlook" (Highet 1985: 531). Various adaptations of antique myths adjusted to the contemporary needs were performed on the stages of theatres in Paris and other cities, thus proving that, thanks to their universal character, the myths survived till modern times. The greatest authors of modernist tragedy are: Jean Anouilh, Jean-Paul Sartre, Jean Cocteau, Jean Giraudoux. Also in the so-called "Theatre of the Absurd" (a term coined by Martin Esslin) we may find playwrights who alluded in many different aspects to Greek tragedy. *Rhinoceros* by Eugène Ionesco is a modern tragedy, which – against the intentions of the author – was adapted to be performed on stage as a comedy. Samuel Beckett's dramas are perceived as remarkably tragic because they fail to provide a clear definition of sin and responsibility "and, above all, the ritual power of ordinary language are features which cannot be found in precisely this way outside the Western theatre, and which were put there by the Greek ancestor of the line" (Rosenmeyer 1981: 123). The reason why these playwrights choose Greek legends as their subjects is the following:

> The central answer is that the myths are permanent. They deal with the greatest of all problems, the problems which do not change because men and women do not change. They deal with love; with war, with sin; with tyranny; with courage; with fate: and all in some way or other deal with the relation of man to those divine powers which are sometimes felt to be irrational, sometimes to be cruel, and sometimes, alas, to be just. (Highet 1985: 540)

Postdramatic legacy

No one is surprised nowadays that ancient tradition has survived till our times in different forms of expression. Ancient theatre enjoys great popularity not only in terms of the very genre of drama, but also when it comes to stage setting (ritual theatrical forms, a particular use of props and costumes, and primarily masks which were later replaced by puppets and marionettes in postdramatic theatre). It is important to stress that this tradition gave rise to postdramatic theatre, which also incorporates certain elements which preceded its birth, because just like in the ancient or Asian theatre, artists in the 20th century looked for a total theatre with a metaphysical dimension that would oppose the causality typical of an ordinary drama. In the new postdramatic theatre you can find "revelation" and not "action", "performance" and not "presentation". "From Strindberg's *théâtre intime* to Wiess's dramatized 'collapse of fictions', the aim is to overcome the inhibitions imposed by Humanist canons and the requirements of a stage that is no longer ours" (Rosenmeyer 1981: 123). The departure from fiction as such (initiated at the end of the 19th century) gave rise to the process of emancipation of theatre perceived as a stage performance of drama which could be treated as a pretext, element, layer and "material" of the stage piece. One could say that the story was replaced by the game. Hans-Thies Lehmann discussed this new phenomenon in his book entitled *Postdramatic Theatre*:

> Theatre is the site not only of 'heavy' bodies but also of a real gathering, a place where a unique intersection of aesthetically organized and everyday real life takes place. In contrast to other arts, which produce an object and/or are communicated through media, here the aesthetic act itself (the performing) as well as the act of reception (the theatre going) take place as a real doing in the here and now. Theatre means the collectively spent and used up lifetime in the collectively breathed air of that space in which the performing and the spectating take place. The emission and reception of signs and signals take place simultaneously. The theatre performance turns the behaviour onstage and in the auditorium into a joint text, a 'text' even if there is no spoken dialogue on stage or between actors and audience. Therefore, the adequate description of theatre is bound to the reading of this total text. (2006: 17)

The main trends in the classical avant-garde of the 20th century contributed to the abandoning of the classical unities of drama, and thus led to establishing the postdramatic theatre. The new current was introduced with Alfred Jarry's *Ubu Roi*, whose premier in 1896 turned out to be a real scandal. Lehmann finds the forerunners of this new theatre also in the works of symbolists who, renouncing the bourgeois mentality, searched for truth in their own individual world. The symbolists (Mallarmé, Maeterlinck, Claudel) were the ones who dreamt of a completely metaphysical theatre. Although they drew their inspiration from Japanese or – more generally – Asian art, they still turned to the ritual, which – just like in ancient theatre – was supposed to illustrate the "destiny of man"; even Maeterlinck himself noticed that his concept of a "static theatre"[1] had already been known in the times before Aristotle. Undoubtedly, such popular genres as

---

1   Maeterlinck cites a number of classical Athenian tragedies in his theorical works. As Toby Cole notes, "it is no longer a violent, exceptional moment of life that passes before our eyes – it is life itself. Thousands and thousands of laws there are, mightier and more venerable than those of passion; but these laws are silent, and discreet, and slow-moving; and hence it is only in the twilight that they can be seen and heard, in the meditation that comes to us at the tranquil moments of life" (1960: 32).

cabaret, vaudeville performance, circus or *variété* must have had a significant impact on the creation of this new theatre, thanks to the element of performance that they contained. Just like Bertolt Brecht, Edward Gordon Craig or Vsevolod Meyerhold, Lehmann emphasises the undeniable contribution to the development of postdramatic theatre made by Gertrude Stein and Stanisław Ignacy Witkiewicz. Still, he does not forget about Expressionism and Surrealism, which were the main currents that initiated the new approach to theatre. The former, though not very radical or avant-garde, was the cornerstone for the future growth of the postdramatic theatre thanks to the introduction of the "play of dreams" and its combination with cabaret elements, as well as the rejection of all linguistic barriers. Similarly, Surrealism, by exploring the "world of dreams", broke away from the reality and gave way to new themes in theatre (such as, for example, exploration of the soul). Yvan Goll started his writing career as an expressionist, however, when this artistic current was declared dead, he immersed himself in Surrealism. Even though Lehmann does not even mention this dramatist or his theatre, Goll should not go unnoticed, as he has also undeniably contributed to the birth of the new theatre.

Goll's case

In his short text entitled *Le Surdrame*, Yvan Goll explains his theory of art with a lot of accuracy and precision. In the introduction he refers explicitly to Greek drama, in which – as he emphasises in accordance with his idea of the ancient theatre – gods struggled with people. In this context, he notices that ancient drama required a great intensification of reality, penetration of the secret land of passions without barriers and a devouring existential pain; it was, as he wrote, "duel divin". Such feelings could only be presented, in his opinion, with the aid of unrealistic means. Therefore, he would often use cinematographic techniques (including screening), which let him revolutionise theatre even a few years before Piscator: "c'est surtout par son exploitation de moyens et d'effets empruntés à la cinématographie que Goll réalise ce bond en avant" (Robertson 2004: 100).

According to Goll, with the disappearance of ancient theatre, man in his desire to explore and explain his own personality focused on psychology, even though words seemed inadequate for this task. Thus, over the centuries, theatre always concentrated on the mind, trying to explain what was inexplicable and what could not be empirically experienced. It is easy to notice in Goll's convictions the anticipation of the Theatre of Cruelty, or of Witkacy's search for what was commonly known as Pure Form. The author of *Les Immortels* expected the coming of a new dramatist who would reject the entire humanist heritage:

Le dramaturge nouveau sent qu'il doit livrer un combat, et affronter, en tant qu'homme, tout ce qui, en lui comme autour de lui, est animal ou chose. C'est une pénétration dans le royaume des ombres, lesquelles s'accrochent à tout et se tapissent derrière toute réalité. Après qu'elles auront été vaincues, la libération sera peut-être possible. Le poète doit réapprendre qu'il existe d'autres mondes bien différents de celui des cinq sens: le monde surréel. (Goll, 1971: 359)[2]

Not trusting psychology or reason, in general, Goll states that the new dramatist must realise that everything that surrounds him and is inside him is either "an animal or a thing". It means that man must discover his own status, which can be found beyond senses that are both limited and limiting: they indeed do not let him spot a world which is different, mysterious, but a world which is real. The new dramatist has to permeate the external world of appearances in order to reach the essence of existence. Therefore, he has to destroy the external form, all rationalism, artistic conventions, morality – in other words, all formalities related to human existence which inhibit the spiritual perception of life. This experience could be compared to a religious one, but it is not associated with any institutionalised religion; it is supposed to be an individual experience. Similarly to Luigi Pirandello, Goll rejected the idea of performance as a consumerist pleasure, believing it was meant to be something exceptional and extraordinary in human everyday life.

Goll argues, therefore, that man and all the things surrounding him should be presented completely "naked", so that they will be freed from the so-called realistic discourse that twists reality, and that in order to contribute to a better effect, everything should be shown in a distorting mirror. Only then the artist would understand that he does not live in just one reality that could only be perceived with his senses – but that there are many realities. That is why, Goll suggests, the world presented on stage should be surrealistic; this term, however, does not always mean exactly the same for him as for the father of Surrealism, André Breton. Goll deplores the fact that since the Renaissance, man has forgotten about the spiritual dimension of his life (the same opinion was also expressed by Witkacy) and about electrifying theatre performances that stirred up his emotions. He gives here an example of the Greeks, who made actors wear platform shoes and masks. For Goll, the mask is a particularly important element symbolizing "hu-

---

2   "The new drama writer feels the must of initiating the struggle and facing as a human being all what is inside and outside him an animal or an object. He ought to enter into the kingdom of shadows which clings to everything and hide behind reality. After they are defeated, liberation is probably possible. The poet should learn again that there exists also another world, differing form the one based on the five senses: the supernatural world" (Translation T.K.).

man destiny". As he explains, everyone wears a mask, which is "called 'guilt' by the Greeks" (Goll 1971: 359). Children are afraid of the mask and scream when they see it; Adults, though so self-confident and rational, should again learn to scream. The mask[3] expresses what is incomprehensible and this is why art must reveal unreality. Man must become a child again, since a child experiences the world more profoundly. To achieve this goal, man must repudiate the mind, which is his worst enemy. Art, thus, must reject the mind, too.

Goll observes that there are many technological devices that replace the mask, such as the phonograph that changes the human voice, the illuminated advertisement or the megaphone. All of these are used to create a strange atmosphere and, at the same time, scare the audience, take away their peace of mind, or simply even to attack them. Actors should wear strange, huge masks, their outfits should also give the impression as if they were being observed through a magnifying glass. All these stage techniques applied by expressionists and surrealists anticipate undoubtedly postdramatic theatre. The artists intended to reject the humanist tradition which, in their opinion, still prevailed in bourgeois theatre, and to create a completely new art that would suit the new times.

> L'art n'est pas là pour la commodité des gros bourgeois, qui secouent la tête, disant: « Oui, oui, c'est comme çà. A présent, allons au buffet nous rafraichaîr! » L'art, dans la mesure où il veut éduquer, améliorer, être efficace d'une façon quelconque, doit supprimer l'homme de tous les jours, l'effrayer comme le masque effraie l'enfant et Euripide les Athéniens, qui sortaient du théâtre en titubant. L'art doit refaire de l'homme un enfant. Le moyen le plus simple, pour y arriver, c'est le « grotesque », dans la mesure où il n'incite pas à rire. La monotonie et la bêtise des hommes sont si énormes qu'on ne peut y remédier qu'avec des énormités. Que le drame nouveau soit donc énorme. (*ibid.*)[4]

Theatre, according to Goll, is not supposed to be merely a pleasant entertainment which the bourgeois audience is accustomed to. A play must appal the audience, shock them, attack all their senses, and be hard to get over – which was also ad-

---

3 Goll, writing about masks, meant the masks of Aeschylus, which were supposed to evoke fear.
4 "The art serves not for the comfort of a fat bourgeois nodding the head while speaking: 'Yes, yes, it is so. And now, let's go to the buffet and get some refreshments!' The art as it wants to educate, improve and be effective in any way must eliminate a regular human being, frighten him in a way a mask frightens a child, as Euripides did with Athenians who upon leaving the theater were still trembling. Art must turn an adult into a child again. The simplest way to do so is through grotesque, as long as it does not encourage laughter. The monotony and stupidity of humans are so enormous that they can be cured only by enormity. Let the new drama be enormous". (Translation T.K.)

vocated by Jarry. Although we do not have any historical evidence reflecting the experiences of the ancient audience, it is obvious that the issues raised in Greek tragedies (such as physical suffering, physical torment, the atrocity of the world, misery and, finally, the inevitable loss of life) must have deeply touched them. It is Euripides, as Goll claims, whom the Greeks "adored to hate" for the feeling of moral insecurity that he evoked in them, which, according to the writer, led the audience to a certain psychological trauma leaving them stunned after the performance. Goll wants to use the grotesque in theatre, however, the grotesque is not there to entertain people, but to illustrate the distorted world. Witkacy perceived the role of theatre in a similar way, saying that the audience was supposed to experience a metaphysical trauma. Antonin Artaud based the Theatre of Cruelty on the same grounds. Goll's artistic motto, therefore, corresponds very well with the avant-garde assumptions of Futurism, Dadaism and Surrealism, which attempted to attack the audience physically, mentally and psychologically. Those movements undoubtedly placed great emphasis on the event (i.e. performance) and not the drama as such. Obviously, the very activity of watching may always lead to an unexpected reaction of the audience, but when it comes to Goll, the reaction and the impact of the drama on the audience became an essential part of the performance. That is why his literary achievement is considered to be the forerunner of postdramatic theatre. It seems reasonable now to analyse Goll's drama in order to see how he intended to put his literary assumptions into life.

Mathusalem

Goll did not write too many dramas and mainly devoted himself to poetry. Certainly, however, his most successful and representative work is the satirical drama *Mathusalem*,[5] which best reflects his poetics. It should be mentioned that while Goll was writing the drama, he was still under the influence of expressionist aesthetics (particularly pacifist and grotesque trends), even though he sensed the oncoming decline of the movement. He was, however, already much attracted to Surrealism, whose manifesto, although not yet announced by André Breton, had already been anticipated by one of the most remarkable poets of the time, Guillaume Apollinaire. It was him who used this word for the first time in the preface to his play *Les Mamelles de Tirésias*. "Goll was a terrific admirer of Apollinaire,

---

5   The play was written in 1919 and published in 1923, in Paris. It was staged fort the first time five years later in Théâtre Michel, directed by Jean Painlevé. The German version appeared in 1922. In 1924 it enjoyed a great success in Berlin – the stage design was made by Georg Grosz himself.

and he particularly championed Apollinaire's idea of Surrealism" (Witkovsky 2004: 4). He often argued about its meaning with Brenton who borrowed the term from Appolinare, but understood it in a much wider context. Just before the announcement of the Surrealist Manifesto (1924), Goll published the first and only issue of his periodical *Surréalisme* (Cf. Stubbs 1997: 69–74). In the periodical, however, Goll rejects the fundamental assumptions of Surrealism, such as automatic registration of dreams or insight into subconsciousness, and concentrates on the satirical aspect of artistic expression. Goll feels attracted to modernist satire which in order to rouse the audience and awake them from the state of torpor has to resort to other exciting stimuli such as grotesque or absurd. This satire can be found in Surrealism and "illogical" dramaturgy, as he firmly acknowledges in the preface written one year after the drama (1920):

> La dramaturgie alogique a pour but de tourner en ridicule nos lois de tous les jours, et de démasquer le mensonge profond de la logique mathématique ou même de la dialectique. En même temps, l'alogique servira à montrer les mille chatoiements d'un cerveau humain qui pense une chose et en dit une autre et qui saute d'une idée à une autre sans la moindre apparence de lien logique. (Goll, 1963: 11)[6]

Illogical dramaturgy makes fun of all aspects and rules of our everyday life, it tears the masks of lies, since our *logical* reasoning is subjected to the tyranny of the mind. A free man must reject the dialectics of reason in order to be able to enjoy genuine freedom. This is, according to Goll, the role of theatre: it was to be a spiritual feast actively involving the audience. His further reflections include an important remark which emphasises the innovative character of dramaturgy and thus anticipates postdramatic theatre:

> L'action du drame? Les événements sont si forts en eux-mêmes, qu'ils agissent d'eux-mêmes. Un homme est écrasé dans la rue: c'est un événement qui fait irruption, dur et irréparable, dans l'existence du monde. Pourquoi ne considère-t-on comme tragique que la mort d'un homme ? Il peut arriver qu'un entretien de cinq phrases avec une inconnue soit plus tragique pour toute l'éternité. (Goll, 1963: 11)[7]

---

6   "Illogical dramaturgy aims to ridicule the everyday laws and to unmask the deep lie of mathematical or even dialectical logic. At the same time, 'the illogical' serves to show thousands of reflections of the human brain that thinks one thing while speaking the other and jumps from one thought to another with no clear logic". (Translation T.K.)
7   "What is drama action? The events themselves are so strong that they seem to act by themselves. [For example] A man is smashed on the street: It is an event that disrupts the world's order. Why is the man's death considered to be tragic? It might happen that a small talk with a stranger will turn to be more tragic for eternity". (Translation T.K.)

The events on stage are to result from themselves, they are to have a life of their own which takes place "here and now", during the performance. It is not necessary to present the death of a man, as if it was the most tragic event. The very word, as August Strindberg would put it, may be more "seminal"; it can also kill. On the one hand, the word has a destructive power, and on the other, it undergoes the process of *autonomisation* and acquires its own life. That is the reason why the grotesque will also be reflected in the language, which will undergo the process of deconstruction, both syntactic and semantic. Language was to be one of the elements of stage setting, employed like other elements to affect the senses of the audience. We can cite here the scene in which guests come to visit Mathusalem to prove that the dialogue bears an apparent resemblance to Eugène Ionesco's style in *La Cantatrice Chauve* (*The Bald Soprano*):

> M. Camphre: Quelle température, ah quelle température !
> M. Jésufils : Si encore il pleuvait !
> M. Assiette : Vous êtes fou ! Et mes souliers qui prennent l'eau !
> Mme Assiette : Assiette ! Assieds-toi ! Et tais-toi ! As-tu besoin de raconter sur les toits que tes souliers prennent l'eau ? Et d'abord, ce n'est pas vrai ! Tes souliers ont été raccomodés l'année dernière.
> M. Assiette : Le cordonnier a dit…
> Mme Assiette : Non ! Les semelles vont encore ! Tant que les trous ne seront pas comme des pièces de deux sous.
> M. Assiette : Mais je t'assure qu'ils sont comme un sou !
> Mme Assiette : Assiette, assieds-toi ! Je les ai mesurés moi-même ! Tu ne me feras rien accroire !
> M. Camphre : Écoutez-moi : d'abord vous achetez un cataplasme…
> Mme Camphre : Vous chauffez de l'eau.
> M. Camphre : Vous prenez de la guimauve.
> Mme Camphre : Vous faites venir le plombier si le gaz ne marche pas.
> M. Camphre : Vous vous lavez les pieds.
> Mme Camphre : Si l'on vous demande un pourboir, répondez: Et moi, pour manger ?
> (Goll 1963 : 55–56)[8]

---

8   "Mr Camphre: It's so hot! Oh, it's so hot!
    Mr Jésufils: If only it was raining!
    Mr Assiette: You are mad! My shoes would get wet!
    Ms Assiette: Assiette, please, sit down and shut up! Do you really have to tell everyone that your shoes are getting wet? Surely, this cannot be true! Your shoes were repaired last year.
    Mr Assiette: The shoemaker said…
    Ms Assiette: No, the soles are quite good! As long as the holes are not the size of a two-sou coin.

Beyond question, Goll's drama is a satire against the bourgeois middle class, their stupidity and greed. The use of surrealist aesthetics allowed the author to create characters which become real puppets. *Mathusalem* is an example of a peculiar, grotesque ballet performance, in which the characters, deprived of individual qualities, represent the vices of the bourgeoisie.

The first scene opens in the apartment of the title protagonist, Mathusalem who is sitting in a big plush armchair, reading a broadsheet newspaper. He has a red face, bald skull and an inseparable attribute of the bourgeois – a big belly on which rests a gold watch with a golden chain that resembles a chain of a convict. The hideous man is accompanied by his wife, who is bedecked with jewellery, wearing golden necklaces, earrings and rings. The two represent a typical bourgeois marriage whose relationship is full of hypocrisy: the husband has a mistress, and the wife spends his "hard-earned" money at night. The dialogue that they engage in immediately brings to mind Ionesco's *jeux de massacres*. It sounds empty, as the words they use carry no meaning, and are only a combination of hackneyed clichés. After a trivial conversation, the wife leaves the husband, who falls asleep. The scenes that follow present his dreams projected on a screen on stage. In the first dream, we see the protagonist walking around the city: it is possible to notice only the shoes of the passers-by. The camera shows then the naked legs of a woman who reminds the protagonist of all the different women in his life. Mathusalem takes off the woman's shoe and suggest that she should buy his shoes instead (he is a shoe seller), and then they will be able to go to bed together. In the second dream, Mathusalem passes a theatre staging *Hamlet*. He enters the building, then gets on the stage, takes away the skull from the actor and puts a shoe into his hands. Hamlet holds the shoe and continues his monologue. In his third dream, Mathusalem is a general and instead of the words "allons enfants de la partie" from *La Marseillaise* sings "allons enfants de la chaussure".

Mr Assiette: I can assure you that these holes are as big as a one-sou coin.
Ms Assiette: Please, sit down! I have measured them by myself. I will not let you suggest anything!
Mr Camphre: Listen to me: first you have to buy a poultice.
Ms Camphre: You have to heat the water.
Mr Camphre: You have to take a marshmallow.
Ms Camphre: You have to call a plumber if the heater doesn't work.
Mr Camphre: You have to wash your legs.
Ms Camphre: If someone asks you for a tip, ask him: "And for me a deep?" [The text contains many untranslatable wordplays. In the last line, the word *pourboir*, meaning "tip", can be literally translated as "for drink", while *pour manger* means "for food"]. (Translation T.K.)

In the drama we can find many other absurd situations like these. In the scene "Animal Revolution" we witness a conversation between a cat, a dog, a cuckoo with a clock, a bear and a parrot, who discuss the topic of a rebellion against the human race. In another scene, the portrait of a grandmother suddenly starts speaking and recalls her first love, and those memories become echoed by the mirror. In scene number IV, we meet Felix, Mathusalem's son, who, as Goll himself explains in the stage directions, is a caricature of a businessman: on his head there is a metal phone with antennas and a small lamp that blinks with red and green lights. He is wearing a mask, and instead of his eyes we see two five-franc coins. He talks all the time in a robotic-like manner about different events that affect the stock market. Similarly, in the scene presenting a feast at Mathusalem's place, the men wear huge masks, whereas their wives wear on their heads a pot of geranium, a stuffed rooster or a cardboard copy of Pantheon. In scene number V, a student in love with Felix's sister, Ida, is presented by means of three different protagonists reflecting different psychical states of someone in love (Me, You, Him). Goll's drama abounds with absurdities. In order to save the family's good reputation, Felix kills the student who dared to fall in love with his sister. On stage, we see the spirit of the infatuated student rising in the air. In the next scene, however, the student talks to an unknown Monica and plots to kill Mathusalem. Later, it turns out that the student, infatuated with Mathusalem's daughter Ida, wants in fact to take control over Mathusalem's bourgeois' property. Paradoxically, his very confession wins Mathusalem's friendship. From this moment on, Mathusalem glorifies the student as a good entrepreneur. This, however, does not stop the student, who in cold-blood shoots Mathusalem dead. The last scene, shows Ida and the student, who are now are a married couple living an everyday life: their child pees on the mother's skirt, and the husband worries that the price of sugar has gone up again. They are now typical representatives of the bourgeois, which is reflected in their bourgeois manners. Towards the end of the play, Mathusalem appears and announces that it is mealtime, which takes us back to the banality of the opening scene.

It seems that a few decades before the arrival of the Theatre of the Absurd, Goll's drama could be regarded as a model of anti-drama. This statement is not legally valid, as the plot could simply be treated as a story of the bourgeois middle class and their obsession with hoarding money. Nevertheless, the drama incorporated Goll's new stage vision. This procedure is obviously nothing new, and many authors wanted to give assistance to directors in this matter. In this case, the author seems to treat his work as a musical score for the concertmaster. In the drama, Goll included certain elements of deformation – or even deconstruction – of the text for the sake of a particular type of performance. The very precise stage directions indicate that Goll paid more attention to how the performance should affect the audience than to the literary value of the text itself – mere reading would not produce the intended effect (Witkacy must have had a similar view on his dramaturgy). It is known that Goll, dissatisfied with the course of action, placed the characters of his play among the audience, wanting to encourage them to participate in the performance.[9] His screenplay – that is how Goll's text should be perceived – predicted (or anticipated) different reactions of the audience. However, as an *avant la lettre* writer, he did not reject the word as such, unlike Antonin Artaud, who probably lost confidence in words as a result of his poetic failures. For Goll, words are important, but to the same extent as decorations, actors' clothes, gestures, lighting and many other factors that contribute to the overall effect of the performance. The word, therefore, does not lose its significance but becomes a part of the stage setting and is no longer its dominant, as it used to be in the past.

Similarly to Alfred Kerr (1919), Goll wishes the word could be replaced by "the external stimulus" (Außenreiz). The word is to give way to grotesque imagery. It is this imagery that triggers off a new artistic form, and not words as such which only help to evoke a certain image. Such an approach inevitably announced the postdramatic theatre. "La dramaturgie du 'Außenreiz' pose comme première condition la scène entièrement ouverte. Les personnages entrent et sortent, ouvrent des fenêtres pour s'adresser à une foule excitée qui s'évanouit aussitôt. A ce va-et-vient endiablé s'ajoutent les projections ou le cas échéant des films faisant pénétrer la réalité tout entière sur le lieu théâtral" (Schlocker 1971: 139).[10] Such considerations could lead to a conclusion that theatre has become an epic form understood in the way suggested by Peter Szondi. Goll, however, while writing his drama thought about a performance that would be a melting pot for many different arts. He was way ahead of his time and he must have subconsciously dreamt of a new theatre, which took shape at the end of the 20th century. One could dare claim that – in Goll's vision – dialogues on stage were only important if they reached the inner emotions of the audience.

---

9   Jean-Victor Pellerin introduced a similar strategy in his play entitled *Terrain vague* (1931).
10 "The dramaturgy of 'Außenreiz' demands as its first condition that the scene is open. The characters come and go, open the windows in order to address speeches to the excited crowd that immediately disperses. This commotion will be accompanied by film projections penetrating the scenic reality". (Translation T.K.)

Conclusion

Yvan Goll was a very original writer and his artistic work could easily parallel the quests of Witkacy and Antonin Artaud. Similarly to them, he created a personal vision of a new theatre that could not be fully accomplished until the 1970s. At the beginning of his literary path, he manifested interest in expressionist aesthetics, he dealt with linguistic innovations (he often adopted a telegram style), he destroyed the uniform perspective on the logic behind human behaviour. Expressionism advocated drama focused on "me" and a sketchy plot (station drama), which enabled to present unconsciousness subjected to the logic of nightmares. It was the imagination that contributed to the destruction of the obsolete drama structure. Surrealism, on the other hand, taught Goll the technique of cuts, collages and multilateralism in associations, and above all, the quest for a public event. Undoubtedly, the assumptions of performance art originated in Surrealism but also in the previously formed futurism. Surrealism intended to activate the audience and stir them in the way Alfred Jarry did. Goll desired the same and, contrary to avant-garde movements that dismissed the tradition *en bloc*, he based his vision of theatre revival, at least to some extent, on ancient theatre. In his manifesto, the author openly indicated Greek drama as an antidote to the "realistic theatre" which became mere entertainment. He wanted to go back to the origins of the theatre and rediscover the techniques capable of shocking spectators by exploring their souls and turning the performance into an "amazing experience". Goll was inspired by the ancient vision of the world where the issues related to life and death were omnipresent, even if they were portrayed in a humorous way. Especially fascinated by the mask, which became in his eyes a symbol of the old theatre and by the modern use of this prop, he wanted to revive the ancient aesthetics and breathe a new spirit into dramatic art. It is hard to say whether the writer managed to fully achieve his artistic goals. Goll, like Witkacy or Artaud, seemed to realise that, despite the originality of his drama, he was still stuck in the literary poetics. His ideas were to be fully accomplished in postdramatic theatre, some elements of which were already unquestionably manifested in *Mathusalem*.

References:

Cole, Toby. 1960. *Playwrights on Playwriting. From Ibsen to Ionesco*. New York: Cooper Square Press.

Goll, Yvan. 1963. *Mathusalem, Les Immortels*. Paris: L'Arche Saint-Amand.

—.1971, "Le surdrame". In: *L'Expressionnisme dans le théâtre européen*. Eds. by Denis Bablet, Jean Jacquot. Paris. Éditions du Centre National de la Recherche Scientifique, 359–360.

Highet, Gilbert. 1985. *The Classical Tradition. Greek and Roman Influences on Western Literature*. Oxford: Oxford University Press.

Lehmann, Hans-Thies. 2006. *Postdramatic Theatre*. Trans. by Karen Jürs-Munby. London and New York: Routledge.

Schlocker, Georges. 1971. "Le cas Ivan Goll". In *L'Expressionnisme dans le théâtre européen*, Eds. by Denis Bablet, Jean Jacquot. Paris. Éditions du Centre National de la Recherche Scientifique. 133–139.

Robertson, Eric. 2004. "Yvan Goll et la poésie cinématographique". *Europe*, n° 899: 95–109.

Rosenmeyer, T. G. 1981. "Drama". In *The Legacy of Greece. A New Appraisal*. Ed. by Moses I. Finley. Oxford: Oxford University Press.

Stubbs, Jeremy. 1997. "Goll versus Breton: The Battle for Surrealisme". In Robertson Eric, Robert Vilain. *Yvan Goll – Claire Goll: Texts and Contexts*. Amsterdam: Rodopi.

Witkovsky, Matthew S. 2004. "Surrealism in the Plural: Guillaume Apollinaire, Ivan Goll and Devětsil in the 1920s". *Papers of Surrealism* Issue 2: 1–14.

Anna Zaorska*

Myths as "Collective Experiences" in the German Democratic Republic on the Example of Chosen Works by Heiner Müller

Abstract: The writers of the German Democratic Republic often reached for myths in order to discuss forbidden issues in an oblique way and deceive the censors. In one of the interviews, Heiner Müller admits that the purpose of these attempts was to raise crucial questions about socialism: "I want neither to write ancient plays today nor to adapt ancient topics. In the early 1960s the plays about Stalinism were forbidden. It was necessary to invent such a model to raise really important issues so that people could realize them at once." The present article, basing on the works *Philoctetes* and *The Horatian* will discuss the reception of two ancient myths in the plays by Heiner Müller. The German playwright employs an interesting strategy: He adopts myths in varied, condensed form, setting the plot in mythical circumstances. Müller does not make an attempt to modernise his dramas by transferring their content into the new setting of time and space, but instead, he draws parallels between past and present. Müller's plays are, in Norbert Otto Eke's opinion, both historical and contemporary drama. Interestingly, according to Bertolt Brecht's idea and his "alienation effect", the spectators should not identify themselves with the events on stage, but only follow and analyse them. For this reason, the works of Müller can be qualified as didactic plays.

Keywords: Heiner Müller, myth in literature, Philoctetes

Despite the pass of time and a wide variety of contemporary issues that the writers get their inspiration from, myths still belong to one of the most popular motifs in literature. It appears that Bertolt Brecht was right in considering mythology a bottomless treasure chest. The creator of the epic theatre did not even feel the need to give references for quotations, because he considered myths to be a cultural heritage that should be obvious for every moderately educated reader. Therefore, according to Brecht, the use of quotation marks in case of many well-known ancient (e.g. Euripides, Sophocles) or world (Shakespeare) dramas was completely unnecessary. Brecht's *oeuvre* and his fundamentals of the epic theatre also appealed to the interests of another German playwright: Heiner Müller.

Heiner Müller, born 1929 in Eppendorf, is one of the most eminent and highly regarded exponents of the German Democratic Republic literature. His first writ-

---

* University of Lodz, Poland.

ing attempts can be dated back to the beginning of the GDR. While his parents Ella and Kurt Müller with his brother Wolfgang decided to emigrate in 1951 to West Germany for political reasons, Heiner Müller resolved to stay in East Germany and start his career as a writer. Although he had many chances to leave the German Democratic Republic, he resolved never to do it, seeing his life as a material for theatre that he wanted to reflect and exploit for the future as a unique experience of divided Germany and divided Europe as well (cf. Muskała 2000: 191). Following the criteria established by Wolfgang Schivelbusch, many literary specialists distinguish three crucial phases of Müller's work and life, namely:

- production plays (Produktionsstücke), 1950s, e.g.. *The Scab (Der Lohndrücker)* 1957, *The Correction (Die Korrektur)* 1957, about work and life conditions in a socialist state,
- ancient plays (Antikenstücke), 1960s, e.g.. *Philoctetes (Philoktet)* 1961, *The Horatian (Der Horatier)* 1968, *Mauser* 1970, *Sophocles: Oedipus the King (Sophokles: Ödipus Tyrann)* 1966/67, *Herakles 5* 1964, *Prometheus* (performed in 1969), *Despoiled Shore Medea Material Landscape with Argonauts (Verkommenes Ufer Medeamaterial Landschaft mit Argonauten)* 1982,
- plays about Germany (Deutschlandstücke), 1970s, e.g. *Germania Death in Berlin (Germania Tod in Berlin)* 1971, *Volokolomsk Highway* I–V (*Wolokolamsker Chaussee* I–V)

As Wolfgang Emmerich emphasised, an overly transparent categorization of Müller's literary output does not reflect its true character, as his works often go beyond the outlined frames (cf. Emmerich: 141). A striking example of such an "inconsistency" is the attention Müller paid to the myth of Medea, adapting it in more than one work. For the first time, this reference appears in the drama *Cement* (*Zement*, 1972) in which one of the scenes is entitled *Medeakommentar*. Two years later, Müller wrote the pantomime entitled *Medeaspie*. Finally, his interest in the myth of Medea became expressed in his trilogy published eight years later, namely *Despoiled Shore Medea-material Landscape with Argonauts*.[1] The common denominator of his works seems to be history, and more specifically, the history of Germany and Europe. Even his plays inspired by the Antique, which apparently do not refer to the present, include many allusions to the political situation that surrounded the author. Müller considers myths as solidified, collective experi-

---

1 The fragment dedicated to the division of work and life of Heiner Müller was taken from the following PhD dissertation: Anna Zaorska: *"My Crimes Are Born from Love". The Myth of Medea in the German Literature.*

ences and, at the same time, as a kind of Esperanto that is nowadays understood in Europe and beyond (Müller 1992: 321). He used this language to provoke reflection and to raise in an oblique way some of the issues that were relevant at the time. The present paper is an attempt to follow the function of a myth on the basis of Heiner Müller's two dramas: *Philoctetes* and *The Horatian*.

The history of Philoctetes, a warrior leader, best known for his participation in Trojan War and the quest of Atreides, has many variations.[2] According to some mythological tales, Philoctetes took part in the quest to reclaim Menelaus' wife, Helen. During the quest, he encountered Heracles and freed him from the suffering caused by his wife Deianira. For lighting the funeral pyre, he received, as an expression of gratitude, a magical bow and arrows poisoned with the blood of the Hydra of Lerna (cf. Chodkowski 2009: 259). It can be assumed that Philoctetes was an excellent archer and a brave warrior. During the sacrificial feast on the Greek island Tenedos he was bitten by a snake, the wound began to fester and reek. Philoctetes' companions unable to stand the stench and his screams, abandoned him on Lesbos disregarding his previous glorious acts. According to a prophecy, the fate of the Trojan War could get changed because of Philoctetes, therefore Odysseus (or, according to other tales, Diomedes) returned to Lesbos and asked him for help. The plot of this history was used by Sophocles in his drama, published in 431 BC and named after the main character *Philoctetes*. It was the work of the ancient dramatist that Heiner Müller based his play upon. The German playwright informed in his autobiography *Krieg ohne Schlacht* (*War Without Battle*) that his interest in the Philoctetes myth dates to the 1950s, when he created a poem dedicated to the mythical hero came into existence (cf. Müller 1999: 188). The first scene is dated back to 1953, the entire work was completed in 1961, but it was published in 1965 in the periodical *Sinn und Form* (*Sense and Form*) (cf. Müller 1999: 189). The premier of *Philoctetes* on stage, however, took place after a certain time.

Creating plays over extended periods of time was not uncommon for Müller. Combining fragments written in different moments gave his works a mosaic or collage-like quality. Because of this, his works are often not homogeneous, and their definitive shape reflects the process of creation determined by different moments of his life; for example, *Despoiled Shore Medea Material Landscape with Argonauts* consists of numerous texts written over the time span of three decades. In this respect, *Philoctetes*, despite the time over which it was written, is quite cohesive and lacks capital letters, which Müller frequently used. The text, however,

---

2   Cf. Segal. 1998 and Winnington-Ingram 1980.

in contrast to other plays, does not contain punctuation marks. On the one hand, the lack of punctuation marks made the reception of the text more difficult; on the other, it acted as an encouragement to reading it in diverse variants. It is significant that Müller restricted mythical motifs and modernised the plot by stripping it from fantastic and religious themes. Instead, He focuses on the story itself and limits the number of protagonists to three: Odysseus, Neoptolemus and Philoctetes. Thus, there is no chorus that would comment the plot, no Hercules and no servants of Odysseus, which additionally emphasises the loneliness of Philoctetes. The limited number of characters and lack of focus on their psychological development allows to focus on the characters' ideological attitudes. According to Uwe Schütte, the removal of the outside characters that draw the attention of the recipients helps to underline the conflict of social classes. In Schütte's opinion, the main conflict, both in the *oeuvre* of Sophocles and Müller, is the one between civil duties and the individual right to autonomy (cf. Schütte 2010: 37).

Müller's text seems to resemble the ancient drama structure[3] with that it opens with a prologue. It is, however, merely an apparent reference to the classical form. In the text there is no parting into stasimons and epeisodions or acts, the text shows a hermetic structure, although the unity of time, place and action is maintained. The prologue contains the only reference to the ancient drama, however, this reference comes to an abrupt end:

[Spoken in a clown's mask by the actor who portrays PHILOCTETES]
Dear audience, the play we are about to show
Will waft you from today to long ago
When man was foe to man, when life was tough,
And every month another bloody war came off.
Our spectacle is grim – let me be plain –
It lacks a Message to take home and frame,
Or useful lesson for a cloudy day.
If you're alarmed – the exit lies that way.
[The doors fly open]
You've had your chance.
[The doors close. The clown unmasks and reveals a death's head]
Our business hereafter
Is meant for something else than laughter. (Müller 1981: 223)

---

3   Heiner Müller is not the only 20th century European writer to refer to Greek mythology and Athenian tragedy. It is also worth to mention the works of Federico García Lorca, which were heavily influenced by Aeschylus and Euripides, as well as Jean-Paul Sartre's *The Flies,* being a French adaptation of Orestes and Electra myth, and *The Cure at Troy* written by Seamus Heaney, refering to *Philoctetes.*

The introduction suggests an innovative approach which will make the text different from typical adaptation of the mythical matter. It uses a typical for ancient literature rhetorical figure known as *recusatio*, which allows the author to pretend humility and become ironic. Already in the beginning, Müller mentions the anachronism and the juxtaposition of other settings. To follow Brecht, the author reminds the public that the situation on the stage they are exposed to is merely a theatre performance, and intrigues with the assertion that the play lacks moral and therefore is useless. The prologue combines the features of comedy and tragedy. The performer of the main role appears in a clown mask and speaks about hatred and wars. He then takes the mask off, revealing that behind it is the head of death. Müller's plays are often based upon contrasts that are additionally underlined and emphasised. It can be assumed that Müller's inclination was to combine settings and to reduce the psychological portrait of the characters, as well as to limit the play only to the plot itself. As he explains in *Three Points with Reference to Philoctetes*, the plot is a model, not a story. Its aim is to show attitudes, not meaning (cf. Müller 1989: 61). In Müller's opinion, the course of events is indisputable only when it does not undermine the system and, as he states, "Only a clown can question the circus" (*ibid.*). Philoctetes, Odysseus and Neoptelemus are defined as clowns and gladiators of his philosophy of life and ideology as well (cf. *ibid.*).

After the modernised prologue, the plot moves to Philoctetes' place of stay, Lemnos. Odysseus and Neoptelemus worked out a plan to convince Philoctetes to leave the Greek island and go with them to Troy. Although Müller adopts from his drama the plot and the names of his characters, he also removed from it many mythological motifs. There is, for example, no mention of the magical bow, and its function was reduced merely to that of a weapon. As Seth Schein notices, in the ancient version of the play, the choir sympathises with Philoctetes (cf. Schein 2013: 19), in Müller's version the lack of choir is emphasising the hero's loneliness.[4] There is also no mention of the fortune-teller Helenus who told the Greeks that they would conquer Troy only with the help of Philoctetes (cf. Chodkowski 2009: 261). Philoctetes in Müller's version is needed as a leader and a hero who could spur the warriors to fight in the battle. Odysseus and Neoptelemus rightly anticipate opposition and reluctance of Philoctetes. Abandoned on the island, he became a distrustful recluse with a hostile attitude towards the Greeks. Uwe Schütte noticed that Müller's drama lacks positive characters (cf. Schütte 2010: 38)

---

4   In Philoctetes' isolation reader can notice autobiographic theme (cf. Hacks 2015: 276). Müller, who was excluded from Writers Association, could feel as abandoned and alienated as the title character.

and Otto Norbert Eke made a note that the drama is based on hatred (cf. Eke 1999: 108). Indeed, Philoctetes hates Odysseus for abandoning and banishing him. Also Neoptolemus hates Odysseus, believing he was responsible for depriving his father of his possessions. Odysseus, cynically takes advantage of the situation and uses it to manage political conflicts. Hence, according to the idea of Müller, three different attitudes emerge: Philoctetes becomes broken as a result of politics; Neoptolemus acting in the name of higher ethical principles, becomes a moralist who abandons the values he used to represent; Odysseus acts for the sake of political aims and, seeing them as the highest priority, follows the principle "the end justifies the means" (cf. *ibid*.: 107). In the centre of attention of Müller's drama are the conflicts between different mentalities, between subjective and objective ethics, freedom and necessity, morals and obligations (cf. *ibid*.: 106). Andreas Moser is right pointing that the problem of structures is more important than the well-being of the individual (Moser 2014: 297), and Ralph Fischer stresses that the wound of Philoctetes signifies a destabilisation of structures and a rupture in the system (cf. Fischer 2012: 87).

The internal conflict is most clearly reflected in Neoptolemus who, on the one hand, follows his moral rules and on the other, tries to achieve his political aims. In a moment of weakness, however, he confesses the truth:

> NEOPTOLEMUS. And let me speak the truth. Troy cannot fall
> Without your soldiers. Your soldiers will not fight
> Unless you lead them. I have plowed the sea
> To fetch you back to Troy where you shall rise
> From long despair to endless glory.
> Myself a dupe, reluctantly I duped
> The victim of too many lies. Duty
> Made me lie: there was no honest way.
> Man of Lemnos, hear the whole hateful truth:
> On the beach Odysseus waits, your foe
> And mine. For this much was no lie: he dies
> Dies by my hand, by ours if you choose
> After Troy falls. Help us speed its destruction
> And therefore his. (…) (Müller 1981: 236)

However, Neoptolemus' turn towards Philoctetes is a temporary one. When he comes into the possession of the bow, he allies with Odysseus again. The turn he makes results from pragmatism: Philoctetes refrains from helping Greeks voluntarily, whereas Neoptolemus is determined to fight against the enemies, even if the price for his fame will be dishonour. If the need arises, he is determined to force Philoctetes to leave the island. Neoptolemus' internal conflict is shown in the scene in which he returns Philoctetes back his bow, saying the following words: "Take it, before his words beguile me again" (Müller 1976: 99). According to Eke, it was not the compassion, but rather the feeling of shame about losing his own moral integrity, and the hatred towards Odysseus who is skilled in persuasion, that make Neoptelemus act righteously and give the bow back (cf. Eke 1999: 109). However, ultimately it is Neoptelemus who maliciously kills Philoctetes to save Odysseus, seeing in him the hope for rescue. Philoctetes dies stabbed in the back with the sword. His death is not a heroic one and turns him from a victim to a martyr. Karol Sauerland aptly notes that the Lemnos quest of Odysseus and Neoptelemus reveals the functioning of the mechanisms of political power. The example of Neoptelemus, exposes the consequences of the system of needs and necessities that, according to Sauerland, all too early gained new "virtues" (cf. Sauerland 1976: 111).

After Philoctetes becomes killed, Odysseus comes up with an idea how the dead Philoctetes could help to execute his plan. He creates a story according to which the Trojans attempted to convince Philoctetes to join their side. Motivated by patriotic reasons, Philoctetes refused to join the enemies and remained faithful to his comrades, for which he was killed by the Trojans:

> Alas the Trojans came ashore before us
> To turn this man against his fellow Greeks.
> But he staunch Greek kept faith with us, not gold
> Nor eloquence nor threats could shake his truth,
> For which they murdered him. We saw him perish
> Saw him from the sea while wrestling for our lives
> With the wild waters: beset upon his rock
> By seven Trojans, till the eight slew him
> From behind and louder than the breakers
> Rang his cry. (…) (Müller 1981: 249)

To this, Neoptelemus responds:

> If Philoctetes can be spared, so can you.
> You showed me how to trample underfoot
> What's best in me. I, thief, liar, killer,
> I saw the Trojans murder not one man but
> Two. (Müller 1981: 249)

The above scene shows lack of respect for individual rights, in this case the right to rest in peace. From Odysseus' cynical perspective, even the corpse of Philoctetes can help his state. In the end, Odysseus manages to dissuade Neoptelemus from murdering him. As the two go away, with dead Philoctetes at Odysseus' back,

Odysseus promises to reveal Neoptolemus, when they reach Troy, how Neoptolemus could have dealt with the situation and killed Odysseus without arousing anyone's suspicions.

While the characters of Philoctetes or Neoptolemus were seen as positive, the evaluation of Odysseus was in general negative. Polish expert, Stanisław Witkowski, emphasised in 1930 that Odysseus, from Sophocles' point of view, is not only a ruthless, cunning master of intrigues, but also the personification of the reason of state.[5] The same receptive tendency was also indicated by Heiner Müller who pointed out that Odysseus was perceived as a scoundrel, an incarnation of evil, a Stalinist. In Müller's opinion, he is a man who unites diverse attitudes.

The outline of the play is generally pessimistic, as hypocrisy, cynicism and lies prevail. The morality of an individual is lost in the political pragmatism, however, it should be emphasised that such results are caused by the people. In Müller's play, deus *ex machina* or transcendental causation factors are not present. Equally disheartening is the depravation of the human from his individuality and the reduction of his role to pragmatic functions.

To summarise, Peter Hacks mentioned three possible variations of interpreting Müller's play (cf. Hacks 2015: 279–280). The first one is interpreting it as an anti-war play and parable of a class conflict. According to him, there is a reason why the readers can find projections of different wars at the end of the play. The second interpretation is in some way an opposition to the first one: it is a modernised version, seeing the drama as showing the problems of socialist reality and dangers connected with communistic politics. Third variant of interpretation focuses on existential motifs and allegory of death.

In the stage directions, Müller also draws attention to the topicality of problems that are issued in the play and suggests how the potential directors should stage it. According to Müller's idea, during the scene in which Odysseus and Neoptolemus go away with the body of Philoctetes, photos of various wars – from the Trojan War to the war in Japan – should be projected in the background. Müller reminds once again that his drama is not about the history, but about the models of behaviour. He describes collective timeless experiences, because "in the previous countries the conditio humana changed not significant. The development of a human as the matter of anthropology is absolute minimal".[6] Hacks emphasises that the play is defined as "Lehrstück" or "learning-play" (cf. Hacks 2015: 275).

---

5   Cf. Kraus 1985.
6   Cited after: Müller 1990: 142.

Another drama, where in spite its obvious ancient references allusions to the political situation of the GDR can be found, is *The Horatian*. In the play, Müller draws on the legend of Horatii and Curiatii form Titus Livius' *Ab urbe condita* and, similarly to Bertold Brecht, he is inspired by Pierre Corneille's *Horace* (cf. Kalb 2001: 28). Müller transposes the plot of myth and significantly changes the ending, in order to modernise its reception. In Livius's version, the decision about killing the sister mourning her fiancé is met with condemnation, and the death sentence is eventually avoided. People appreciate the hero's commitment and the pardon given by the monarch. Müller, however, emphasises the moral consequences of a deed.

The story begins from the power struggle between Rome and Alba. To avoid bloodshed, both city-states decide to choose their representatives for a duel. The drawn lots indicate the Horiatian to fight for Rome and the Curiatian for Alba. Because the two men are connected to each other by family ties (the Curiatian is the fiancé of Horiatian's sister), they are asked whether they want the lots to be drawn again, but both of them strongly oppose. The conflict becomes settled by the Horiatian for the benefit of Rome. In spite of being implored by the Curiatian ("Spare the conquered man. I am/ Betrothed to your sister"), the Horiatian declares "My bride is Rome" and "thrust[s] his sword into the Curiatian's throat, so that the blood drop[s] to the earth in a stream to the ground". In Müller's work, blood will be shed many times. Having returned to his home city, the Horiatian kills his sister who bewailed her dead fiancé:

> With quick strides his sister
> But the sister recognized the bloodied mantle
> Work of her hands, and wailed and let her hair down. And the Horatian scolded the mourning sister:
> Why do you wail and let down your hair.
> Rome has conquered. The conqueror stands before you.
> And the sister kissed the bloodied mantle and screamed:
> Rome.
> Give back to me what was clothed in this mantle.
> And the Horatian thrust the sword
> Into the breast of the weeping girl.

In Müller's work there is neither a character list nor the usual division into roles, and all dialogues are integrated into the corpus of the text. Thanks to this solution, the work resembles the very initial ancient version of the myth conveyed in an oral form. The murder committed on the sister leaves the Romans dumbstruck. The question about the moral overtone of the character and the following conveyance of his history arises ("To the conqueror the laurel, to the murderer the axe"). The assembled come to the conclusion: The Horiatian should be honoured as a winner and executed as a murderer. The question about the way in which he should be called in the future was answered in unison:

> He shall be called the conqueror of Alba
> He shall be called the murderer of his sister
> Within one breath his merit and his guilt.
> And whoever speaks of his guilt and not of his merit Shall dwell where the dogs dwell, as a dog.
> And whoever speaks of his merit but not of his guilt He, too, shall dwell among dogs.
> But he who speaks of his guilt at one time
> and at other times speaks of his merit
> Differently speaking with one mouth at different times Or differently to different ears
> His tongue shall be torn from his mouth.
> Since the words must be kept pure. Because
> A sword may be broken and also a man
> May be broken, but words
> They fall into the wheels of the world, irretrievably Making things known to us or unknown.

Müller raises an important question about dealing with history. Uwe Schütte called Müller's drama a political diagnostics of the time in the mythological border (cf. Schütte 2010: 36), hence pointing to the analogy between the plot and to the forbidden subject of Stalinism (cf. *ibid.*). Schütte recognizes in the work the voice of the author himself who seems to appeal to not allow political success overshadow the victims who pave the way for the political (*ibid.*: 41). On the one hand, it shows that there is no clear distinction between offence and merit; and on the other hand, that after victory, the fate of the victims and negative results of politics cannot be left unsaid in the collective memory (cf. *ibid.*). The crux here is that honouring a ruthless murderer and executing the hero who rendered great service to his state do not constitute a satisfying solution. As Schütte concludes, it is a paradox that one should get accustomed to (cf. *ibid.*).

Also in *The Horatian*, there are no deep psychological portraits of the characters, but the emphasis is put on the attitudes and ideas. According to Müller's instructions, the characters appearing in the drama – the citizens of both state-cities and their representatives – should wear masks, as the author wanted to prevent identifying them with one of the parties. The actors who finished performing their roles should stay on stage and impersonate other characters (cf. Müller, 1978: 101).

The writers of the German Democratic Republic often reached for the myths to convey forbidden issues in an oblique way and to deceive the censors. In one of the interviews, Müller admits that it was an attempt to raise crucial questions about socialism:

I want neither to write ancient plays today nor to adapt ancient topics. In the early 1960s the plays about Stalinism were forbidden. It was necessary to invent such a model to raise really important issues so that people could realize them at once.[7]

Müller's works raise the question of the *conditio humana* in the contemporary world, criticising the imperialistic and capitalistic politics. Reaching for the myth of Philoctetes, the author managed to show his pessimistic vision of the world: on the one hand, Philoctetes, who wanted freedom from solitude and stagnation; and on the other, Odysseus with Neoptolemus, representing the politics of terror and hypocrisy. Philoctetes tries to become free and independent as a human, but his efforts remain ineffective. The oppositions – the dialectics of reason versus terror, individual versus authorities, truth versus lie, and morality versus pragmatism – determine the work on the whole. The same oppositions are also evident in the play *The Horatian*, which will also raise the question about the form of transmitting memory. Müller's plays are, in Norbert Otto Eke's opinion, both historical and contemporary drama (cf. Eke, 1999: 114). Setting of the plot in mythical circumstances is apparent, because, as Joanna Jabłkowska notes:

> Müller uses myth as a type of alienation effect (Verfremdungseffekt). He does not adapt myths but quotes them as archetypical examples of recurring social situations and exposes not only the cynical and pragmatic GDR system, but also the Western instrumentalisation of values for political or economic purposes on ad hoc basis. (Jabłkowska 2014: 139)

Müller does not make an attempt to modernise his dramas by transferring their content into the new setting of space and time, but he draws parallels between past and present. In this way, the public is forced to participate actively and to interpret the plot. Interestingly, according to Brecht's idea and his "alienation effect", the spectator should not identify with the events on stage, but only follow and analyse them. For this reason, the works by Müller can, in a certain sense, be qualified as didactic plays.

Translated by Łukasz Plęs

References:

Chodkowski, Robert R. 2009. "Filoktet. Wstęp". In *Sofokles: Tragedie. Tom I. Ajas, Trachinki, Philoctetes, Edyp w Kolonos*. Trans. by Robert R. Chodkowski. Lublin: Towarzystwo Naukowe Katolickiego Uniwersytetu Lubelskiego Jana Pawła II. 259–302.

Eke, Norbert Otto. 1999. *Heiner Müller*. Stuttgart: Philipp Reclam.

---

7   Cited after, Emmerich, Wolfgang 1990.

Emmerich, Wolfgang. 1990. "Der vernünftige, der schreckliche Mythos. Heiner Müllers Umgang mit der griechischen Mythologie". In *Heiner Müller: Material. Texte und Kommentare.* Ed. by Frank Hörnigk. Leipzig: Reclam Verlag. 138–156.

Hacks, Peter. 2015. *Heiner Müller und das antagonistische Drama des Sozialismus.* Berlin/Boston: Walter de Gruyter.

Jabłkowska, Joanna. 2014. "Antique Dramas by Heiner Müller. Adaptation of myths or a new dramatic aesthetics". *Collectanea Philologica XVII*: 137–148.

Kalb, Jonathan. 2001. *The Theater of Heiner Müller.* New York: Limelight Editions.

Kraus, Manfred. 1985. "Heiner Müller und die griechische Tragödie". *Poetica* 17: 299–339.

Moser, Andreas. 2014. *Utopiekonzept und Geschichtsauffassung im Werk Heiner Müllers.* St. Ingbert: Röhrig Universitätsverlag.

Müller, Heiner. 1976. "Filoktet". *Literatura na Świecie* 1/76: 74–107.

—.1989. "Drei Punkte zu Philoktet". In: *Heiner Müller: Material. Texte und Kommentare.* Ed. by Frank Hörnigk, 61. Leipzig: Reclam Verlag.

—.1978. "Horacjusz". *Dialog nr 2*: 96–102.

—.1999. *Krieg ohne Schlacht. Leben in zwei Diktaturen.* Köln: Kiepenheuer & Witsch.

—.1965. "Philoctetess". In *Philoctetess and the fall of Troy. Plays, Documents, Iconography, Interpretations.* Trans. by Oscar Mandel. Lincoln and London: University of Nebraska Press. 214–250.

—.1990. *Material. Texte und Kommentare.* Ed. by Frank Hörnigk. Leipzig: P. Reclam.

Muskała, Monika. 2000. "Tłumacz, ten 'sprawca zza biurka'". In *Heiner Müller: Makbet, hamletmaszyna, anatomia Tytusa.* Trans. by Jacek St. Buras, Elżbieta Jeleń, Monika Muskała. Kraków: Księgarnia Akademicka.

Sauerland, Karol. 1976. "Smutna prawda". *Literatura na Świecie* 1/76: 108–111.

Schütte, Uwe. 2010. *Heiner Müller.* Köln: Böhlau Verlag.

Segal, Charles. 1998. *Sophocles' Tragic World. Divinity, Nature, Society.* Cambridge MA: Harvard University Press.

Sophocles. 2013. *Philoctetess.* Ed. by Seth L. Schein. Cambridge: Cambridge University Press.

Winnington-Ingram, Reginald. 1980. *Sophocles: An Interpretation.* Cambridge: Cambridge University Press.

Rossana Zetti[*]

The Re-staging of *Antigone* in Twentieth-Century Europe: an Irish Example

Abstract: This paper will explore the impact of the Antigone myth on modern thought, which has been persistent over the past decades in Europe, primarily from a political point of view. *Antigone* is, in fact, a paradigmatic play for exploring the clash between the state and the individual person, and for vindicating the human right to rebel against a repressive authority. Several politically oriented adaptations of *Antigone* have been written and staged around the globe and have been used to fight for the recognition of human rights. But how are the plays from the classical *repertoire* to be made to live for an audience of today? Why has the Antigone myth been so fruitful and how does it affect our modern imagination? In this paper, I will focus on two Irish adaptations of the play: Tom Paulin's *The Riot Act* (1984) and Brendan Kennelly's *New Version of Antigone* (1986). Written at a particularly turbulent time, when Ireland was facing the tragedy of the Civil War, the Irish playwrights exploit the Antigone myth to raise modern issues of human right, justice and rebellion against the State. Both plays are particularly interesting, since they claim a transposition to the political situation in Northern Ireland. Such parallel is achieved through specific choices of language and by giving clear hint to the characters. By modifying the play in this way, Paulin and Kennelly tend to appropriate the myth, rather than translate its every detail, and to remake it into something new.

Key words: Greek tragedy, Antigone, Sophocles, Irish history and theatre, Tom Paulin, Brendan Kennelly

Sophocles' *Antigone* has had a major influence upon writers, translators and theatre practitioners of all periods. The question formulated by George Steiner in very clear terms is: "Why a hundred 'Antigones' after Sophocles?" (1984: 121). In order to elucidate such a question, it must be noted that, in the twentieth century, there seems to have been more translations and versions of Greek tragedy written and performed in the island of Ireland than in any other country in the English-speaking world.[1] At the beginning of the century, the Abbey directorate commissioned a translation of *Antigone* from Robert Gregory, intended for production in 1907, together with a translation of *Oedipus the King*. Irish poet William But-

---

[*] University of Edinburgh, Scotland.
[1] By "island of Ireland" I refer to the entire island and to the Irish, the British, and the Northern Irish residing there.

ler Yeats' version of *Oedipus the King* was staged at Dublin's Abbey Theatre in December 1926, soon after the Irish Civil War (Clark & McGuire 1989: 11–12). Since then, Irish writers "have produced eleven translations and loose adaptations of Sophocles" (Arkins 2010: 22). Especially *Antigone* returns again and again in Ireland, and continues to fascinate the Irish.

It is interesting to analyse the reason why the Antigone myth has been so fruitful in Ireland and why it has been readapted to the modern Irish stage, in front of contemporary Irish audiences. It will become all the more evident that the political framework of twentieth-century Ireland provided an ideal background for a re-proposition of the play on the stage, and influenced the shaping of most of the modern Irish adaptations of the play. That the underlying idea of neverending strife, the burial and political issue regrettably suit the Irish landscape will become even clearer by analysing two influential Irish representations of the play. In my paper, I will focus on two modern Irish interpretations of *Antigone* – Tom Paulin's *The Riot Act* (1984) and Brendan Kennelly's *New Version of Antigone* (1986) – in their receptive context. They are particularly relevant since they invoke the political questions raised by Sophocles' play and the largely political legacy of its performance tradition. Moreover, in different ways and with emphasis on different issues, they are able to turn Sophocles' tragedy into something new and to pose questions concerning modern issues (i.e. war, society, the relation between the individual and the state). In this article, I will analyse the differences between these interpretations: the various ways in which they modify the original play to communicate something personal, the degree of creativeness and divergence from the original adopted by the authors, and the influence of the very specific framework in which they operated.

According to Fiona Macintosh, "the perceived links between Ireland and ancient Greece have a very long ancestry, and the links between Ireland and *Antigone* are equally deep rooted" (2011: 2). One of the reasons for Ireland's inexhaustible attraction to *Antigone* is its political tradition: the play, interpreted as a history of resistance and rebellion, is revealed particularly apposite because of Ireland's past, steeped in injustice and oppression. But there are also other themes present in *Antigone* that find an immediate resonance in Ireland: the violent measures adopted by an autocratic government, the urge to revolution, justice and the law, the opportunity of burying political opponents (Polyneices, as well as the hunger strikers), respect for the dead and the needs of the living, the sexual dialectic of male and female. As Julie Barber, administrator of Field Day at that time, writes to Kevin McCaul of the Derry City Council on April 9th, 1984:

> Antigone may seem rather an odd choice, but it is a play about justice and power and is as relevant to Northern Ireland in 1980s as it was to Greece in 400 BC. It is amazing to realise how little human behaviour has actually changed. (1984)

The early 1980s were indeed a tough time for the Irish because of the problems with the North, the country's poor financial situation, the conservatism of the Catholic Church: all these issues troubled Irish society at the moment when the first set of *Antigone* was written in 1984. These plays were profoundly engaged with the political and cultural crisis in Ireland. 1984 was in fact a crucial year. Tom Paulin's *The Riot Act* was first presented by the Field Day Theatre Company in Derry/Londonderry on the 19th of September 1984. Significantly, this is the city in Northern Ireland where the Bloody Sunday events had taken place on the 30th of January 1972, when paratroops opened fire on civil rights protesters killing 13 unarmed civilians. Moreover, *The Riot Act* appeared just three years after the 1981 hunger strike, when ten Republicans had starved themselves to death to protest the British government's prison policy that would deny Republicans the status of political prisoners. The play is profoundly focused on the historical problems tormenting the country in the 1980s. Northern Ireland had in fact experienced a history of violence, disorders and rioting since the 1960s, mainly because of the contrasts between the Catholic minority in the North and the Protestant majority. At the same time, paramilitary groups, such as the IRA (Irish Republican Army), posited themselves as the protectors of the working class Catholics who were vulnerable to police and civilian brutality. The late 1960s and early 1970s saw a prolonged period of civil strife and political turbulences, known as The Troubles. Coming in the wake of these events, Paulin's remaking of *Antigone* is inevitably a highly engaged, angry and subversive play. Paulin was raised in Belfast, in the North, as a Protestant Unionist, and he was actively engaged in the political Irish situation. In his version, he remains generally faithful to the structure of the original. Nevertheless, Paulin does not offer a simple translation of Sophocles' work: the ancient play serves rather to camouflage his contemporary concerns and his critique of contemporary politics and insincere politicians.

As the title itself makes it clear, the core of Paulin's drama is a "riot act".[2] The cause of the riot which troubles the city is an individual person: Antigone. She challenges the authority of her κύριος and of the male order, while her sister Ismene considers any attempt to rebel against established authority as useless.

---

2   The Riot act was an 18th century law which prohibited gatherings of more than 12 people; it was read by law enforcers as a way of requiring crowds to disperse; hence 'reading the riot act' became a metaphor for giving someone a final warning.

At the beginning of Paulin's play, the two young women present an immediate contrast: Antigone, single-minded and intransigent, devoted to the body of her beloved brother, rejects her sister Ismene, who is more circumspect and conventional. Exactly as in the ancient play, Antigone's self-assertion stands in opposition to Ismene's submissive conformity. The two in conflict represent two different tragic choices. In the dramatic years of The Troubles, the same tragic choice between acting and rebelling (as Antigone) or passively accepting the reality (as Ismene) was presented to Irish people. To make such a choice also meant to take a stance on larger political and religious issues, and on questions of justice. Antigone claims that she will "only do what's right / and sanctioned by the gods" (Paulin 1984a: 14). However, according to Ismene, by acting against the law, they will surely encounter death (*ibid.*: 12):

> Some scraggy, smelly crowd,
> us dragged before them –
> oh they'll spit,
> they'll sleg us then,
> shout all the dirt
> till the first stones go whap!
> and go on thumping us.
> Don't tell me it's not right –
> that's what is!

Ismene's speech has a contemporary political reference: it evokes mob rule and protest, as well as sectarian violent hostility against a rebellious minority. What is more, the debate about "what is right" emerges in these crude words and insistently recurs throughout Paulin's play. Each character has his own notion of justice to bring to the stage; the Chorus leader believes that "no one in their right mind / would choose to die" (Paulin 1984a: 18). Creon claims that only Eteocles "knew the difference / between right and wrong" (*ibid.*: 29). Later, in the στιχομυθία with his son Haemon, he asserts: "There's only one sentence / and it's the just one" (*ibid.*: 36).

It should be questioned, however, whether such boundaries between right and wrong can be clearly outlined, and whether Antigone's "riot act" is legitimate. One might ask whether it is right to defend to the death a deeply-felt conviction (her brother and the gods below *must* be honoured) or to conform to authority (Creon's edict). On the one hand, Antigone's decision may seem a disputable one. Creon's anger over her is not wholly unprovoked: she transgresses his law, she overtly challenges his legitimate power, she "betray[s] the state" (Paulin 1984a: 37), and therefore she has to be punished. In a crucial point of Paulin's tragedy, the Chorus leader asks whether Antigone's death "is…worth it / for a handful of dust on Polynices" (*ibid.*: 34). Conor Cruise O'Brien, Irish diplomat and writer, as well as one of the first to apply the story of Antigone to the Northern Irish situation, believes that "after four years of *Antigone* and her understudies and all those funerals – more than a hundred dead at the time of writing – [one begins] to feel that Ismene's common sense and feeling towards the living may make the more needful, if less spectacular element in dignity" (O'Brien 1972: 159). Such an interpretation of the play, expressed in his book *States of Ireland*, stimulated Paulin's reaction. In 1980 he responded in an article entitled "The Making of a Loyalist" in the *Times Literary Supplement*, in which he denounced O'Brien's "crude and straightforward Unionist reading of *Antigone* in his book *States of Ireland*", according to which Antigone becomes responsible for "all those funerals" leaving the Unionist state "virtually absolved…and Creon's hands apparently to be clean" (*TLS*, 14 Nov. 1980, repr. in Paulin 1984a). The argument with O'Brien proves the controversial nature of the play and its openness to different (even opposite) interpretations. As Anthony Roche points out, such a debate was an incentive, but "Paulin's dramatic articulation of the issues gives them a range that transcends mere personal polemic" (1988: 224).

Paulin's version distances itself from the original *Antigone* since it claims a transposition to the political situation in Northern Ireland. Such a parallel is achieved by Paulin through specific choices of language and by giving recognizable features to his characters. Significantly, in Paulin's script, there are inescapable allusions to both British and Northern Irish politicians. Creon, for example, carries marked political connotations and is turned by Paulin into an exemplar model of politician familiar to the Irish of contemporary Ireland, and having overtones of both UK and Northern Irish figures. The similarities are pointed out by a number of scholars.[3] Roche associates Paulin's Creon with British or Northern Irish politicians of the time, such as Hurd or Paisley. When Creon appears for the first time, he is appointed by the Chorus as "the big man", which is a clear reference to the Reverend Ian Paisley, Northern Ireland leader and politician. Paulin himself writes: "I wanted Creon to be a kind of puritan gangster, a megalomaniac who spoke alternately in an English public school voice and a deep menacing Ulster growl" (Paulin 2002: 167). He also says that he imagined Creon "partly as a Northern Irish secretary" (*ibid.*: 166).

Likewise, in the original Greek text, Creon's opening *rhesis* sounds confident and assertive; Sophocles employs the language typical of contemporary Athenian

---

3 Younger 2006: 155; Roche 1988: 224–225; the same associations with Thatcher, Paisley and Hurd are evoked in Harris 1988: 257–258.

political debate ("the ship of state" sounds traditional, as well as the references to "straight", "upright" government). Drawing on the Sophoclean text, Paulin employs a politically engaged language; he chooses a Northern Irish vernacular that clearly hints at certain parallels with contemporary public figures. In marking such parallels Paulin's modes of characterization at times tend towards caricature. Creon's language, for example, is characterised by savage and brutal words (Paulin 1984a: 36):

> I've seen children
> Chuck both parents over –
> blood on the walls
> and the whole street laughing!
> I've watched good men wrecked,
> By some hard-nosed bitch!

Also the conversation with the guard exemplifies the typical attitude of politicians. Here, Paulin's Creon is vigilant, cynical, judgemental and impatient in his immediate accusation to the guard (*ibid.*: 22):

> Go you, dead quick,
> and find who done it,
> else I'll tear the skin
> off o' the whole pack o'ye
> and roast you real slow.

Paulin adopts a short verse line, whose language includes terms such as "scraggy", "sleg", "pobby" (Roche 1988: 226). The disjunction between the elevated classical style we expect from the Greek original and Paulin's "pared, minimal style, conversational yet urgent" (*ibid.*: 225) creates an interesting effect. Paulin's originality resides here in a peculiar choice of a heavily colloquial, slangy, often humorous language.

Throughout the play, Paulin's Creon – despite his assertion that "I shall be doing a very great deal of listening" (Paulin 1984a: 16)[4] – is an utterly intransigent, quick to wrath person, who can "neither bend nor listen" (p. 56) and becomes violent towards Ismene calling her "the sneaky, sleaked one" (*ibid.*: 30), and Antigone, to whom he refers to as the "dirt-watcher" (*ibid.*: 26) or "hard bitch" (*ibid.*: 34). He hardly believes that his law has been broken by a woman: "As long as I draw

---

4 Creon also says to Tiresias (Paulin 1984a: 49): "Did I turn a deaf ear ever?" Such assertions are contradicted by Haemon (*ibid.*: 42): "You'd speak, you'd mock; / but you never, never listen".

breath / I'll not be bested by a woman" (*ibid.*: 30).[5] Creon's "shallow rhetoric, his glad-handing, power-broking, self-interested politicking" (Goldhill 2007: 142), as well as his refusal to listen and his obsession with female rivalry, alienate the public sympathies. He is depicted as a hard man of violence, "a self-appointed leader of a gang of bullyboys deciding who shall live or die: 'Go on boys…Bring out the dirty bitch / and let's be rid of her'" (Roche 1988: 225). Paulin's depictions of Antigone as a political heroine and of Creon as a brutal man make any hint of "reconciliation" (in Hegelian terms) apparently vain. Such a radically negative depiction of the latter, suggests Paulin's personal views. Coherently to his political ideals, he seems to tell his audience that it is just to rebel against authority, if the authority is abusive and oppressive. Antigone's rebellion is preferable to Ismene's passivity. In this regard, Paulin's view is clear and impartial, radically opposed to O'Brien's interpretation.

Nevertheless, in the end, Creon is forced to change his mind, "his Unionist viewpoint has altered to take account of the republican position; his state has to find room for the genuine Dissenters in Northern Ireland" (Arkins 2005: 38). The reversal is sudden in both the ancient and modern play. In lamenting the death of his wife and son, this "blind and thin, / a wretched, sinful man" (Paulin 1984a: 59) takes full responsibility for what happened. This ambiguity is certainly due to the essence of tragedy itself, which "chimes with the fact that suffering is pervasive in human life" (Arkins 2010: 7). It is also possible that Paulin takes pleasure in such a dramatic display of failure, which recalls the failure of the Irish and the British to find a solution to the conflict and to prevent innocent deaths. Therefore, Paulin's version is more ambiguous than it may seem; and even if Antigone is the indisputable heroine, much attention is concentrated on Creon and on his language of politics, employed as a primary means to express a link with modern Ireland.

At the same time, Antigone's subordination of her own personal life to the cause that compels her is absolute. From an Irish viewpoint, she is a representative of the potency of individual resistance denied to the Irish by the British. Her characterizing epithet is "wild", meaning that she is untamed, exuberant, outside of the system. Yet from the perspective of Creon, Antigone's behaviour is "wild" only in the sense that it is unruly, potentially anarchic, threatening the stability of civic order. In reality, Antigone is prepared to pay any price, since she sees as her obligation to put her own life "right there on the line and show no fear of him".

---

5   For the insistence of not being defeated by a woman, cf. Paulin 1984a: 27: "If she was a man, now, / she'd maybe stick"; *ibid.*: 37: "You'll find I'm tougher / nor a shrieking woman".

For her, the rejection of the political system means that she will die, and do so following the tradition of Republican martyrs. In Ireland, patriotic martyrdom has a political power and it is linked with Irish history and religion. The hunger strikers' death recalled this tradition: it was seen as a sacrificial martyrdom and served to increase public protests and rioting (Foster 2001: 43–66).

Another important aspect stressed by Irish playwrights, which partly explains *Antigone*'s political immediacy in Ireland, is the issue of the burial of the dead that is tackled in the play. Ireland is a country where ritual lamentation and public burial are live traditions. Religion has a central role in Ireland, and permeates public life to the point that Ireland has been called "one of the most funeral-conscious countries in the world" (Ó hEithir 1986: 152). In Ireland, the burial is directly associated with significant political events. Funerals of political figures – mainly related to the IRA – have offered an opportunity for huge crowds to gather and express their political sentiments. For example, hunger striker Joe McDonnell's funeral in July 1981 was followed by arrests and rioting in the streets; in the same year, more than 100,000 people attended Bobby Sands' funeral in Belfast. Therefore, the burial in Ireland has a strong political implication – especially when it involves burial of war dead.

Significantly, the very day Brendan Kennelly's *Antigone: a New Version* opened at the Peacock Theatre "saw a huge funeral for a dead IRA man in Monaghan" (Toibin 1986: 1). According to Kennelly, *Antigone* is "a truly haunted play; the presence of the dead in the hearts and minds of the living is a fierce, driving and endlessly powerful force" (McDonald 2005: 128). The same power endows Irish people, sensitive to the innumerable deaths of famous politicians as well as common people in the prolonged period of civil strife which had started in the 1960s. Like Paulin's version, Kennelly's *Antigone* also has a deep contemporary significance, and situates itself in the political tradition that the Sophoclean original has spawned. Nonetheless, Kennelly shifts the focus of her play from politics to *gender* politics, emphasising the issues of gender and sexuality, and thus contributes to the emergence of a *feminist* (rather than a political) Antigone. In fact, he opts to emphasise the dialectic of genders in his version: his *Antigone* "is a play for and about women" (McCracken 1996: 63) and it is labelled by the author himself as a "feminist declaration of independence" (Kennelly, quoted in Roche 1988: 242). When the play was first performed in 1986, Ireland was convulsed by debates concerning women's rights and their sexual identity. Written at this time, against the background of failed attempts on the part of the liberal and feminist lobbies to introduce legislation on abortion and divorce, Kennelly's version sounds a feminist note in contrast to Sophocles' original. Since the 1970s, Irish women were claiming a new role in society: debates on the political rights of women and their role in public life were raised, equal-pay and the elimination of discriminatory practices were demanded. Such crucial issues related not only to women's social position, but also to their rights of sexual self-determination and control of their fertility, which were first tackled at the time of the feminist movement during the late 1960s and early 1970s.

Moreover, in the Irish imagery Antigone was associated with Bernadette Devlin, a Republican political activist and member of the UK Parliament who fought for civil rights and equality in Northern Ireland. The connection is not a surprising one, since Antigone, being the first female voice raised against an unjust law, became a feminist icon and a model of an active, brave woman in a particularly relevant moment in Ireland. Kennelly's celebration of women reflects Irish freedom fighters such as Bernadette Devlin or Countess Constance Markievicz, officer in the Citizen Army in the Rising of 1916. Therefore, while in Paulin's *The Riot Act* much attention is given to Creon, in Kennelly's version Antigone is the central heroine, "a Romantic-Idealist / Existentialist Antigone of fairly familiar stamp" (Cairns 1998: 142) who expresses a feminist consciousness. Likewise, it has been noted that in Kennelly's Antigone there is a distinctive reflection of the mythical figure of Deirdre, symbolic of the rebellion against patriarchy (Macintosh 2011).

Kennelly's progressive move into a "woman-centred space" is demonstrated by his three versions of Greek tragedies, *Antigone, Medea* and *The Trojan Women*, in which the central characters are female rather than male. Kennelly's Irish versions of these Greek tragedies celebrate the spirit of women in adverse circumstances: "they become symbols of Ireland at the same time as they represent Greek heroines" (McDonald 2005: 124). Kennelly's aim is in fact to work towards the fusion of the voices of Irish women today with the voices of women in fifth-century Athens. In the *Antigone,* in particular, the male/female confrontation is centralised, and "female rights, whether to despair, to connive, or to rage, are exposed as elemental to both the impact of the performance and to human nature" (Pine 1994: 124). Kennelly unearths the subtle clash between masculine and feminine discourse, between "gendered ways" of seeing and saying the world. His *Antigone* becomes the "empowering emblem of the collective strength, courage and potential of Ireland's women" (*ibid.*: 123).

Such a shift of focus has been often criticised: the poet has been accused of transforming Sophocles' play "into a piece of pseudo-feminist propaganda that foregrounds a simplistic opposition between the individual and the state" (O'Rawe 1999), or of switching "the emphasis from the clear, majestic discussion of politics to a vague psychosexual drama" causing the play to suffer from "a consequent failure of energy" (O'Toole 1986). But to criticise this would be to criticise Kennelly for "not doing what he did not set out to do" (Cairns 1998: 143). Kennelly's *Antigone* is "new" and different from the original insofar as it is able to voice a female perspective. His aim is to vindicate women's struggle and rage against exploitations by men and the Church. In his essay "Poetry and Violence", Kennelly speaks of "[t]he hypocrisy engendered by the violence of the institution of the Church, directed against its members, especially women. Some four thousand Irish girls go to England every year to have abortions there" (Kennelly 1994: 39). Also in his book *The Irish: Priests and the People* Kennelly writes: "by putting women on pedestals, by turning Irishwomen into docile provincial versions of the mother of God, the Church of Ireland, the entire male-infested institution, has used women to further and establish its own power" (Kennelly 1985: 115). Kennelly's prime battle is therefore fought against the Irish society's "closed minds" and clericalism.[6]

Indeed, the chief problem of Kennelly's version of Antigone can be located in his ambivalent desire "to be true, to be loyal" both to his "understanding of the Greek world" and also to his "experience of life in Ireland, in the modern world" (Kennelly 1996: 50). On one hand, Kennelly greatly manipulates the text in order to make it speak to his contemporary society; on the other hand, he fully confronts its Sophoclean original. His translation, though contemporary in its language, does indeed stick closely to the original. As Douglas Cairns points out in his review, "the translation is often stunning in its accuracy; where he compresses or rewrites, Kennelly generally remains faithful to the conceptual structure of the original." (Cairns 1998: 141). He adopts a short, simple line and he often employs repetitions and anaphora in order to reinforce the immediacy of each statement; his words are "like drum beats with which he punctuates his lines" (McDonald 2005: 127).

Yet, even if his *Antigone* is, in Kennelly's own words, "a straight translation", it departs from Sophocles' text in a number of ways. The author compresses and expands the original freely.[7] Both Douglas Cairns and Brian Arkins remark that his version omits much of the cultural material that is specifically Greek in favour of what is abstract and universal;[8] it rewrites or reduces some of the Choral Odes

---

6   Defined as "acceptance of the view that the teaching of the Catholic Church possesses such authority that it should be reflected in State legislation" (Coackley 2005: 61).
7   For example, the Eurydice-scene is significantly expanded (Kennelly 1986: 44–46).
8   In Kennelly, some mythical examples are elided, for example the reference to Niobe (line 825 in the original), Danae (line 945) and Lykourgos (lines 955–65). I refer throughout to Griffith 1999 edition of *Antigone*.

and Antigone's laments;[9] significantly, it privileges the male/female conflict in the play (Cairns 1998; Arkins 2010).

By writing a "truly feminist *Antigone*" Kennelly's aim is to "restore the centrality of women to the culture" (Roche 1988: 250). His Antigone has no fear of challenging the male authority as she proclaims (Kennelly 1986: 35):

> I am a woman
> And must go my way alone.
> I am a woman without fear
> In a hole in the rocks
> Where no man or woman dare venture.

In Kennelly's hands, Antigone is a republican whose crime is "love" (*ibid.*: 34). She is also an Irish woman who is devoted to her values – not war (if it can be avoided), not money or power, but love (*ibid.*: 10):

> I have more love
> For the noble dead
> Than for the ambitious living.

Sophocles' Antigone says she was born to share in love, not to share in hate (line 523: οὔτοι συνέχθειν ἀλλὰ συμφιλεῖν ἔφυν) while Kennelly's Antigone claims: "It is no shame to love a brother. / It is my love that makes me different" (Kennelly 1986: 23). This difference is expressed by a rebellion of "a woman who chooses love over hate and to be true to her sexual difference, which Kennelly correlates with a woman's value system" (McDonald 2005: 129). Moreover, in Kennelly's version, Antigone's heroism and integrity are never in doubt: more evidently than in the original, she is admired by the guard ("Something about her is so / Noble, so unafraid" (Kennelly 1986: 21)) and by the chorus ("Antigone, / Whose fiery heart would never let her tell a lie" (*ibid.*: 34)). Her unmovable conviction became a model for the strength required in contemporary Irish society in the 1970s and 1980s, in order to face the oppressive forces of patriarchy and the Church. Just as the Church or the government, so Creon (*ibid.*: 9)

> Has no right
> To stop me doing what is right.
> I will do what I believe is right.

---

9   Some see that reducing the choruses increases dramatic effectiveness. Paulin (2002: 165) quotes Stephen Rea telling him to "Go easy on the choruses. . . They can be a bit of a bore".

Kennelly's Antigone is unable to conform to the prescription of what she sees as an unjust law, therefore she challenges the masculine *ethos* embodied by Creon. Her death is a high price to pay for rebellion and the Irish understand both the glory of the rebellion and its cost in human lives.

Antigone proclaims that is better to "be true, not *silent*" (Kennelly 1986: 16). Also Creon claims that he would never "be *silent* if [he] saw / [His] people threatened / Who can be *silent* if he understands the law?" (*ibid.*: 13) and the guard asserts that "Only a bad guard would be *silent* on such a matter" (*ibid.*: 17). Towards the end of the play, Eurydice says that her heart is "Happy to speak out of its own *silence* / To the listening *silence* of [her] god" (*ibid.*: 45).[10] Silence and voice oppose one another in Kennelly's play, but words prevail over silence in the dynamic enactment of opposite points of view they represent. In particular, the words of men contrast with the truth of women: more explicitly than in the Greek original, Kennelly stresses the fact that Antigone rebels against Creon's word because it is the "word of a man, not of a god". Overall, words are central in Kennelly's play, and every character is urged to express his own μῦθος. As Cairns notes, there is a "profuse repetition of the notion of the 'word' (seven occurrences in the first page of the translation alone)" (Cairns 1998: 143). There is Antigone's "blind, servile, murderous word" (as she herself defines it at the beginning of the play). There are also Eurydice's "merciless words" (Kennelly 1986: 44) as well as Tiresias' "cutting words" (*ibid.*: 42), which he claims to be true "The accusing words of the dead" stand against "the words of the living" (*ibid.*: 48). To accommodate everyone, Haemon advocates a pluralist approach: "the world is full of different words, different voices. / Listen to the words, the voices" (*ibid.*: 29). Creon asserts that "With these words, you [Antigone] differ / From all the other people in this city" (*ibid.*: 22) whilst Antigone claims "It is my love that makes me different". She says to Creon, "You fear the thoughts of difference", and Haemon vainly tells him to listen to "different voices" (*ibid.*: 23).

Kennelly's advocacy to pluralism of words and tolerance of difference is central. Indeed, in both the modern and the ancient play, the collision between such opposite words remains unbridgeable. The insistence on female subservience appears in the original text as Ismene says to Antigone: ἐννοεῖν χρὴ ἐν γυναῖχ'ὅτι / ἔφυμεν, ὡς πρὸς ἄνδρας οὐ μαχουμένα (lines 61–2). In Kennelly's play, the gap between man and woman comes under special scrutiny. It emerges in the first dialogue as Ismene reminds her sister (Kennelly 1986: 9):

---

10 Italics mine. The notion of "silence" also recurs in the original: lines 86–7; 185–6; 509.

> Remember this, Antigone:
> You and I were born women.
> We must not go against men.

And also (*ibid.*: 11):

> A woman against the State
> Is a grain of sand against the sea.

For Ismene being female means being marginalised, uninformed. Nonetheless, Kennelly does not condemn her; he is rather able to depict the tension between the sisters' love on one side, and the difficulties in understanding each other's position on the other. He emphasises "not only Antigone's rebellious quest for articulate action, but her sister Ismene's inability to rebel", which offers us different models of femininity (Younger 2006: 153). Behind their disagreement lies a larger debate, about "the position of women in the governance of the city state and, by extension, the amount of actual control they are free to exercise over their own lives" (McCracken 1996: 56–57). Further, Michael Walton quotes Kennelly describing the aims of his adaptation of *Antigone*: "I wanted to explore sisterhood, the loyalty a sister will show to a brother, against law, against marriage, against everything" (Kennelly 1991: 22).

In opposition to Ismene traditional conformity, Kennelly's Antigone expresses a deep feminist consciousness. Rather than by the transgression itself, Creon is especially afraid of being ashamed by a woman; in fact, when he discovers the subversive agent is female, he makes it clear that he is punishing her for usurping the prerogatives of his sex. Just as in the ancient play (line 525: ἐμοῦ δὲ ζῶντος οὐκ ἄρξει γυνή), he asserts (p. 24):

> While I live, no woman
> Will tell me how to think and feel;
> Above all, how to rule.

Creon constantly stresses his innate superiority as a man, he attacks Haemon to "put a man below a woman" and so tells him to be a "woman's slave" (Kennelly 1986: 32; in the original, line 756: γυναικὸς δούλευμα). As the play progresses, it becomes all the more evident that Creon is primarily threatened as a man rather than as a King, challenged by what he describes as a "mere girl" or (*ibid.*: 29) "disobedient woman". In the original, Creon is addressed by Antigone simply as "mortal" (line 455: θνητὸν) and Antigone is variously referred to as "woman" (line 395: κόρη), "child" (line 694: παῖδα), "girl" (line 525: γυνή), or addressed through personal pronouns (σέ, αὐτή). In Kennelly, Creon and Antigone classify each other in terms of gender as "girl" and "man": the author puts a particular emphasis on these words to highlight the difference of gender between the characters. Terence Brown suggests that Antigone chooses to address Creon as man "at her moment of pure rebellion. An uncompromising female spirit declares itself in radical opposition to Creon's male authority" (Brown 1986b: 53). But Creon, as already remarked, is unwilling to accommodate the resulting concept of difference. Kennelly, in an interview, sees the salvation of the world coming as something that comes from an understanding of both sexes:

> We have a duty to be women if our kind is to survive, to produce this human being, this man-woman, who in the future will not declare war on women, or on men, and who will save the world. Just as Antigone shows us how a just society has to consider the individual and her needs, so the human race would be better off declaring peace in its war between the sexes (Pine 1994: 182).

Indeed, the words of men and women appear as mutually incomprehensible as Antigone asks (Kennelly 1986: 35): "What man / Knows anything of women?" Despite her incredible integrity and self-assertion, Antigone is ultimately a victim, a "mere woman", led by "men" to her death (*ibid*.: 38):

> Men are leading me to death.
> Men made the law that said I'm guilty.
> Men will place me
> In a black hole among the rocks.

The two worlds ultimately fail to achieve reciprocal recognition and dignity. Her story "reminds us of the difficulties involved in making a lace for women in established male-centred codes" (McCracken 1996: 62).

The conflict between Creon and Antigone symbolises a battle of principle and its failure to achieve a solution; it also concretises Kennelly's belief that "Ireland's difficulties are rooted in the failure of 'close minds' to embrace that which is other and opposite" (McCracken 1996: 55). His reworking of *Antigone* has a peculiar significance for a society "undergoing a protracted and often fraught adjustment of its fundamental attitudes to sexuality" (McCracken 1996: 55). What the play does, in both its Greek original and the modern version, is "show Antigone acting for and, in the perspective of prevailing conventions of society and of politics, as a man" (Roche 1988: 242). Sophocles' timeless tragedy is therefore given new life through Kennelly's powerful articulation of female tragic voice. His translation reflects the contemporary society and politics. As Gabriel Fitzmaurice points out, "what Kennelly translated is experience, the feel of a thing. He translates the spirit of a poem or play; he is no slave of the literal. Yet his approach is faithful and powerful as mere imitations are not...Poetry is made in the translation, too" (Fitzmaurice 1994: 34).

Thus, the Irish playwrights exploit *Antigone* to mediate the contemporary reality and to comment on Irish politics and society. They exploited the play's contemporary and political significance in order to evoke the turbulent situation of their country. At the same time, they were able to transform Sophocles' play into something new and personal. The differences between the two versions also show the flexibility of the Antigone myth: Paulin is able to raise its contemporary political implications, while Kennelly focuses on the articulation of a powerful, rebellious female voice. Also the peculiar use of the dialect forms indicates Paulin's intention to subtly relate the action to contemporary Northern Ireland and to represent (or satirise) the North. By modifying the play in this way, both Paulin and Kennelly tend to appropriate the myth, rather than translate its every detail: their originality resides in this direct association between the ancient myth and the reality of modern Ireland. They retain the original conflicts present in the *Antigone,* because these conflicts have distinct Irish parallels. The Irish playwrights succeed in re-experiencing Sophocles' tragedy in order to create a poetic version of Ireland's dilemma. In their hands, the play becomes a vehicle to express a collective memory, to reflect on the dramatic Irish past, and to gain self-knowledge of that past, since (Paulin 1984a: 35):

> The world is a very,
> very old place, but the people in it, they're very young
> still, and if you've never grieved then you're lucky.

Written at a traumatic time for the country, both versions reflect the authors' concerns and personal experiences. They also emphasise the potential within Greek tragedy for illuminating our contemporary "tragedy".

The Irish examples show how effectively Greek drama – and especially the *Antigone* – has been used to communicate messages about the pressing, both political and of gender, issues of today. Many of the changes made to the source text are to be located in the particular socio-political and cultural context that produced the reworking of the story. The peculiar Irish context enhances our appreciation of the tragedy's reception as well as sheds some light on the reasons why both Irish authors chose to make certain changes to their source.

References:

Arkins, Brian. 2005. *Hellenising Ireland: Greek and Roman Themes in Modern Irish Literature*. Newbridge: Goldsmith.

—.2010. *Irish Appropriation of Greek Tragedy*. Dublin: Carysfort Press.

Barber, Julie. 1984. "Letter to Kevin McCaul." In *Field Day Theatre Archieves*, I.v.5, T/39/B, 9 Apr.

Bartlett, Thomas. 2010. *Ireland: A History*. Cambridge: Cambridge University Press.

Brown, Terence. 1986a. "The Twentieth Century". In *Ireland Past and Present*. Ed. by Brendan Kennelly, 81–103. Dublin: G&M.

—.1986b. "An Uncompromising Female Spirit". In *Sophocles* Antigone: *A New Version by Brendan Kennelly*. Newcastle upon Tyne: Bloodaxe Books. 52–53.

—.2004. *Ireland: A Social and Cultural History, 1922-2002*. London: Harper Perennial.

Bruce, Steve. 2007. *Paisley: Religion and Politics in Northern Ireland*, Oxford: Oxford University Press.

Cairns, Douglas. 1998. "Sophocles' *Antigone* by Brendan Kennelly Review by: Douglas Cairns". *Classics Ireland* 5: 141–146.

Clark, David. James, McGuire. 1989. *W. B. Yeats, the Writing of Sophocles' King Oedipus: Manuscripts of W.B. Yeats*. Philadelphia: American Philosophical Society

Cleary, Joe. 1999. "Domestic Troubles: Tragedy and the Northern Ireland Conflict". *The South Atlantic Quarterly* 98.3: 501–537.

Coakley, John. 2005. "Society and Political Culture". In *Politics in the Republic of Ireland*. Ed. by John Coakley and Michael Gallagher. London: Routledge. 32–70.

Conrad, Kathryn. 1998. "Women Troubles, Queer Troubles: Gender, Sexuality, and the Politics of Selfhood in the Construction of the Northern Irish State". In *Reclaiming Gender: Transgressive Identities in Modern Ireland*. Ed. by Marilyn Cohen and Nancy Curtin. New York: St Martin's Press. 53–68.

Deane, Seamus. 2002. "Field Day's Greeks (and Russians)". In *Amid our Troubles: Irish Versions of Greek Tragedy*. Ed. by Marianne McDonald and Michael Walton. London: Bloomsbury Methuen Drama. 148–164.

Ferriter, Diarmaid. 2004. *The Transformation of Ireland, 1900-2000*. London: Profile Books.

Fitzmaurice, Gabriel. 1994. "Becoming Song: The Translated Village". In *Dark Fathers into Light: Brendan Kennelly*. Ed. by Richard Pine. Glasgow: Bloodaxe Book. 27–35.

Foley, Imelda. 2003. *The Girls in the Big Picture: Gender in Contemporary Ulster Theatre*. Belfast: Blackstaff Press.

Ford. Alan. 2001. "Martyrdom, History and Memory in Early Modern Ireland". In *History and Memory in Modern Ireland*. Ed. by Ian McBride. Cambridge: Cambridge University Press. 43–66.

Foster, Fitzroy Robert. 1989. *The Oxford History of Ireland*. Oxford: Oxford University Press.

—.2001. "Martyrdom, History and Memory in Early Modern Ireland". In *History and Memory in Modern Ireland*. Ed. by Ian McBride. Cambridge: Cambridge University Press. 43–66.

Goldhill, Simon. 1986. *Reading Greek Tragedy*. Cambridge: Cambridge University Press.

—.2007. *How to Stage Greek Tragedy Today*. Chicago: University of Chicago Press.

Hall, Edith and Fiona, Macintosh. 2005. *Greek Tragedy and the British Theatre 1660–1914*, Oxford: Oxford University Press.

Hall, Edith. 2010. *Greek Tragedy: Suffering Under the Sun*. Oxford: Oxford University Press.

Harkin, Hugh. 2008. "Irish Antigones: Towards Tragedy Without Borders?" *Irish University Review* 38: 292–309.

Harris, Claudia. 1988. "The Martyr-Wish in Contemporary Irish Dramatic Literature". In *Cultural Contexts and Literary Idioms in Contemporary Irish Literature*. Ed. by Michael Kenneally. Gerrards Cross: Colin Smyth. 251–268.

Hayes, Bernardette and McAllister, Ian. 2013. *Conflict to Peace: Politics and Society in Northern Ireland Over Half a Century*. Manchester: Manchester University Press.

Innes, Catherine Lynette. 1993. *Woman and Nation in Irish Literature and Society 1880–1935*. Athens: University of Georgia Press.

Jackson, Alvin. 2014. *The Oxford Handbook of Modern Irish History*. Oxford: Oxford University Press.

Jackson, Conroy. 1993. "Managing the Mothers: The Case of Ireland". In *Women and Social Policies in Europe: Work, Family and the State*. Ed. by Jane Lewis, 72–91. Aldershot: Edward Elgar.

Jones, Richard. 1997. "Talking amongst Ourselves: Language, Politics, and Sophocles on the Field Day Stage". *International Journal of Classical Tradition* 4.2: 232–246.

Kennelly, Brendan. 1985. "The Irish: Priests and the People". In *Ireland, Past and Present*. Ed. by Brendan Kennelly, 106–121. Dublin: Gill and Macmillan Ltd.

—.1986. *Sophocles' Antigone: a New Version*. Newcastle upon Tyne: Bloodaxe Books.

—.1991. "Q and A with Brendan Kennelly". *Irish Literary Supplement* 9 (1).

—.1994. "Poetry and Violence". In *Journey into Joy: Selected Prose*. Ed. by Åke Persson. Newcastle upon Tyne: Bloodaxe Books. 5–28.

—.1996. "Doing Justice to Antigone". In *Sophocles' Antigone: A New Version by Brendan Kennelly*, edited by Brendan Kennelly, 50–51. Newcastle upon Tyne: Bloodaxe Books.

Kitto, Humphrey Davey Findley. 2003. *Greek Tragedy*. London and New York: Routledge.

Lane, Warren. 1986. "The Politics of Antigone". In *Greek Tragedy and Political Theory*. Ed. by Paul Euben. Berkeley and Los Angeles: University of California Press. 162–182.

Levine, June. 1982. *Sisters: The Personal Story of an Irish Feminist*, Dublin: Ward River Press.

Long, Joseph. 2002. "The Sophoclean Killing Fields: An Interview with Frank McGuinness". In *Amid Our Troubles: Irish Versions of Greek Tragedy*. Ed. by Marianne McDonald and Michael Walton. London: Methuen. 263–277.

Macintosh, Fiona. 1994. *Dying Acts: Death in Ancient Greek and Modern Irish Tragic Drama*, Cork: Cork University Press.

—.2011. "Irish Antigone and Burying the Dead". In *Antigone on the Contemporary World Stage*. Ed. by Erin Mee and Helene Foley. Oxford: Oxford University Press. 1–15.

McDonald, Marianne. 2002. "The Irish and Greek Tragedy". In *Amid Our Troubles: Irish Versions of Greek Tragedy*. Ed. by Marianne McDonald and Michael Walton. London: Methuen. 37–86.

McCracken, Kathleen. 1994. "Rage for a New Order: Brendan Kennelly's Plays for Women". In *Dark Fathers Into Light*. Ed. by Richard Pine. Glasgow: Bloodaxe Books. 114–147.

—.1996. "Site of Recovery: Brendan Kennelly's *Antigone*". In *Sophocles' Antigone: A New Version by Brendan Kennelly*. Ed. by Brendan Kennelly. Newcastle upon Tyne: Bloodaxe Books. 54–63.

McDonald, Marianne. 2005. "Rebel Women: Brendan Kennelly's Versions of Irish Tragedy". *New Hibernia Review* 9: 123–136.

—.2009. "Classics as Celtic Firebrand". In *Theatre Stuff: critical Essays on Contemporary Irish Theatre*. Ed. by Eamonn Jordan. Jefferson-London. 16–26.

Murray, Christopher. 1991. "Three Irish Antigones". In *Perspectives on Irish Drama and Theatre*, edited by Jacqueline Genet and Alan Cave, 115–129. Gerrards Cross: Colin Smythe.

O'Brien, Connor Cruise. 1972. *States of Ireland*, London: Hutchinson.

Ó hEithir, Brendan. 1986. *The Begrudger's Guide to Irish Politics*. Dublin: Poolbeg Press.

O' Rawe, Des. 1999. "(Mis)Translating Tragedy: Irish Poets and Greek Plays". In *Open University: Classical Receptions in Drama and Poetry in English from c.1970 to the Present*. http://www2.open.ac.uk/ClassicalStudies/GreekPlays/Conf99/Orawe.htm (Accessed 10.10.15)

O' Toole, F. "Struggling with the Greeks". In *The Sunday Tribune*, 4 May.

Roche, Anthony. 1988. "Ireland's Antigones: Tragedy North and South". In *Cultural Contexts and Literary Idioms in Contemporary Irish Literature*, Ed. by M. Kenneally. Totowa, NJ: Barnes & Noble Books, 221–250.

Paulin, Tom. 1984a. *Ireland and the English Crises*. Newcastle upon Tyne: Bloodaxe Books. 9–22.

—.1984b. *The Riot Act: A Version of Sophocles' 'Antigone'*, London: Faber & Faber.

—.2002. "Antigone". In *Amid our Troubles: Irish Versions of Greek Tragedy*. Ed. by Marianne McDonald and Michael Walton. London: Bloomsbury Methuen Drama. 165–170.

Pine, Richard (ed.). 1994. *Dark Fathers into Light: Brendan Kennelly*. Newcastle upon Tyne: Bloodaxe Books.

Steiner, George. 1984. *Antigones*. New Haven: Yale University Press.

Tóibín, C. 1986. 'Oh, oh, Antigone'. *Sunday Independent*, 4 May.

Younger, K. 2006. "Burying the Colonial Symptom". *Colloquy: Monash University Postgraduate Journal* 11, 148–162.

Magdalena Hasiuk[*]

"As if he was not a grandson but the child of the Greeks":[1] Wajdi Mouawad's Dialogue with Antiquity

Abstract: The article attempts to define references to Antiquity in a versatile Lebanese artist Wajdi Mouawad's work process on *Scorched* and in the text itself. The analysis of mythical references, their functions and the meanings acquired through them let us realise how the playwright's personal experiences connected with civil war, exile and the search for his own identity found their roots in the cosmos of Greek references. The myth of Oedipus present in *Scorched* appears not only as a thematic repetition or the model of the drama structure. It is a tool permitting to recover the meaning of the world after a personal and social trauma. Metaphysical values, and "the mythical core" they are connected with, make it possible to return to "the situation of positively primary experience of the world" (Kołakowski). This feature of Mouawad's text links it to Jerzy Grotowski's *Tu es le fils de quelqu'un* on many levels.

Keywords: Biography, Sophocles, Myth of Oedipus, socially engaged theatre, "the mythical organization of the world", Grotowski

Too shallow breath?

Eugenio Barba, Italian director and founder of a more than half-century-old international company Odin Theater, in his lecture given in Wrocław in October 2011 on the occasion of the release of the Polish translation of his then latest book entitled *Spalić dom* (*On Directing and Dramaturgy: Burning the House*), stressed the importance of "two lungs" in the work of a director. Obviously, it was not the condition of internal organs that Barba had in mind. As he claims, one of the lungs is theatre, which comprises not only the whole theatrical tradition but also the cultural heritage that the particular artist belongs to and which he consciously chooses, forms and dialogues with. Jerzy Grotowski, Barba's former teacher, called such kind of a dialogue "the dialogue with ancestors"; To be more precise, a dialogue with "ancestors from the same profession". "It is obvious that I do not agree with my ancestors. But at the same time it is impossible to deny them.

---

[*] Polish Academy of Science, Institute of Art, Warsaw, Poland.
[1] Gruszczyński 2012: 160.

They are my foundation, my source. It is a personal matter between me and them", wrote Grotowski (1997: 292).[2] The second, and equally important, lung of the director is, according to Barba, "biography" or "origins" (Barba 2009).[3] It is only by combining the work of both lungs that the theatre artist can completely, in an organic way, develop his work in response to the challenges of the contemporary world and talk about "the problems of present days".[4] If the director, for whatever reason, ignores the work of one of the lungs in favour the other, his breath becomes limited, unbalanced and too shallow.

War infected?

There is hardly any other contemporary theatre creator who more than Wajdi Mouawad deserves to be called "the theatre artist", in the sense that Edward Gordon Craig uses the term. Mouawad is a playwright, director, actor, group leader, visual artist and at the same time a filmmaker, a novelist and an essayist. A particularly important feature of his theatre work is its connection to his biography. Mouawad's formative experience was the ordeal of the 1975 Lebanese Civil War, which broke out when Wajdi Mouawad was seven years old. It was one of the most horrifying types of wars – the conflict between the Muslims and Christian groups, with the involvement of army forces of Syria, Israel and Palestine Liberation Organization, involved military actions full of bloody massacres, retaliations and pogroms. For this reason, the Christian and Francophile family of Mouawad decided to leave the country. The war made the future playwright a refugee, or even double-refugee. Mouawad, left Beirut in 1979 when he was eleven and settled with his mother and siblings in Paris. The family was subsequently joined by their father, who earlier tried in vain to save the family business in Lebanon. Four years later, after Mouawad's family had been refused French citizenship, they moved to Canada. Apart from the difficulties connected with the status of a

---

2 Jerzy Grotowski called himself a great-grandson of Calderon. Barba, in turn, saw himself as the grandson of Meyerhold (Barba 2003: 17–21). The search of artistic belonging, professional roots, an attempt to situate their own work (not only that of a director) against masters, teachers, guiding spirits are increasingly frequent in the theatre of the twentieth and the twenty-first century.
3 It is worth pointing out that while the English title of Barba's book emphasises the work of a director *On Directing and Dramaturgy: Burning the House* (2009), its Polish translation stresses the importance of the creator's biography *Spalić dom. Rodowód reżysera* (2011) (*Burning the house. The director's origins*).
4 Cf. Jerzy Grotowski's notes on "the dialogue with ancestors": "I talked to Mickiewicz. But I talked with him about present day problems." (Grotowski 1997: 292)

refugee, Mouawad had to deal with the premature death of his mother who died from cancer when he was sixteen. Thus, it is impossible to read his works without bearing in mind those traumatic experiences of his childhood and early youth. Years later he himself mentioned, "I didn't live through the tragedy in its fullest but I was so close to it not knowing about it" (Mouawad quoted in Bouchez 2011).

At the time of Mouawad's exile, which Josif Brodski described as "a metaphysical state (…) or [something that] has a very strong, very clear metaphysical dimension" (1996: 27), there appeared a bright light in his life which "reversed [his] destiny. And that light was theatre" (Mouawad 2009: 6). The playwright wrote that he had to "find the thing which would let him recreate the [lost] state of happiness, let [him] keep in touch with Nature and its fundamental constituents, which used to be present daily in his childhood" (*ibid.*).

Having mentioned the above experiences, it is not surprising that exile, wandering and agony of protagonists searching for their roots presented against the background of war are central motifs of Mouawad's numerous drama pieces. This holds particularly true for the tetralogy *Blood Promises* (*Le Sang des promesses)*, the cycle which not only scandalised the Avignon audience in 2009, but also opened up many professional doors for Mouawad. *Tideline* (*Littoral*, 1999), *Scorched* (*Incendies*, 2003), *Forests* (*Forêts*, 2006) and *Heavens* (*Ciels*, 2009) let the author, as he claims, restore the lost contact with the basic elements of life. Mouawad added: "*Tideline* was snatched from the sea, *Forests* from mountains and *Heavens* from birds" (Mouawad 2009: 6). The author also pointed out that "the abyss of his father's eyes" (Mouawad 2009: 7) inspired the sentences of his dramas. In Lebanon, where he received the Fenix Award in 2012, he talked about writing as a return to his father's always wet eyes. "I don't need to describe him to you", he said in an eulogy. "We all know him, we all have the same father whose eyes always shed tears (…) Words, imagination, the need to tell stories might be the appropriate way to give back to our parents, at least my father, what he suffered for the sake of children (…) this painful and numb light as my father had no words to express this experience" (Mouawad 2013). On the same occasion, Mouawad also described the process of writing as dealing with the ashes of those who left and thus serving to highlight all possible shades of pain, suffering and every kind of mourning which we, as people, carry.

Considering roots

Theatre as "a sudden bright light reversing destiny" (Mouawad 2009: 6), in case of Wajdi Mouawad, was inseparably connected with the thorough reading of Greek texts. When he was twenty-three – as he himself points the moment – following his friend Francois Ismert's advice, he read *The Iliad* and *Odyssey*, and all works by Aeschylus, Sophocles and Euripides. As he later recalled, "Reading the Greeks saved [him]" (Mouawad quoted in Bouchez 2011), allowing to finish the theatre school in Montreal without going astray but instead discovering his own literary path[5] and putting together "separate pieces of puzzle" comprising war suffering, emigration and mourning. "Thanks to Greek authors", commented Mouawad, "I heard the call 'Don't assume, don't claim: I would have never committed such appalling deeds.' Because all heroes, despite constantly showing their own virtues, commit those acts in the end. Who would I have become, as a Christian Maronite, if I had stayed in Lebanon? Would I have joined the police forces and be held responsible for massacres in Sabra and Shatila?[6] I don't know. Being familiar with Greek tragedies made me circumspect in answering such questions" (*ibid.*). But in Greek texts Mouawad found much more – the traces of mythical homeland from which we all come (cf. Mnouchkine [in] Féral 1998: 16), as phrased by another director Ariane Mnouchkine, who was also preoccupied with the representations of civil wars. What the Lebanese playwright took from the Greeks were, as Piotr Gruszczyński suggests, "mythical rules, grand tragic epics, which one can refer to, like to scientific mechanisms. They can possibly help to put life in order, to add meaning by placing individual cases on the map of great narratives" (Gruszczyński 2012: 161).

From the three previously mentioned Greek tragedy writers, it is Sophocles – "who experiences doubts, oscillates between hope and despair to reconcile with the world nearing the end of one's days in *Oedipus at Colonus*" (Mouawad quoted in Bouchez 2011) – that is undoubtedly the closest to Mouawad. Referring to seven tragedies by Sophocles (*The Trachiniae, Antigone, Electra, Oedipus the King, Ajax, Philoctetes* and *Oedipus at Colonus*), all of which he staged in July 2015 in Mons, Belgium, Mouawad points out that what strikes him in their author is "the obsession of presenting how the tragedy gets at those who blinded by themselves don't realise that they had overstepped the mark". As he confesses: "That made me, ponder over what I don't see in myself, what our world doesn't see in itself and what once revealed might tear the tangled web of my life" (Mouawad quoted in Savigneau 2011). In another place Mouawad adds:

---

5 Mouawad's first literary fascinations came earlier. It was Franz Kafka's novel *The Metamorphosis*, which he read at the age fifteen, that made the future playwright discover his artistic calling. Years later, Mouawad mentioned that it was the knowledge of literature that made him take up art and not the traumatic experiences of childhood and early youth.
6 Bestial murders committed by Christians on Palestinian civilians.

One cannot be sure of themselves. The thought not to express such belief never stopped striking its poetic and spiritual roots in me, entering each story I try to tell. Because it is the base of Sophocles' tragedies, like an echo, his epoch preserved from even more ancient times (…) when pain, suffering and violence were given thought. (Mouawad 2014)

For the playwright, self-awareness is not an invitation to psychoanalysis but "getting to know your own standards: if you think that you are God, it is an exaggeration", stresses Mouawad, "if you think you are nobody, you underestimate yourself. Between nobody and God, where are you? (…) The Greek protagonist overdoes it thinking that he is God. When Athena shows Ajax his lack of standards, he becomes a tragic figure, the truth about him appears with such clarity that instead of dazzling him, it destroys him (…) Ajax cannot accept it and commits suicide" (Mouawad quoted in Bouchez 2011).

Third road

In the space of Wajdi Mouawad's personal dialogue with both ancient Greek and contemporary theatre, there are also other frequent inspirations: meetings, stories, images. It was thanks to them that the playwright experienced that "at the junction of two roads, there might appear the third one" (Mouawad 2009: 7). During the work on *Scorched*, this third road appeared as a result of meeting women and listening to their stories.

From Josée Lammbert, a Canadian photographer who spent five years in Lebanon (1995–2000) and while travelling further to the south of the country managed to take photos of the leaving Israeli troops, Mouawad learnt about Khiam Prison. For the Lebanese director, the Non-Lebanese woman unveiled a shocking aspect of his own country's contemporary history. The prisoner-of-war camp organised in the former army barracks, held thousands of Lebanese, the majority of which were women, brutally tortured in interrogations to reveal the hiding places of their fathers, brothers, husbands and sons. Their interrogators were Lebanese in the pay of Israel and – what Mouawad stressed very strongly – spoke the same language as their victims. Amnesty International repeatedly appealed against the methods used in the prison, yet with no success. It was the very place that inspired the playwright's idea for the play.

In *Scorched*, Khiam was transformed into Kfar Rayat and appeared twice – as an orphanage in which the protagonist, Nawal Marwan, to no avail, looked for her son taken from her by force, and as the prison in which she served her long sentence for political activity.

Josée Lammbert, while telling Mouawad about her Lebanese journeys, admitted that during her work there were photos which she deliberately decided not to take. It was because she was afraid that they might be used by other people against her intentions. This unusual story of seen but untaken pictures inspired Mouawad to organise in the Théâtre de Quat'Sous, which he ran, an exhibition of non-existent photos of Josée Lammbert. Preparing for the show, opened in February 2001 and consisting of her stories, Lammbert shared with Mouawad the confessions of tortured women that she heard in Khiam.

In one of such confessions, a young woman, imprisoned in Khiam with other Lebanese women, described the tortures and humiliations – many of which involved sexual torment. The act of breaking the silence by the woman and the detailed account of her own life were a breakthrough in discovering the mysteries of Khiam Prison. Thanks to the help of UNICEF, Josée Lammbert, conducting a private investigation, traced the Lebanese torturer who for over a year sexually abused the women prisoners in there. The photographer also found that the man immigrated to Montreal and obtained a Canadian citizenship. None of his acts classified as crimes against humanity had been ever prosecuted. This story allowed Mouawad to fill some scenes in the future play.

But it was the story of an elderly woman that gave the actual framework for *Scorched*. To make her reveal the hiding place of her sons, she was tortured in front of her own daughter. The tormented woman challenged her interrogator with the final argument: "Look at me, how can you do this to me, I could have been your mother" (Mouawad 2011).[7] At that particular moment of Lammbert's story, Mouawad had an epiphany, envisioning the whole plot of *Scorched*. It came not as an idea but a deep insight. Thus, the untaken photo gave rise to the story. In turn, it was thanks to Randa Chahal Sabbagh, a French-Lebanese camera operator, that the playwright met Nawal Marwan – the woman who was the direct inspiration for the main protagonist of the drama.

From the evoked – yet authentic – images, testimonies and accounts, in the process of rehearsals and cooperation with the troupe, the fictitious story was born, and the characters and situations emerged. The acquired facts immersed Mouawad in an emotional and intellectual turmoil and in reflection upon complex ethical issues. The "chemistry" of the theatre group, its technique and cooperation, suggestions and inspirations from the actors, let "the text be created". *Scorched* would not have been written, as the author stresses in the introduction to the play, but for the ideas, presence and involvement of each member of theatre company working together for ten months.

---

[7] "Each man who tortures a woman, tortures potentially his own mother" (Mouawad 2011).

Mirror of the myth

Although the life story of Nawal Marwan and her children was rooted in the contemporary history of Lebanon and, to a certain extent, in the history of every civil conflict, its true dimension appears in its relation to the story of Oedipus. Only after applying the mythological perspective and seeing the drama in this light, one can free the story of "exaggerated bravura originality calculated for the sake of plot which bursts with tragic coincidences" (Gruszczyński 2012: 161). It is the myth that unveils the mechanics of dramatic precision constructed by Mouawad.

> CHAMSEDDINE Can you hear my voice (…)? It sounds like the voice of centuries past. But, no, (…) it is the voice of today. (Mouawad 2005: 127)

This phrase from the drama's dialogue is a self-commenting sign of the myth's presence in this text.

The story of Oedipus was not the starting point for the playwright, and it was not the need to reinterpret it that made Mouawad start working on *Scorched*. The myth appeared by itself with the story of Nawal Marwan. Her words, quoted above – "I could have been your mother" (Mouawad 2011) – led the playwright to the Greek sources of inspiration. The immense amount of suffering experienced on a personal level (individual and family fate) but also on the social one (a country brutally torn by civil war) in the retold story intrinsically demanded giving it a mythological dimension.

In theory, the earth, which becomes the setting and a dramatic persona of Mouawad's drama, is not burdened with a curse. The suffering that exists on it, however, suggests the opposite. In litanies of crimes cited in *Scorched* and based on cause and effect, one can recognize Sophocles' poetics, who "never shrinks from physical image of agony" (Kott 1974: 166). The curse put on the earth is not as much untold as it is inexpressible.

The search for help in a myth turns out, in this situation, to be fully justified. In the face of prevailing atrocities, the mythical source of energy in a human being present in the conscious approach to the world is growing (or might grow) even more (cf. Kołakowski 1994: 8). The needs "to live through the world of experience in a meaningful way", to notice the "purposeful order of the world" and affirmation, as well as the need to believe in stability of human values (*ibid*. 8–9) become more prominent. Contemplating the mythological form of time soothes the feeling of hopelessness, impotence and futility of inflicting and enduring agony. The introduced perspective allows us to see that the facts, no matter how cruel, are

> not only the facts but the elements building the world of values, which can be saved regardless of irreversibility of events. The faith in purposeful order (…) gives us the right

to think that what passes gives soil for things that do not pass (…), decay and destruction touch only the visible layer of existence (…) passing and extermination might appear as phenomenal layer of humanity, but observed from mythological perspective, they become the phases of the growth of values. (Kołakowski 1994: 10–11)

Awakening, discovering mythical awareness in the times of crisis seems inevitable, valuable and liberating, as the myth becomes the cure that allows the humans to inhabit the world after destruction.

In *Scorched*, the Oedipus myth is not limited to a fictional reminiscence exclusively, although Mouawad's text is one. The firstborn son of the teenage Nawal Marwan – Nihad Harmanni / Abou Tarek, the fruit of the forbidden love between her and Wahaba, the refugee from the south – is taken away from her soon after his birth. Many years later, he returns as a prison torturer, and not recognizing his own mother rapes her, giving her twins.

What is more meaningful is the fact that the Oedipus myth got interwoven into the well-structured drama. *Scorched* is a kind of investigation, which the twins are forced to undertake. They are accompanied by the notary Alphonse Lebel, who – to a certain extent – fulfils the role played in classical dramas by the chorus (the role of an adviser, ally, but also an opponent and commentator offering a transcendental perspective).

In the play by Mouawad, just like in Sophocles' work, everything had already happened before the beginning of the play. Now, the characters only have to discover the truth of their fate. In *Scorched*, the truth will not be discovered by the father-brother, the man with a broken identity, the torturing and killing machine Nihad Harmanni / Abou Tarek. In the drama, he subsequently plays the roles of a victim, an executioner, a prosecutor and the accused. Not only is he a devilish, inhuman automaton, but also, to a certain extent, the great absent character of the text who is unable to discover his own truth. The truth is to be discovered by the twins, Jeanne and Simon (or Jannaane and Sarwane), who became obliged to do it by their mother's will. They approach the task their mother left them with anger. Like in the case of Oedipus, it is not the twins own will to solve the mystery of their origin. However, from revolt and total rejection of the imposed investigation, they turn to action. Step by step, they discover more and more about their tragic inheritance. In the process, the secrets of their mother's life come to light. "There are truths that can only be revealed when they have been discovered" (Mouawad 2005: 135) – she tells them in the final letter. Like Oedipus, they have to discover who their father and brother are by themselves. "Silence awaits everyone in the face of truth" (*ibid.*: 130). The shattering discovery that their father and brother are one and the same person has to be accepted by Jeanne and Simon, because it cannot be explained. The revelation, however, does not cause a catastrophe in Mouawad's play. It might be because it directly results from fulfilling the promise given by the sixteen-year-old Nawal to her dying grandmother: the promise that she would break the thread of anger, learn to read, write and speak to tear herself away from poverty and the web of anger, and that she would do anything "to preserve love" (*ibid.*: 132). It is also the vow Nawal told her born of love, first son: "No matter what happens, I will always love you" (*ibid.*: 31).

"This is your grandmother's song" (Grotowski 1997: 302)

The insignificance of humans, the fragility of their happiness, the uncertainty of their fate, the immensity and cruelty of their suffering, and the meanders of their mistakes and falls are balanced by a human, or possibly superhuman, strength. It lies in a decision not to repay suffering with suffering and retaliation with retaliation. Such an approach lets us trust that it is possible to live through the worst agony and still preserve humanity. There is, though, one condition that must be met: the person who adopts such an attitude has to be in touch with their own roots. The awareness of one's roots becomes the precondition for the defence of humanity, Wajdi Mouawad seems to claim. Nawal Marwan, tortured in Kfar Rayat Prison, referred to by her prison torturers as "whore number seventy-two" or "cell number seven", was also called by them "the woman who sings". She sang her songs over the screams of other inmates, but also responded with songs to inflicted tortures. Prison guards respected her, for even they noticed her strength.

Nawal Marwan, the woman who sung to the tortured and while being tortured, belonged to the world of the Greeks. It was in this world where reality meant complementarity overcoming binary contrapositions. One of the older versions of the myth of Sisyphus tells that while he was rolling a huge boulder up a steep hill, Orpheus was singing.

What did Nawal Marwan sing in prison? Were they not by any chance ancient religious songs or traditional songs her grandmother used to sing? If it was so, the fifteen-year-long prison sentence became the time of singing the song which Jerzy Grotowski wrote about in his text *Tu es le fils de quelqu'un* (Grotowski 1997). Nawal Marwan was definitely "une fille de quelqu'un" (after Magnat 2011) – the daughter of a certain place, countryside, neighbourhood, related to a certain situation and an ancient love story consummated at dawn among the rocks and white trees. An ancient song, like in the practice of Jerzy Grotowski, allowed Nawal not to lose herself but head for the source of humanity. "The woman who sings" remained a human being after all.

Translated by Anna Mirowska-Przybył

References:

Barba, Eugenio. 2003. "Dziadkowie i sieroty". Trans. by Monika Gurgul. *Didaskalia* 54–56: 17–21.

—.2009. *On Directing and Dramaturgy: Burning the House*. London and New York: Routledge.

—.2011. *Spalić dom. Rodowód reżysera*. Transl. by Anna Górka. Wrocław: Instytut im. Jerzego Grotowskiego.

Bouchez, Emmanuelle. 2011. "Wajdi Mouawad sauvé par Sophocle". *Télérama*, 2 July. http://www.telerama.fr/scenes/wajdi-mouawad-sauve-par-sophocle,70687.php (Accessed 28 January 2016).

Brodski Josif. 1996. *Pochwała nudy*. Trans. by Anna Kołyszko, Michał Kłobukowski. Kraków: Wydawnictwo Znak.

Féral, Josette. 1998. *Trajectoires du Soleil autour d' Ariane Mnouchkine*. Paris: Éditions Théâytales.

Grotowski, Jerzy. 1997. "Tu es le fils de quelqu'un". Trans. by James Sloviak. In *The Grotowski Sourcebook*. Eds. by Lisa Wolford & Richard Schechner. London, New York: Routledge, 292–303.

Gruszczyński, Piotr. 2012. "Słowa utkane z pyłu". *Dialog* 4: 160–163.

Janion, Maria. 1998. "Na rozstajach dróg". In *Sofokles. Edyp Król. Program spektaklu*. Łódź: Teatr im. Stefana Jaracza. http://www.eteatr.pl/pl/programy/2013_12/57835/krol_edypteatr_im_jaracza_lodz_1998.pdf (Accessed 28 January 2016).

Kołakowski, Leszek. 1994. *Obecność mitu*. Wrocław: Wydawnictwo Dolnośląskie.

Kott, Jan. 1974. *The eating of the gods: an interpretation of Greek tragedy*. Trans. by Boleslaw Taborski and Edward J. Czerwinski. London: Eyre Methuen.

Magnat, Virginie. 2011. "La fille de quelqu'un: twórcze poszukiwania kobiet w diasporze Grotowskiego". Trans. by Kosińska, Olga. *Performer* 1. http://www.grotowski.net/performer/performer-1/la-fille-de-quelqu-un-tworcze-poszukiwania-kobiet-w-diasporze-grotowskiego (Accessed 30 January 2016).

Mouawad, Wajdi. 2003. *Incendies*. Montréal: Leméac, Arles: Actes-Sud Papiers.

—.2005. *Scorched*. Trans. by Linda Gaboriau. Toronto: Playwrights Canada Press.

—.2009. *Le sang de promesses. Puzzle, racines, et rhizomes*. Montréal: Leméac, Arles: Actes-Sud Papiers.

—.2011. *Sur la question de la violence dans „Incendies"*. https://www.youtube.com/watch?v=XWIY3gwhc6k (Accessed 28 January 2016).

—.2013. *L'émotion de Wajdi Mouawad à Beyrouth*. (Laudation speech, Phénix Award 2012). https://www.youtube.com/watch?v=26UZt0PnkU8 (Accessed 28 January 2016).

—.2014. "Wajdi Mouawad et Sopholcle". *La Chuoette. Le Blog de la Comédie de.. Genève*, 22 January. http://comediedegeneve.blogspot.com/2014/01/wajdi-mouawad-et-sophocle.html (Accessed 28 January 2016).

Savigneau, Josyane. 2011. "Raconter la manière avec laquelle je regarde le monde". *Le Monde*, 24 June. http://www.lemonde.fr/idees/article/2011/06/24/wajdi-mouawad-raconter-la-maniere-avec-laquelle-je-regarde-le-monde_1540516_3232.html (Accessed 28 January 2016).

Stephen Wilmer[*]
Greek Tragedy as a Window on the Dispossessed

Abstract: The exiled character in need of asylum is a recurrent theme in ancient Greek tragedy. In many of these plays, we see uprooted and homeless persons seeking sanctuary, and for the ancient Greeks hospitality was an important issue. Many of these plays have been updated to comment on the current social and political conditions of refugees. This essay considers Elfriede Jelinek's play *Die Schutzbefohlenen* as an emblematic case of the appropriation of Greek tragedy to reflect on the refugee situation in Germany and Austria. It will consider several productions of the play, including Nicholas Stemann's that was first presented as a reading in St Pauli Church in Hamburg in September 2013, and features asylum seekers from Lampedusa who beg the audience for the right to remain in Germany. It will also consider other reappropriations of Jelinek's text including *Schutzbefohlene Performen Jelineks Schutzbefohlene* by the Silent Majority and its disruption by right-wing activists.

Keywords: *Die Schutzbefohlenen*, refugees, Jelinek, Stemann, *The Suppliants*

It has become common practice for writers and directors to appropriate the text of an ancient Greek tragedy for a new play or production. The new work often retains some of the structural elements of the original narrative and perhaps the characters' names, but strays so far from the Greek text that it seems like a completely new script. This essay will discuss several adaptations that highlight the plight of the dispossessed. In particular, it will focus on Elfriede Jelinek's *Die Schutzbefohlenen* as an emblematic case of the appropriation of an ancient Greek play to comment on the problems facing refugees in Europe. It will consider how her play has been directed in a variety of ways in Germany and Austria, and how, in turn, it has been reappropriated for new dramatic performances to further investigate the conditions for refugees.[1]

The refugee is a familiar character in ancient Greek tragedy. Medea, Orestes, the Children of Herakles, Oedipus in *Oedipus at Colonus*, and the daughters of Danaos in Aeschylus' *The Suppliants* all seek asylum. In Aeschylus' *The Suppliants*, the fifty daughters of Danaos ask King Pelasgos for protection in Argos. Likewise, the Children of Herakles flee to Athens to get away from Eurystheus,

---

[*] Trinity College Dublin, Ireland.
[1] An earlier version of this essay appeared in Wilmer 2016.

who is determined to kill them. Medea, who refers to herself as *apolis* or stateless, persuades Aegeus to grant her asylum in Athens before she wreaks vengeance on Jason. In *Oedipus at Colonus*, Oedipus asks King Theseus for sanctuary in Colonus and succeeds in finding a final resting place. Similarly, writers and directors have used other plays such as *Antigone*, *The Trojan Women* and *Hecuba* to focus on the rights of the dispossessed, the vulnerable and the disenfranchised.

These plays not only depict uprooted and homeless persons seeking protection, but also demonstrate the importance of hospitality (*xenia*) and the ritual of supplication (*hiketeia*) as a moral practice in ancient Athens.[2] It is significant that in *Oedipus at Colonus*, Oedipus provides a kind of sanctuary for Athens in return for being granted one. By allowing Oedipus to be buried in Colonus, Theseus ensures that Athens will be protected in the future. The play thereby emphasises the potential benefit of looking after asylum-seekers. Thus, these ancient Greek dramas easily lend themselves to the issue of refugees today and have often been appropriated to legitimise the concept of hospitality, as a social duty which not only the ancient Greeks revered, but which has also been stressed as fundamental to ethics by both Emmanuel Levinas and Jacques Derrida.[3] As Judith Butler writes, "Emmanuel Levinas offers a conception of ethics that rests upon an apprehension of the precariousness of life, one that begins with the precariousness of the Other" (Butler 2004: xvii–xviii). Moreover, Greek tragedies about refugees and the dispossessed have carried all the more resonance as the world has been experiencing, according to António Guterres, the United Nations' High Commissioner for Refugees, "the highest levels of forced displacement in recorded history".[4]

Antigone is a play that sometimes serves as a vehicle for calling attention to the position of the stateless person and has been adapted to comment on the current refugee situation. Hegel regarded Antigone as an "internal enemy"[5] opposing the legitimate role of the state, but modern productions frequently

---

2   For a discussion of the supplication process, see Gould 2006 and Naiden 2006.
3   See for example, Derrida and Dufourmantelle 2000: 151, and Levinas 1991.
4   Opening remarks at the 66th session of the Executive Committee of the High Commissioner's Programme, Geneva, 5 October 2015 Press Releases, http://www.unhcr.org/cgi-bin/texis/vtx/search?page=search&docid=561227536&query=refugees%20october%202015, Accessed 30 October 2015.
5   From her example, he generalised the position of women who placed the interests of the family before the needs of the state as "the everlasting irony [in the life] of the community." Hegel 1977: 288.

represent her as a righteous character who is condemned to death by a tyrannical ruler. She has been used as an emblematic figure to embody the excluded, the dispossessed or the Other in society. While the chorus refers to her as *autonomos* because she favours her own laws instead of those of the state, she refers to herself as *metoikos* (cf. S. *Ant.* 850–53; 867–68). It is interesting that, despite being a member of the royal household of Thebes, she uses the term *metoikos* which Liddell and Scott translate as a "settler from abroad, alien resident in a foreign city". One wonders in what way she considers herself to be a foreign settler or an alien resident, in other words situated somewhere between being accepted and not accepted in society. Is it because her father, Oedipus, has been exiled from Thebes and she therefore feels half-exiled? Or is it because she is caught between the laws of the state and the laws of the gods in wanting to bury her brother? Or is it because her ontological status is uncertain, given her unusual family background? Or is it because she is in a liminal state between life and death as she goes off to be buried alive? In any case, it seems that she is referring to a psychological rather than a political status, a state of vulnerability and precariousness in her attempt to mourn for the ungrievable body of her brother.[6]

Emotionally charged versions of *Antigone*, such as the very much transformed *Antigona Furiosa* by Griselda Gambaro, featured in the Argentinian theatre in the 1970s and 1980s, at a time when opponents of the state were disappearing and mothers were parading in the Plaza de Mayo, calling on the state to disclose the whereabouts of their missing sons and daughters. In Janusz Głowacki's *Antigone in New York* (staged at the Arena Stage[7] in Washington, D.C. in 1993), Anita, the Antigone figure, tries to reclaim the body of Paulie, her dead lover, who has been removed by the authorities to be buried in an unmarked grave. Anita, a homeless immigrant from Puerto Rico, wants to bury him in a Manhattan public park where she lives. As both a homeless person and an immigrant, her legal and ontological status is ill defined. Her friend Sasha tells her: "We have to get indoors. When you live outdoors no one thinks you are a person" (Głowacki 1997: 72). Moreover, because it is dark when her friends retrieve the body and mistake another corpse for Paulie's, Anita ends up ironically burying someone else instead of her lover in the park. Eventually, the police close down the park, erecting a ten-foot high barbed wire fence around it, and rendering her status even more insecure. Anita

---

6   See Butler 2004: 36 and 46.
7   It was also staged at the Off-Broadway Vineyard Theatre in 1996 and in various parts of Europe, and translated into more than twenty languages.

hangs herself on the main gate of the park after trying unsuccessfully to climb over the fence to return to Paulie's grave. The authorities take the woman, sadly rejected by civil society, to be buried in an unmarked grave.[8]

In 2014, a workshop production entitled *Antigone of Syria* took place in Beirut. It featured displaced women from the civil war in Syria who recounted aspects of their experience, such as the loss of their homes and their relatives, and how the play *Antigone*, which is also about a civil war, spoke to them. Mona, a 28 year old woman who had fled from Damascus, addresses the audience in a monologue, comparing her experiences to that of Antigone's fame: "We are not princesses… No one knows of us and no one would speak of us if we died. Even in death, there are lucky people" (Fordham 2014).

Likewise, Euripides' *Medea* has been adapted to address the lifestyle and circumstances of the dispossessed. Marina Carr's *By the Bog of Cats* (1998) transposed the play to the Irish midlands with the Medea character, represented by Hester Swane, a member of the ostracised Travelling Community. The Travelling Community in Ireland, like the Roma in other parts of Europe, adopt lifestyles that do not coincide with the private property obligations of the capitalist system. In order to maintain the rights of a citizen in the nation-state, one must provide an address, "a fixed abode". Having no "fixed abode" reduces one virtually to the status of the refugee. Thus, those who choose a nomadic lifestyle are frequently deprived of human rights by the exclusionary policies of governments and by the hostility of local residents. In Carr's version, the structure of the ancient Greek play is retained, but the names are changed and many new scenes, characters and back stories are added, so that it seems like a new play. Hester Swain, the Medea figure, is evicted from her home by her partner's father, Xavier Cassidy. Unlike in the original, however, there is no Aegeus character who will provide her with a place of exile. Threatened with social exclusion and the dispossession of her young daughter, she takes her own life as well as that of her child.

Carr's latest project, a version of *Hecuba* for the Royal Shakespeare Company, opened in September 2015 at the Swan theatre in Stratford-upon-Avon. By contrast with her other versions of Greek tragedies, it is the first one that she has set in ancient times. She explained her purpose in altering the text: "I always thought Hecuba got an extremely bad press. Rightly or wrongly I never agreed with the verdict on her… No doubt she was as flawed as the rest of us. But to turn a flaw to a monstrosity smacks to me of expedience" (Carr 2015: x). Accordingly, Carr provided the Stratford audience with a Hecuba who doesn't kill the children of

---

8   For a discussion of this play, see Kott 1993.

Polymestor, but appears as a much more ambiguous and damaged character than in the original.

Carr's adaptation of *Hecuba* comes across as very political and anti-militarist. She created a visceral image of the aftermath of the Trojan War, with the gory signs of battle evident from Hecuba's first speech:

> So I'm in the throne room. Surrounded by the limbs, torsos, heads, corpses of my sons. My women trying to dress me, blood between my toes, my sons' blood, six of them, seven of them, eight? I've lost count, not that you can count anyway, they're not complete, more an assortment of legs, arms, chests, some with armour still on, some stripped, hands in a pile, whose hands are they? (Carr 2015: 211)

The production of *Hecuba* at the RSC conjured up images of the present crisis in the Middle East. While lamenting her lost status as the former queen of Troy and expressing her grief over the death of her children, Hecuba recounts her earlier lavish lifestyle in Troy and the types of treatment she misses. She reveals her disgust at the Greeks, whom she regards as barbarians and who are depicted as the malignant forces in the play, killing Hecuba's as well as Polymestor's and Hector's children, and menacing her entourage. Echoes of the current civil war in Syria, as well as the inhuman practices of Daesh or ISIS, come to mind as the brutality of the Greeks is recounted in the play, especially the numerous beheadings and the suggestion of genocide that accompanies Agamemnon's execution of Polydorus. This is reinforced by the unusual casting of white actors for the victimised Trojans and black actors for the malevolent Greeks, creating an us-and-them discourse that was physically represented by the bodies of the actors on stage. As Cassandra says of the Achaeans, "They were the wild dogs, the barbarians, the savages who came as guests and left an entire civilization on its knees and in the process defiled its queen and her memory" (Carr 2015: 259–260).

Moreover, as Hecuba recounts her search for her nine-year old son Polydorus amongst a group of bodies next to the sea, the media images of the current exodus from the Middle East are evoked, with hundreds of thousands fleeing across the Mediterranean, and bodies piling up on beaches. She says:

> And there he is, on his side looking past me, they didn't even close your eyes. I gather him up, he resists me, doesn't want my embrace now, will never want it again, no breath, none... Hold his hard little body, his lips when you touch them are ice. Who did this? Who did this to my war baby, born in the first year of these unimaginable times. I must bear this too it seems. (Carr 2015: 256)

A journalist for the *Independent* newspaper commented on the topicality of the production in her interview with Erica Whyman, the director of the production: "The day I speak to Whyman is the day this newspaper runs the image of little

Aylan Kurdi's body washed up on the shore of a Turkish beach; discussing the murder of Polydorous [sic], a nine-year-old thrown off a boat, feels distressingly close" (Williams 2015). Another reviewer wrote, "As a human, a mum and a witness to the refugee crisis, I found this two-and-a-half-thousand-year-old story about the horror of war delivered a painfully profound comment on our world today" (Sutherland 2015).

Hecuba represents a culmination of Carr's adaptations in reinterpreting the classics and transforming what Slavoj Žižek calls the monstrous qualities of these women into more vulnerable and passionate attributes. Hecuba and Medea, in Carr's treatment, become more passionate and sympathetic mothers who act ecstatically because they have been dispossessed. Rather than becoming bloodthirsty and calculated murderers who commit acts of revenge (Medea killing her children to spite Jason, and Hecuba murdering Polymester's children because of the loss of her own Polydorus), Carr's female heroines react to the loss of their children in ways to which the audience can react more sympathetically. Hester, threatened with losing Josie as well as her home, intends to commit suicide but takes her daughter with her in a moment of unforeseen passion. Rather than calculating this act, she acts in an ecstatic state of passion. According to Butler, "To be ec-static means, literally, to be outside oneself, and thus can have several meanings: to be transported beyond oneself by a passion, but also to be *beside oneself* with rage or grief" (2004: 24). Thus these females are transformed by their grief or inability to mourn, becoming characters outside themselves. Likewise, rather than committing a crime of passion, as in the ancient Greek play, Hecuba in Carr's version seems to be beside herself with grief after the loss of her last child. Cassandra describes her ecstatic state:

> All day she sits, Polydorus at her feet, another pyre burns, she refuses to put him on it, twines her fingers in his long brown hair, tries to warm his feet, his hands she holds against her cheek, gathers his stiff arms around her neck, they fall away, his eyes won't close. She walks around with him, will let nothing past her lips, she's dying in front of us, nothing consoles or ever will again. (Carr 2015: 257–258)

Thus, Carr transforms these female figures from monstrous murderers into precarious beings who suffer irreparably from the loss of their children and, like Antigone, consider their kin as more important than themselves.

With Germany alone receiving approximately a million refugees in 2015, many pro-immigration plays have begun to appear in their theatre repertories, often using ancient Greek tragedies as a vehicle to comment on the issue. Perhaps the most noteworthy is Elfriede Jelinek's *Die Schutzbefohlenen*, which she based on

Aeschylus' *Suppliants*. Nicholas Stemann, who was employed by the Thalia Theatre in Hamburg, staged a first reading of Jelinek's play in the St Pauli Church in September 2013 with professional actors as well as refugees from Lampedusa who had been given sanctuary in the church. The play then toured to the Ruhr Triennale in Mannheim and the Holland Festival in Amsterdam before finally opening at the Thalia Theatre in Hamburg in September 2014. It was later invited to open the prestigious Theatertreffen in Berlin in May 2015, apparently on political grounds as well as for artistic reasons, given the increasing importance placed on the refugee question by the theatre community.

Jelinek based *Die Schutzbefohlenen* on Aeschylus' *The Suppliants* in which fifty women, who describe themselves as "a dark, sun-burned race" (cf. A. *Su*. 154–155), have crossed the Mediterranean from Egypt and arrived in Argos to ask for asylum from fifty men, the sons of King Aigyptos. Pelasgos, the King of Argos, after deliberating over the consequences of protecting them and asking his subjects' approval, agrees to give them shelter. Thus, the tragedy ends happily, but with the ongoing fear of a possible attack. Jelinek used the original Greek play as little more than a pretext for her version, which aimed to confront the policies of the Austrian government towards refugees. Little remains of the original play in Jelinek's adaptation, other than some intertextual links and allusions, and the representation of vulnerable and powerless immigrants coming to a foreign land and asking for asylum. Jelinek related the Greek tragedy to the plight of refugees who had arrived from the Pakistan/Afghanistan border area and had been confined in the Traiskirchen refugee centre outside Vienna. About sixty of these refugees occupied the Votiv Church in Vienna in 2012 and went on hunger strike to demand better conditions, but they were later moved to a monastery and many were subsequently jailed or deported. Like the women in Aeschylus' *Suppliants*, who plead "May Zeus who guards suppliants look graciously upon our company, which boarded a ship and put to sea from the outlets of the fine sand of the Nile" (cf. A. *Su*.1–4), Jelinek's play depicts the refugees seeking asylum from the Austrian government and indicating the threat to their lives and the hazards of returning home.[9]

---

9 The title, *Die Schutzbefohlenen*, is a play on words of *Die Schutzflehenden* (literally, "those who beg for protection"), which is the usual German title for Aeschylus' drama. This altered title is somewhat subversive in that it means "those who are under protection or control", rather than "those who are seeking asylum". Thus, its meaning is ambivalent as to whether it implies that the government is protecting the refugees or simply controlling them (like children).

Fig. 1: Michael Thalheimer's production of Die Schutzbefohlenen at the Burgtheater. Photo by Reinhard Werner

The text is quite playful, parodying governmental and popular attitudes about immigration and ethnicity, and calling attention to Austrian political issues such as the unequal treatment of those seeking permission to remain. It also refers to the dangers for specific refugees who have fled from war-torn countries and whose families have been slaughtered, and their difficulty in providing evidence that will convince the Austrian authorities that they require protection. Jelinek's text also explores the role of church and government authorities who can decide the future of the refugees, and it conflates images of church sanctuary with national asylum, and ancient Greek gods with the Christian God on whom the refugees call for protection.

Jelinek's version is not structured in a dialogue form like the original ancient Greek text, and has no characters or divisions of roles. It reads like a long, rambling monologue, or like a choral diatribe (sometimes in the first person singular and more often in the first person plural), heavily nuanced with classical references and current political issues, a postmodern bricolage of images. Jelinek leaves it to the theatre director to decide how to allocate speeches and create characters on stage, and so the play has been directed in very different ways in its many productions in Germany and Austria in the last two years.[10]

---

10 These included Mirko Borscht's production premiered at the Theater Bremen and Michael Simon's at the Theater Freiburg, in November 2014, Peter Carp's at the Theater Oberhausen and Michael Thalheimer's at the Burgtheater, Vienna in March 2015, Erick Sidler's at the Deutsches Theater Göttingen in September 2015, Sebastian Nübling's (*In unserem Namen*)

Greek Tragedy as a Window on the Dispossessed 199

For example, Michael Thalheimer at the Burgtheater in Vienna approached the play like an ancient Greek drama with masked actors performing largely like a chorus (*Fig. 1*). The actors entered through a thin, cross-shaped doorway at the back of the stage and struggled through water that filled the stage as though they were actual refugees striving to cross the Mediterranean. They spoke sometimes in chorus and sometimes singly, as in Jelinek's text. Thalheimer's approach seemed somewhat conservative and straightforward, emphasizing the choral aspect in a performance of high culture without the presence of actual refugees.

Fig. 2: Nicolas Stemann's production of Die Schutzbefohlenen at the Thalia Theatre. Photo by Christian Kleiner

Mirko Borscht staged his version of Jelinek's play at the Theater Bremen amidst a year-long series of some fifty refugee-related events at the theatre called "In Transit". By contrast with Thalheimer's somewhat refined classical approach, which might seem quite appropriate for an ancient Greek play, Borscht's production which opened in November 2014, spoke to the immediacy of the refugee problem and the failed response by local politicians to the refugees. The spectators were photographed as they entered the theatre and had to find a place to sit on the stage, rather than in the auditorium because cardboard cut-outs of refugees had been placed there. Photos of European politicians also decorated the room. The photos of the spectators later replaced the photos of the politicians and the faces

---

in November 2015, Bettina Bruinier's at the Staatstheater Nürnberg in February 2016 and Hermann Schmidt-Rahmer's at the Schauspielhaus Bochum in April 2016.

of the refugees in the cardboard cut-outs so that the spectators became individually implicated in the events.

By contrast, as the audience entered the Thalia Theater for Stemann's production in Hamburg, they saw actors on a mostly bare stage acting like journalists interviewing some Lampedusa refugees about their ordeal in coming to Germany and their current vulnerable status. The faces of the refugees were projected onto a back screen as they spoke. Underneath the screen appeared a series of numbers in the thousands, continuously increasing throughout the performance, indicating something sinister to do with the fate of refugees. Then, three white German actors with scripts in their hands advanced towards the auditorium and began to read the Jelinek text: "We are alive. We are alive. The main thing is we live and it hardly is more than that after leaving the sacred homeland" (Jelinek 2014: 2).

As the performance progressed, it incorporated musical numbers that added an ironic touch to counterpoint the harrowing images projected onto the back screen of refugees struggling to survive in perilous Mediterranean voyages, dead bodies lying in rows on beaches, and children's coffins decorated with teddy bears. The production merged imagery from the occupation of the church in Vienna with the situation of the asylum seekers on stage who had received sanctuary in the St. Pauli church in Hamburg after their disastrous journey from Libya. This was emphasized by a huge crucifix descending onto centre stage that resonated with the refugees' experiences in gaining *kirchenasyl*, or asylum in a church, as a temporary measure. The performance offered the opportunity for the refugees to address the audience and state their need for asylum, raising awareness amongst the audience of their individual plight and vulnerability.

The question of who can speak for or on behalf of the refugees was raised repeatedly throughout the performance. Stemann felt uneasy about the permanent company of white German actors at the Thalia Theater representing asylum seekers. He wanted the refugees to be able to represent themselves. And so he developed a kind of compromise concerning who and what was represented, with the actors and the refugees alternatively representing asylum seekers. While most of Jelinek's text was performed by German actors employed by the Thalia Theater (most of whom were white),[11] acting often with the script in their hands as a metatheatrical indication that they were standing outside the roles that they were playing (*Fig. 2*), the actual asylum seekers appeared and reappeared many times on stage during the performance, both as witnesses and as symbolic presences (*Fig. 3*).

---

11   The Thalia Theater also employed two black professional German actors for the production on guest (short term) contracts.

Stemann further destabilised characterisation, identity and gender identification, by the use of cross-dressing, desubjectivation, and cross-racialization, having at one point a white actor in black face, a black actor in white face, another black actor in yellow face, and another white actor in red face. This allowed the audience the space to become politically engaged, however, it caused other problems. When Stemann's production opened the Theatertreffen in Berlin in May 2015, Wagner Carvalho, the artistic director of the Ballhause Naunynstrasse, walked out in protest during a blackface scene. He considered the scene to be racist and later took part in a heated debate in the Theatertreffen about the production and about the continued use of blackface in German theatre.[12] Despite a response from members of the Thalia company that the production was trying to expose black facing as an issue rather than simply practicing it, others considered it offensive. For example, a critic had argued, in response to a blackfacing controversy at the Deutsches Theater in 2012, that it was inappropriate for a white director to try to deconstruct blackfacing.[13] This incident fomented a general discussion about institutionalised racism in German theatre, especially since the jury for the Theatertreffen was all white and mostly male, and the majority of German theatres hire only white actors.

Fig. 3: Nicolas Stemann's production of Die Schutzbefohlenen at the Thalia Theatre. Photo by Christian Kleiner

---

12 Wagner later explained: "Blackface ist Rassismus pur" (Blackface is pure racism). See http://theatertreffen-blog.de/tt15/gehts-noch-ein-zwischenruf-von-wagner-carvalho/
13 See Otoo 2012: 11–13

Stemann's production was therefore controversial on several levels. It made visible those who are normally invisible in society and provided them with the opportunity to confront the audience with stories of their actual day-to-day suffering. Jelinek's text, which discussed the situation of being illegal in Austria (and Germany) and living with the constant threat of deportation, connected with the actual presence of asylum seekers on stage. By law, the asylum seekers were not allowed to be employed in Germany when the play opened in September 2014.[14] Consequently, most of the twenty-eight refugees on stage were not only inhabiting a liminal space of uncertainty as to whether they could remain in the country, but also they were walking a legal tightrope with a state theatre engaging them in a performance and paying them an allowance — an act that also could be considered illegal.[15] At the end of the play, the male and female refugees once again took centre stage and advanced on the audience stressing their bodily presence and the denial of their human rights. They related how some of their fellow refugees had been deported since the initial preparation for the play and how one of the refugees who was in the show had died in a parking lot in Amsterdam where he took shelter.

The performance, through its recontextualisation of a Greek tragedy about supplication by refugees that used the actual physical presence of refugees threatened with deportation, created an imaginative space where the possibility for re-evaluation, reflection and creation opened up. It not only questioned where people should be allowed to live but specifically what should happen to those refugees on stage, and to what extent the state and the members of the audience should act as host and provide for their visitors.

In addition to productions of *Die Schutzbefohlenen* that stuck quite closely to the text by Jelinek, I want now to consider two productions that have used her text as a pretext for further dramaturgical development: Sebastian Nübling's piece titled *In unserem Namen* ("In Our Name") at the Maxim Gorki theatre in Berlin November 2015, and *Schutzbefohlene performen Jelineks Schutzbefohlene* (which can be translated as "Wards perform Jelinek's wards") devised by a Viennese group called The Silent Majority. For *In unserem Namen*, Nübling removed all the seats from the main auditorium of the Gorki theatre so that the audience entered into a bare arena and had to find a place to sit on the floor. The spectators discovered

---

14 This law was later relaxed, with asylum seekers allowed to work after three months, with the proviso that any job has to be offered to a German citizen first.
15 The Intendant of the Thalia Theatre had made a prior arrangement with the Mayor of Hamburg that the theatre would not be prosecuted for engaging refugees in the production.

that actors, dressed like them, had entered the theatre with them and sat next to them in the audience. The actors, who were from a variety of countries, including three refugees, stood up individually to deliver specific monologues from Jelinek's text in their own language (and sometimes spoke as a chorus). They also made personal pleas to the spectators for help. Nübling's production also included extracts from a debate in the Bundestag on a new law to limit the rights of refugees. Rather than presenting a conventional staging of Jelinek's text (like Thalheimer's or Stemann's), Nübling's performance developed an intimate relationship between the actors and the audience that, through various forms of bricolage, stressed the ongoing and ever-changing political situation for refugees in Berlin.

A second production that reappropriated and recontextualised Jelinek's play was developed in Vienna from September 2015 by an activist team of theatre makers called The Silent Majority. The group visited the refugee reception centre in Traiskirchen (outside of Vienna) and invited about thirty refugees of all ages from Syria and Afghanistan to participate in a production called *Schutzbefohlene Performen Jelineks Schutzbefohlene*. The performance was presented as a German class in which a German character teaches German to the refugees by using parts of Jelinek's play as the class text. The show, which also interpolates interviews and interrogations with the individual refugees, toured to various venues and won a special prize at the Austrian Nestroy theatre awards. But during the 2016 presidential campaign in which the far-right presidential candidate won 49% of the vote, a group of about thirty agitators from the extreme right-wing Identitarian Movement broke into The Silent Majority's performance at the University of Vienna, stormed the stage, sprayed fake blood at the audience, and hurled leaflets saying "multiculturalism kills". Eight people were injured in the fray, including a Kurdish woman who was five months pregnant. One of the refugee actors expressed her horror at the attack: "I had … worried about my children: This is the end, they will kill us now".[16] After members of the audience had chased the demonstrators from the university auditorium, and the organisers announced that they would continue the show, the actors received a minute's standing ovation before finishing the performance with "trembling knees".

The extremist Identitarian Movement, who videoed their attack and released it on the internet, claimed that their action was to remind the audience of the Paris and Brussels terrorist attacks: "You've chatted up rapists and brought terror to Europe. People had to die because of your ignorance and hypocrisy…The blood of Bataclan and Brussels is on your hands" (Reuter 2016).

---

16 See Silent Majority website at: http://www.schweigendemehrheit.at/wo-werden-wir-unsere-eigenen-knochen-vergraben-koennen/#more-1442.

After this event, the President of the Austrian National Assembly invited the theatre group to perform in the Burgtheater under her personal protection. Seeing this as a provocation, the right wing Identitarian Movement then invaded the Burgtheater, which was performing Thalheimer's more classical version of *Die Schutzbefohlenen*. The Identitarians filmed themselves climbing to the top of the theatre, like in a scene from *Mission Impossible*, unfurling a banner that read "Hypocrites!", and also publicised this video on the internet.

In conclusion, theatre artists in various parts of the world have been responding to the changing social dynamics and demographics by staging productions about displaced people, often appropriating ancient Greek drama to do so. Some, such as the Thalia Theatre in Hamburg, have used a Greek text as a pretext whose intertextual links help to legitimise the values that they are conveying, while others have transformed the source text by an even more radical use of bricolage. Certain productions have made visible those who are normally invisible in society and have provided a voice to those who normally do not have one. In so doing, they have generated new experiences, interpretable by spectators in relation to their own memories and presuppositions, and encouraged them to question their own place and identity in the nation state, and their responsibility to those who have been excluded. Such performances have raised questions whether to simply pity those on stage or become actively involved with them in solidarity. Moreover, they have illuminated the mechanism of power behind social discourses on immigration, uncovering and exposing power structures and nationalist ideologies. Ironically, the discussion at the Theatertreffen about Stemann's use of blackfacing also illuminated the mechanisms of power within the theatre world itself and raised questions about how to rid the German theatre of racism.

References:

Aeschylus. 1926. *Suppliant Women*. Trans. by Herbert Weir Smyth. Cambridge, MA: Harvard University Press. http://www.perseus.tufts.edu/hopper/text?doc=Perseus:text:1999.01.0016 (Accessed 31 July 2016).

Butler, Judith. 2004. *Precarious Life: The Powers of Mourning and Violence*. London: Verso.

Carr, Marina. 2015. *Plays 3*. London: Faber and Faber.

Derrida, Jacques and Anne Dufourmantelle. 2000. *Of Hospitality*. Trans. by Rachel Bowlby. Stanford: Stanford University Press.

Fordham, Alice. 2014. "Syrian Women Displaced By War Make Tragedy Of 'Antigone' Their Own". *National Public Radio*, 13 December 2014, http://www.

npr.org/sections/parallels/2014/12/12/370343232/syrian-women-displaced-by-war-make-tragedy-of-antigone-their-own (Accessed 14 July 2016).

Głowacki, Janusz. 1997. *Antigone in New York*. Trans. by Janusz Głowacki and Joan Torres. New York: Samuel French.

Gould, John. 1974. "Hiketeia". *Journal of Hellenic Studies*, 93: 74–103.

Hegel, Georg. W. F. 1977. *Phenomenology of Spirit*. Trans. by A.V. Miller, Oxford: Oxford University Press.

Jelinek, Elfriede. 2014. *The Charges*. Trans. by Gitta Honegger, London: Goethe Institute.

Kott, Jan. 1993. "Antigone Hangs Herself in Tompkins Square Park". Trans. by Jadwiga Kosicka. *Slavic and East European Performance* 13 (1): 44–47.

Levinas, Emmanuel. 1991. *Totality and Infinity: An Essay on Exteriority*. Trans. by Alphonso Lingis, Dordrecht: Kluwer.

Liddell, Henry G. and Robert Scott. 1891. *Greek-English Lexicon*. Oxford: Oxford University Press.

Naiden, Fred S. 2006. *Ancient Supplication*. Oxford: Oxford University Press.

Otoo, Sharon. D. 2012. "(R)evolutionary vocabulary". In *The Little Book of Big Visions: How to Be an Artist and Revolutionize the World*. Ed. by S. Micossé-Aikins and S.D. Otoo, Münster: Edition Assemblage.

Reuter, Benjamin. 2016. "'Right-Wing Hipsters' Increasingly Powerful In Austria", *Huffington Post*, 20 April, http://www.huffingtonpost.com/entry/right-wing-hipsters-increasingly-powerful-in austria_us_573e0e07e4b0646cbeec7a07 (Accessed 14 July 2016).

Sutherland, Gill. 2015. "REVIEW: Hecuba at the RSC". *Stratford-upon-Avon Herald*, 7 October, http://www.stratford-herald.com/42748-review-hecuba-at-the-rsc.html (accessed 19 May 2016).

Williams, Holly. 2015. "The RSC's new 'Hecuba': A vengeful queen with a difference". *Independent* (London). 23 September, http://www.independent.co.uk/arts-entertainment/theatre-dance/features/the-rscs-new-hecuba-a-vengeful-queen-with-a-difference-10513125.html (Accessed 17 May 2016).

Wilmer, Stephen. E. 2016. "Cultural Encounters in Modern Productions of Greek Tragedy", *Nordic Theatre Studies* 28 (1): 15–26.

Withnall, Adam. 2015. "If these extraordinarily powerful images of a dead Syrian child washed up on a beach don't change Europe's attitude to refugees, what will?" *Independent*. 22 September, http://www.independent.co.uk/news/world/europe/if-these-extraordinarily-powerful-images-of-a-dead-syrian-child-washed-up-on-a-beach-don-t-change-10482757.html (Accessed 30 October 2015).

Małgorzata Budzowska[*]

Death in Theatre.
Between Word and Image[1]

Abstract: As Horace explained in his *Ars Poetica*, one of the phenomena that should not be seen on stage is death, or more precisely, the act of dying (*AP* 182–184). In tragedy, death was always connected with violence of others (murder) or with self-aggression (suicide). This rule of *decorum*, already existing in ancient Greek theatre as *prepon*, arose from the conviction that seeing death onstage would be a break of an aesthetic order. In the article, this aesthetic issue is considered on the basis of the assumption that the act of dying could not be shown and seen because of the sympathetic and ethical nature of mimetic *diegesis* in theatre, as it was discussed by Aristotle, Cicero and Horace. Tragedy on stage pretended to be a mimesis of life on the edge of death, therefore the performance could consist only of signals of approaching death and, subsequently, of post-mortem signs. Nevertheless, death was staged by shouting out from the *skene* or, more often, in extended messengers' reports in Greek tragedy and in pathetic *ekphraseis* in Roman drama. Furthermore, in Roman drama, against *decorum*, the death scenes were acted out on stage as it is epitomised in Seneca's dramas. All these cases are studied on the example of Euripides', Aeschylus' and Seneca's tragedies and scholia commentaries. In the second part, the paper focuses on stage procedures employed in death scenes in contemporary Polish productions of ancient tragedies. Based on case studies from performances of *Phaedra* by Maja Kleczewska, *Iphigenia. New Tragedy* and *Oresteia* by Michał Zadara, the article considers the ancient notion of *prepon/decorum* within the postmodern version of the aesthetics of "wet" and "dry" theatre, as described by Patrice Pavis. Defined as such, aesthetic issues to be discussed in the article provide the philosophical framework of cogitating death as the most invisible, unpresentable and unspeakable phenomenon of human life.

Keywords: *prepon*, *decorum*, death, the unpresentable, Polish theatre, scholia

Making the invisible believe

The true goal of the art of theatre is described by the Japanese director Tadashi Suzuki as follows:

---

[*] University of Lodz, Poland.
[1] This article is part of the research projects: *Ancient theatre and drama in the works of scholiasts* (DEC-2012/07/B/HS2/01475) and *Reception of ancient myth from Mediterranean culture in Polish theatre of XXI century* (DEC-2012/07/D/HS2/01106) funded by the National Science Centre within the programs OPUS and SONATA respectively.

Some people think that theatre makes visible something which is invisible. However, the situation is the opposite: theatre, through visible things, enables one to intuitively feel and imagine what is invisible. This is the nature of the theatrical expression. (…) in the place where there is nothing, actor behaves as if there was something and s/he makes spectators feel the same. (Suzuki 2012: 97, 77; trans. M.B.)

In this definition, the director accurately depicts the essence of ancient *hypokrisis* – the art of acting which aims at explaining and making believe what is shown on stage. Within this context, acting out a death scene seems to be extremely challenging. Residing in the source of the European theatre, Greek tragedy explored the phenomenon of death as being an essence of theatre *per se*, since tragedy on stage pretended to be a mimesis of life on the edge of death. Therefore, the performance could consist only of signals of approaching death and, subsequently, of post-mortem signs. The forthcoming danger of loss of life evoked fear, whereas post-mortem signs of death could generate fear by the emotion of pity when a killed character was perceived as partially or fully innocent.

If theatre is the art of making one feel, imagine and believe in what is invisible, death furnishes the best occasion for scrutinizing the problematics of representation. As Simon Critchley pointed out: "Since direct contact with death would demand the death of the person who entered into contact, the only relation that the living can maintain with death is through a representation, an image, a picture of death, whether visual or verbal" (Critchley 2004: 86). And next: "Thus, representations of death are *misrepresentations*, or rather they are representations of an absence" (*ibid.*, emphasis in the original). Death as the ungraspable experience is the most invisible thing that theatre can perform – acting out a death is acting out "not being", as Critchley continues:

The paradox at the heart of the representation of death is perhaps best conveyed by the figure of *prosopopeia*, that is, the rhetorical trope by which an absent or imaginary person is presented as speaking or acting. Etymologically, *prosopopeia* means to make a face (*prosopon* + *poien*); in this sense we might think of a death mask or *memento mori*, a form which indicates the failure of presence, a face which withdraws behind the form which presents it. In a manner analogous to what Nietzsche writes about the function of *Schein* in *The Birth of Tragedy*, such a prosopopeic image allows us both to glimpse the interminability of dying in the Apollonian mask of the tragic hero, and redeems us from the nauseating contact with the truth of tragedy, the abyss of the Dionysian, the wisdom of Silenus: 'What is best of all is . . . not to be born, not to *be*, to be *nothing*. But the second best for you is – to die soon'". (*ibid.*, emphasis in the original)

Aesthetics of visuality – Greek *prepon*

Visual or verbal representations of death or, more precisely, the act of dying in Greek tragedy was ordered in terms of aesthetics, which privileged word over image. It seems to be a natural consequence of the whole previous oral tradition of Greek literature with the Homeric foundation of *pathos* created by words, and the following practice of *aoidoi*, which can be compared with performative reading of literature.[2] Interestingly, at its very beginning, Greek literature had the form of a performance while existing only in collective memory improved by *aoidoi*, performers being a medium between authors and recipients. This background has to be recalled constantly so as to understand the priority of the word over the image, since the word for Greeks was a tool to paint a picture. And it never was a word read in silence, but it was always a word performed by *aoidos*, or by an actor. Within this view, we can observe that literature was delivered and perceived through the human body as a whole, with modulated voice, mimicry and gestures.

However, the highest value of literature, and even of tragedy in Antiquity, was to create proper verbal construction of an action that is seen as a "dramatically shaped structure of events" (Halliwell 2011: 226). Considering the significance of *opsis* (visuality) in drama in the *Poetics* by Aristotle, Stephen Halliwell underlines that for the ancient thinker visual aspects of tragedy were just a foil for the theoretical principle of organizing the plot's structure (*ibid.*). Aristotle himself notes that "spectacle, while highly effective, is yet quite foreign to the art and has nothing to do with poetry. Indeed the effect of tragedy does not depend on its performance by actors (…)" (Arist. Poet. 1450b17-19)[3] and he goes on to indicate that:

> (…) fear and pity sometimes result from the spectacle and are sometimes aroused by the actual arrangement of the incidents, which is preferable and the mark of a better poet. The plot should be so constructed that even without seeing the play anyone hearing of the incidents happening thrills with fear and pity as a result of what occurs. So would anyone feel who heard the story of Oedipus. *To produce this effect by means of an appeal to the eye is inartistic and needs adventitious aid, while those who by such means produce an effect which is not fearful but merely monstrous have nothing in common with tragedy.*

---

2   Cf. Powell 2007.
3   ἡ δὲ ὄψις ψυχαγωγικὸν μέν, ἀτεχνότατον δὲ καὶ ἥκιστα οἰκεῖον τῆς ποιητικῆς· ἡ γὰρ τῆς τραγῳδίας δύναμις καὶ ἄνευ ἀγῶνος καὶ ὑποκριτῶν ἔστιν (…). All quotations from Aristotle's *Poetics* hereinafter I provide on the basis of the edition: Aristotle 1966 (ed. Kassel) and English translation hereinafter on the basis of the edition: Aristotle 1932 (trans. by Fyfe).

> For one should not seek from tragedy all kinds of pleasure but that which is peculiar to tragedy, and since the poet must by 'representation' produce the pleasure which comes from feeling pity and fear, obviously this quality must be embodied in the incidents. (Arist. *Poet.* 1453b1-14; emphases added)[4]

Nevertheless, it must be emphasised that Aristotle does not underestimate *opsis* in the making of tragedy, but he considers visuality in terms of the mimesis of human experience: "Since the representation is performed by living persons, it follows at once that one essential part of a tragedy is *the spectacular effect*, and, besides that, song-making and diction. For these are the means of the representation" (1449b31-32; emphases added).[5] Song-making (*melopoiia*) and diction (*leksis*), as Aristotle further explains, concern "metrical arrangement of the words" (1449b35),[6] "rhythm and tune" (1449b29-30).[7] And all of these are important factors for the understanding of the nature of ancient Greek tragic performance that was mainly based on audial semiotics of musical declamation (melorecitation):

> Yet it is well-known that not just words are recited in the theatre. Ancient Greek tragedies based their recitations on trochaic tetrameters, while comedy used iambic and anapestic verses in the parabases. Both were accompanied by the flute. All text segments written in lyrical form were sung with an alternating chorus and partly with virtuoso solo arias. The tragedy's ritualistic death lamentation known as *commos* is an example of this practice. Hence, *we can hardly speak of a dominance of a spoken language*. (Fischer-Lichte 2008: 121; emphases added)

Then, *opsis* in Aristotle's theory should be seen as a feature indicating "visual language" that is able to create mental images, which, consequently, can be performed on stage to achieve congruency between picture imagined by means of the

---

4 ἔστιν μὲν οὖν τὸ φοβερὸν καὶ ἐλεεινὸν ἐκ τῆς ὄψεως γίγνεσθαι, ἔστιν δὲ καὶ ἐξ αὐτῆς τῆς συστάσεως τῶν πραγμάτων, ὅπερ ἐστὶ πρότερον καὶ ποιητοῦ ἀμείνονος. δεῖ γὰρ καὶ ἄνευ τοῦ ὁρᾶν οὕτω συνεστάναι τὸν μῦθον ὥστε τὸν ἀκούοντα τὰ πράγματα γινόμενα καὶ φρίττειν καὶ ἐλεεῖν ἐκ τῶν συμβαινόντων: ἅπερ ἂν πάθοι τις ἀκούων τὸν τοῦ Οἰδίπου μῦθον. τὸ δὲ διὰ τῆς ὄψεως τοῦτο παρασκευάζειν ἀτεχνότερον καὶ χορηγίας δεόμενόν ἐστιν. οἱ δὲ μὴ τὸ φοβερὸν διὰ τῆς ὄψεως ἀλλὰ τὸ τερατῶδες μόνον παρασκευάζοντες οὐδὲν τραγῳδίᾳ κοινωνοῦσιν: οὐ γὰρ πᾶσαν δεῖ ζητεῖν ἡδονὴν ἀπὸ τραγῳδίας ἀλλὰ τὴν οἰκείαν. ἐπεὶ δὲ τὴν ἀπὸ ἐλέου καὶ φόβου διὰ μιμήσεως δεῖ ἡδονὴν παρασκευάζειν τὸν ποιητήν, φανερὸν ὡς τοῦτο ἐν τοῖς πράγμασιν ἐμποιητέον.
5 ἐπεὶ δὲ πράττοντες ποιοῦνται τὴν μίμησιν, πρῶτον μὲν ἐξ ἀνάγκης ἂν εἴη τι μόριον τραγῳδίας ὁ τῆς ὄψεως κόσμος: εἶτα μελοποιία καὶ λέξις, ἐν τούτοις γὰρ ποιοῦνται τὴν μίμησιν.
6 μέτρων σύνθεσιν
7 ῥυθμὸν καὶ ἁρμονίαν

heard words and the picture seen as performed on stage[8]. This issue is appositely recognized by Coleen Chaston, who notes that "as a necessary part of dramatic poetry *opsis* too may have a share in the cognitive potential of mimesis and the realising of universals. If this is the case then Aristotle's support for the importance of visual effect may imply a function for *opsis* in the intellectual experience of the spectator of tragic drama" (2010: 8).

The theoretical considerations of Aristotle from the end of the 4th century BC (c. 335 BC), however, were based on the theatrical practice of the Attic tragedy of the 5th century BC. As such, they were postscriptive observations aimed at developing an aesthetic theory of drama. Nonetheless, the Aristotelian approach to the art of creating drama initiated an extensive discussion about the aesthetics of both writing dramatic poetry and acting. One of the most significant issues originated by Aristotle's rhetorical reflections was the notion of *prepon* (appropriateness), which was strongly connected with what can or should be shown by words or by acting. In *Rhetoric*, Aristotle indicates that:

> Propriety of style will be obtained by the expression of emotion and character, and by proportion to the subject matter. Style is proportionate to the subject matter when neither weighty matters are treated offhand, nor trifling matters with dignity, and no embellishment is attached to an ordinary word. (…) Appropriate style also makes the fact appear credible; for the mind of the hearer is imposed upon under the impression that the speaker is speaking the truth, because, in such circumstances, his feelings are the same, so that he thinks (even if it is not the case as the speaker puts it) that things are as he represents them; and the hearer always sympathizes with one who speaks emotionally, even though he really says nothing. (Arist. *Rhet*. 3.7.1–2; 3.7.4)[9]

---

8   Cf. Sifakis 2013: 52–53: „The execution of the visual aspects is credited to the art of mask-maker which is clearly stated to be distinct from, and unrelated to, the art of the poet. The poets, however, were also called didaskaloi (and tragōidodidaskaloi or kōmōidodidaskaloi, respectively) with reference to the function many of them performed as producers (or stage directors) of their own plays well beyond the fifth century; and the art of didaskalos – literally teacher, master – could hardly be thought to be unrelated to opsis. Therefore, it is necessary for us to assume that the same person – the dramatic poet – often had to be master of two different, though overlapping, trades, corresponding to the composition of his plays and their stage presentation."

9   τὸ δὲ πρέπον ἕξει ἡ λέξις, ἐὰν ᾖ παθητική τε καὶ ἠθικὴ καὶ τοῖς ὑποκειμένοις πράγμασιν ἀνάλογον. τὸ δ' ἀνάλογόν ἐστιν ἐὰν μήτε περὶ εὐόγκων αὐτοκαβδάλως λέγηται μήτε περὶ εὐτελῶν σεμνῶς, μηδ' ἐπὶ τῷ εὐτελεῖ ὀνόματι ἐπῇ κόσμος. (…) πιθανοὶ δὲ τὸ πρᾶγμα καὶ ἡ οἰκεία λέξις· παραλογίζεταί τε γὰρ ἡ ψυχὴ ὡς ἀληθῶς λέγοντος, ὅτι ἐπὶ τοῖς τοιούτοις οὕτως ἔχουσιν, ὥστ' οἴονται, εἰ καὶ μὴ οὕτως ἔχει ὡς λέγει ὁ λέγων, τὰ πράγματα οὕτως ἔχειν, καὶ συνομοπαθεῖ ὁ ἀκούων ἀεὶ τῷ παθητικῶς λέγοντι, κἂν μηθὲν λέγῃ. All quotations from Aristotle's *Rhetoric* hereinafter I provide on the basis

As can be noticed, considering the idea of *prepon*, Aristotle appeals to the principle of verisimilitude that is connected with mimesis. Indeed, he seems to refer the art of rhetoric both to the art of creating dramatic plot and to its enactment. This assumption is confirmed by Cicero's reflection on *prepon* in rhetoric and art. Substituting the Latin name *decorum* for the Greek one, he underlines that "observing decorum is the main thing about art, but it is also the one thing that cannot be passed on by means of art" (Cic. *De Oratore* 1.132),[10] and goes on to stress elsewhere that "failure to appreciate it leads to mistakes not only in life, but also quite often in poetry and oratory. Moreover, the orator must observe decorum not only in his thoughts but in his language. For he must not use the same language and thoughts for portraying individuals of every condition, status, position, or age, nor in every place, or at every time, or before every audience. In every part of an oration as in life, decorum must be taken into account" (Cic. *Orator* 21.70–71),[11] in order to conclude that "appropriateness' [*decere*] covers what is fitting to and consistent with an occasion and a person. (…) If even the actor seeks appropriateness, to what standard shall we hold the orator?" (Cic. *Orator* 22.74).[12] Consequently, the ethical aspect of this concept is obvious, as Walter Beale rightly noted: "so seamless is the fabric of Ciceronian humanism that it is difficult to say whether . . . decorum is an aesthetic principle applied to life or a moral principle applied to art. In either case decorum is properly associated with harmony, grace, and comeliness as well as timeliness and appropriateness, just as the beauty of nature is associated with its rational design" (1996: 169).[13]

---

of the edition: Aristotle 1959 (ed. Ross), and English translation hereinafter on the basis of the edition: Aristotle 1926 (trans. by Freese).

10 [(…) sed etiam ipsi illi Roscio,] quem saepe audio dicere caput esse artis decere, quod tamen unum id esse, quod tradi arte non possit. All quotations from Cicero's *De Oratore* hereinafter I provide on the basis of the edition: Cicero 1902 (ed. Wilkins), and English translation hereinafter on the basis of the edition: Hughes 2002 (trans. by Hughes).

11 (…) huius ignoratione non modo in vita sed saepissime et in poematis et in oratione peccatur. est autem quid deceat oratori videndum non in sententiis solum sed etiam in verbis. Non enim omnis fortuna, non omnis honos, non omnis auctoritas, non omnis aetas nec vero locus aut tempus aut auditor omnis eodem aut verborum genere tractandus est aut sententiarum semperque in omni parte orationis ut vitae quid deceat est considerandum; All quotations from Cicero's *Orator* hereinafter I provide on the basis of the edition: Cicero 1911 (ed. Wilkins), and English translation hereinafter on the basis of the edition: Hughes 2002 (trans. by Hughes).

12 decere quasi aptum esse consentaneumque tempori et personae; (…) si denique histrio quid deceat quaerit, quid faciendum oratori putemus?

13 Cf. also: "[to prepon] represents the formal aspect of the epistemological content expressed in *kairos*" (Untersteiner 1954: 198).

Thus, *opsis* and *prepon* meet each other in the considerations of staged images. Within this particular context, this question is discussed extensively in Horace's *Ars poetica*,[14] however, the principle of *prepon* was common already in the staging of Greek tragedy. Although we do not have stage directions regarding Greek dramatic performance, we do have a lot of commentaries (scholia) written by ancient scholars, which provide a considerable amount of valuable remarks regarding the staging *praxis* of Greek theatre.[15] In relation to death scenes from different tragedies, ancient scholiasts always give the same direction, as it was the common rule in performative practice. Discussing the fragment from Euripides' *Hecuba* (484), the scholiast first implicitly suggests that "Polyxena is killed in silence (κατὰ τὸ σιωπώμενον)" and next, more explicitly, points out that "tragedians used to not kill [sc. the character] before the eyes of an audience (τὸ μὴ ἐπ' ὄψει τῶν θεατῶν), since the viewers could be grieved by such a view".[16] The expression κατὰ τὸ σιωπώμενον, then, indicates the *prepon* of silent – so neither heard nor seen – death that can be later described by the messenger. Similarly, the death of Cassandra is silent, as specified by hypothesis to Aeschylus' *Agamemnon*: "(…) Cassandra's death is silent and [Aeschylus] showed only her corpse, (…)".[17] The scholiast describes here the staging procedure in which the audience does not witness the actual death of the character, however the viewers can see its post-mortem signs such as a corpse. Apparently, sudden and often cruel death, as it occurs in tragedy, cannot be performed directly, but its signs, even silent, become important props on stage. Ancient playwright, apart from the rule of *prepon*, seemed to be aware that silent props of death sometimes work more effectively than direct, affective performance. On the other hand, in the same tragedy Aeschylus constructs a different death scene for Agamemnon. His death is not silent, however it is still not seen. As scholiast aptly observes: "Aeschylus, as he used to, made Agamemnon's murder inside the palace (*skene*) (…)",[18] however, the audi-

---

14 Considered in detail in the next sections.
15 Cf. Easterling and Hall 2002; Nünlist 2009.
16 Sch. vet. E. *Hec.* 484: κατὰ τὸ σιωπώμενον ἐσφάγη ἡ Πολυξένη. ἔθος γὰρ τοῖς τραγικοῖς τὸ μὴ ἐπ' ὄψει τῶν θεατῶν ἀναιρεῖν· ἠνιάθησαν γὰρ ἂν ὁρῶντες τοιαύτην θέαν. Scholia to Euripides' plays are quoted hereinafter on the basis of the edition: *Scholia in Euripides* 1887, 1891. All English translation of all scholia hereinafter are mine.
17 Sch. vet. hypothesis Aes. *Ag.* 14: τὸν δὲ Κασσάνδρας σιωπήσας θάνατον νεκρὰν αὐτὴν ὑπέδειξεν (ί). Scholia to Aeschylus' plays hereinafter are quoted on the basis of the edition: *Scholia in Aeschylum* 1976, 1982.
18 Sch. vet. hypothesis Aes. *Ag.* 13–14: ἰδίως δὲ Αἰσχύλος τὸν Ἀγαμέμνονα ἐπὶ σκηνῆς ἀναιρεῖσθαι ποιεῖ (…).

ence could hear Agamemnon's screams: "Alas! I am struck deep with a mortal blow! (…) And once again, alas! I am struck by a second blow" (Aes. *Ag.* 1343, 1345).[19] The evaluative commentary to this scene in the scholia reads as follows: "This part of the play is highly valued, since it causes fear (ἔκπληξιν) and pity (οἶκτον)."[20] According to this *scholion*, it can be seen that stage *prepon* regarding death scenes in Greek theatre was strictly connected with visuality (or rather its lack). It was the question of *opsis*, so of a specific performative procedure, that was described by Aristotle as of secondary importance in the making of plays. However, the visuality of language remains primary, hence the audience can hear the victim describing his own death by screaming out.

Evidently, ancient playwrights left an extensive field for imagination of spectators, conscious of the fact that nothing should be shown directly if it is to be captivating and intriguing. Furthermore, it seems that they did not employ *opsis* in the performance of death in pursuance of the principle of mimesis, as was pointed out by the scholiasts commenting the Orestes' matricide in *Choephoroi* (904): "Persuasively (πιθανῶς) [did it], to the murder occur not in sight (ἐν φανερῷ)."[21] It is interesting how *prosopopeia* of the act of dying, which means making death mask using silence or cries without any simultaneous visual signs, is strongly connected with mimesis, that is imitating somebody's presence. It is significant, that the trope of *prosopopeia* is frequently described by scholiasts as a purely mimetic type of acting,[22] where one character imitates the one which is gone not by describing his/her behaviour but by imitating it. Most often in ancient drama, this is the case with the messenger's speech, which describes (*diegesthai*) and quotes (*mimesthai*) the moment of death. Nonetheless, in both situations, when death is silent or just heard, and when it is described or imitated by the messenger, we deal with the semiotics of spoken words, as Aristotle noticed, with "arrangements of words", "rhythm and tune". Regarding the verbally created scenes of death, modern linguist Michel Arrivé indicates that: "[Languages] have an extremely large inventory of words to designate death and especially the act of dying" (2010: 614).

This superiority of verbality over visuality in death scenes was enormously extended in Roman drama, where great *ekphrases* employ extremely gruesome

---

19 ὤμοι, πέπληγμαι καιρίαν πληγὴν ἔσω. (…) ὤμοι μάλ' αὖθις, δευτέραν πεπληγμένος. All the quotations from Aeschylus' *Agamemnon*, together with the English translation, hereinafter I provide on the basis of the edition: Aeschylus 1926 (ed. and trans. Smyth).
20 Sch. vet. hypothesis Aes. *Ag.* 13: θαυμάζεται ὡς ἔκπληξιν ἔχον καὶ οἶκτον ἱκανόν.
21 Sch. vet. Aes. *Ch.* 904: πιθανῶς δὲ ἵνα μὴ ἐν φανερῶι ἡ ἀναίρεσις γένηται.
22 Cf. the expression: ἀπὸ τοῦ διηγηματικοῦ ἐπὶ τὸ μιμητικὸν μετέβη.([s/he] passes from narration to acting) Cf. e.g. Sch. vet. E. *Ph.* 1225; Sch. vet. E. *Hipp.* 1240.

and naturalistic language to visualise both acts of dying and post-mortem signs. Obviously, if we talk about Latin tragedy, we can have in mind only Seneca's dramas – the only *corpus* that survived. Senecan aesthetics, though, were contradictory to Horatian *Ars poetica*, in which we can read:

> The things which enter by the ear affect the mind more languidly, than such as are submitted to the faithful eyes, and what a spectator presents to himself. You must not, however, bring upon the stage things fit only to be acted behind the scenes: and *you must take away from view many actions*, which *elegant description* may soon after deliver in presence [of the spectators]. (Hor. *AP* 180–184; emphases added)[23]

As could be noticed, Horace makes a quite interesting observation, which stands in obvious opposition to Greek aesthetics as formulated by Aristotle, indicating visuality as more effective (*segnius*) than verbality. Nonetheless, he evidently follows the Greek notion of *prepon* by indicating that many actions should be taken away from spectators' view and replaced by "elegant description" (*facundia*[24]). In the following lines (185–189)[25] he provides examples of such actions that are noticeably connected with cruelty, death or supernatural events. Latin tragedy, though, as epitomised by Seneca's works, employed both verbality and visuality *in extremum*. Death scenes in his dramas are usually meticulously described by messengers and sometimes even acted on stage. Counter to Horace's protocol of "elegant description", Seneca creates extended ghastly *ekphrases* full of anatomical details, blood, deformity etc. The sample of such explicit descriptions can be found

---

23 segnius inritant animos demissa per aurem
quam quae sunt oculis subiecta fidelibus et quae
ipse sibi tradit spectator: non tamen intus
digna geri promes in scaenam multaque tolles
ex oculis, quae mox narret facundia praesens: (w. 180–184)
All quotations from Horace's *Ars poetica* hereinafter I provide on the basis of the edition: Horace 1836 (ed. Smart), and English translation hereinafter on the basis of the edition: Horace 1863 (trans. by Smart and Buckley).
24 Horace uses the word *facundia* which belongs to rhetoric qualities. According to Lew is & Short (1879), *facundia* means *eloquence, fluency*.
25 Ne pueros coram populo Medea trucidet,
aut humana palam coquat exta nefarius Atreus,
aut in auem Procne uertatur, Cadmus in anguem.
Quodcumque ostendis mihi sic, incredulus odi.
("Let not Medea murder her sons before the people; nor the execrable Atreus openly dress human entrails: nor let Progne be metamorphosed into a bird, Cadmus into a serpent. Whatever you show to me in this manner, not able to give credit to, I detest.")
(Hor. *AP* 185–189)

in his *Agamemnon* when the act of killing the king is reported by Cassandra: "He has it [sc. wound]! the deed is done! The scarce severed head hangs by a slender part; here blood streams over; his headless trunk, there lie his moaning lips. And not yet do they give over; he attacks the already lifeless man, and keeps hacking at the corpse; she helps him in the stabbing" (Sen. *Ag.* 901–906).[26] However, the most disgusting are his *ekphrases* of corpses being post-mortem signs of death, bethinking description of little Astyanax's dead body from *Trojan Women*:

> His bones were crushed and scattered by the heavy fall; the familiar marks of his noble form, his face, the illustrious likeness of his sire, have been disfigured by his body's weight plunging to earth below; his neck was broken by the crash upon the rock, his skull was crushed, his brains dashed out – he lies a shapeless corpse. (Sen. *Tr.* 1110–1116)[27]

Seneca's extensive gruesome death reports became great *ekphrases* of death, being the resplendent – however, subversive – achievement of Horatian "ut pictura

---

26 habet, peractum est. pendet exigua male
    caput amputatum parte et hinc trunco cruor
    exundat, illic ora cum fremitu iacent.
    nondum recedunt: ille iam exanimem petit
    laceratque corpus, illa fodientem adiuvat.
    uterque tanto scelere respondet suis: (901–906)
    All quotations from Seneca's *Agamemnon* I provide on the basis of the edition: Seneca 1921 (ed. Peiper and Richter), and English translation on the basis of the edition: Seneca 1917 (trans. by Miller).
    In Greek tragedy we can find similar death reports (Hecuba's description of Astyanax' death in Euripides' *Hecuba*), however not so much naturalistic. We can also find examples of death acted out before the eyes of audience – the best known example being the scene of Ajax' suicide from Sophocles' tragedy (*Ajax*), but this case is considered an exception.

27 ossa disiecta et gravi
    elisa casu; signa clari corporis,
    et ora et illas nobiles patris notas,
    confudit imam pondus ad terram datum;
    soluta cervix silicis impulsu, caput,
    raptum cerebro penitus expresso— iacet
    deforme corpus, (1110–1116)
    All quotations from Seneca's *Trojan Women* I provide on the basis of the edition: Seneca 1921 (ed. by Peiper and Richter) and English translation on the basis of the edition: Seneca 1917 (trans. by Miller).
    Actually, the "shapeless corpse" was Seneca's obsession, and he used this phrase in the meticulous and naturalistic descriptions of different characters' death. Cf. description of Hippolytus' body in *Phaedra* (1080–1104).

poesis" (*AP* 361). Paradoxically, in his tragedies, Seneca applied aesthetics of disgust and cruelty not to be *merely monstrous* (cf. Arist. *Poet.* 1453b1-14, quoted above), as it could seem, but to bring direct negative moral *exemplum* to fulfil the same edifying demand of poetry as Aristotelian *psychagogia*.[28]

In Seneca's dramas there are also several death scenes written to be acted directly onstage with the most diabolical crime scene ever found in ancient drama – the scene of Medea's murder of her sons – which reads as follows:

MEDEA
O brother, bid the avenging goddesses depart from me, and go in peace to the deep-buried ghosts; to myself leave me and use this hand, brother, which has drawn the sword – [*She slays the first son.*] With this victim I appease thy ghost. – What means that sudden noise? 'Tis arms they are making ready, and they seek me for my slaying. To the lofty roof of our palace will I mount, now the bloody work hath been begun. [*To her remaining son.*] Do thou come with me. [*To her dead son.*] Thy corpse also will I take hence with me. Now to the task, O soul; not in secrecy must thy great deed by lost; to the people approve thy handiwork. [*Exit MEDEA, carrying the body of her dead son and leading the living. Enter JASON in the street below shouting to the citizens.*] (Sen. *Med.* 967–977)
(…)
MEDEA
Thou biddst me pity – [*She slays the second son.*] 'Tis well, 'tis done. I had no more atonement to offer thee, O grief. Lift thy tear-swollen eyes hither, ungrateful Jason. Dost recognize thy wife? 'Tis thus I am wont to flee. A way through the air has opened for me; two serpents offer their scaly necks bending to the yoke. Now, father, take back thy sons. [*She throws the bodies down to him.*] I through the air on my winged car shall ride. [*She mounts the car and is borne away.*] (Sen. *Med.* 1018–1025)

Medea doses the crime, performing the triumphant dialogue with Jason in the break between two murders. What seems to be the most significant in this scene is the fact that Medea murders her children in front of Jason, and Seneca, putting this scene on stage, allows the audience to feel (almost) the same thing that a father watching his children being killed can feel. Distinctively, unlike the atrocity and macabre of Senecan messenger's death reports, this death scene, when seen

---

28 Cf. Budzowska 2012: 115–116: "Seneca, as the follower of cognitive concept of poetry, accuses poets of being indifferent to the ethical truths about man (*De beneficiis* I.3.10). In Seneca's opinion, poets play with the audience's (spectators') emotions by telling false stories (…). On the other hand Seneca admits: *Quam multi poetae dicunt quae philosophis aut dicta sun taut dicenda* (*Ep.* VIII, 8, 7–8), and this way reveals the supremacy of poetry over philosophy in terms of the propagation of moral norms. A poetic writing, though, referring to the spectators' emotions, inspires them to analysis themselves and to engage in deliberations about their value system (*Ep. Mor.* 108.8–12)".

onstage, lacks any descriptions of gore. Considering this stage procedure, which apparently stays in opposition to Horatian *decorum*, M.J. Mans indicates that "Medea's 'bloodless' child-murders are an indication that Seneca does not always need blood and the physically spectacular consequences of violence in order to express the macabre results of unrestrained emotions. He therefore confines the macabre to the repugnant deed itself" (1984: 114). Furthermore, Mans points out that it was unnecessary to create great *ekphrases* here, since the infanticide performed by the mother before the eyes of the father was a sufficiently dreadful deed:

> Did Seneca really let slip this golden opportunity to describe the infanticide (and the death of Creon and his daughter) in the same gruesome terms as in his other tragedies? It would seem that the actual macabre element lies in the type of deed itself and in the fact that Medea (before the eyes of her husband) first murders one child and then at a later stage the other. For this view we find support in Seneca's *De Beneficiis* 2.5.3 where he argues that the most cruel way of punishing a victim consists in postponing and protracting the act of vengeance. (*ibid.*: 105–106)

Medea's infanticide remains one of the most horrible death scenes in the European theatre. Interestingly, it is also provided as a proof that Senecan tragedies were designedly written not to be staged but just to be recited. This supposition, though, should be considered as a sign of still operating *decorum* rule, since commentators and critics could hardly imagine this particular death scene to be staged. Although the issue of the nature of Senecan tragedy is not resolved, it is obvious that in Seneca's dramas death is acted out mainly in words.[29] Doubtlessly, the aesthetics of death reports differs from the death scenes performed onstage in terms of language. Seneca unmistakably recognized that his protocol of horror evoking disgust and fear works through word and through image respectively, therefore it was pointless to employ simultaneously atrocity of verbality and visuality. Appalling *ekphrases* work out as warning moral *exempla* themselves, and staged death scenes were visually dreadful enough on their own to evoke desired emotions followed by proper moral learning.

---

29 Although the *prepon/decorum* rule seems to be common in Greek and Roman tragedy's performance (with exceptions), different rules operated in regard to pantomime, as Alessandra Zanobi notes: "(…) ancient writers attest that violence and death were a central focus of pantomimic performances, listing violent actions such as dismemberment, tecnophagy, killings, and both self-mutilation and mutilation of others as recurring topics of pantomimic performances" (2014: 13). Further, she tries to explain this situation: "A dancer may have mimed such a scene in a more allusive way than an actor onstage; the allusiveness of the art of the dancer would have added even more *pathos* to the scene." (*ibid.*: 137)

Staging the unpresentable today

Ancient poets and thinkers seemed to be aware of the radical unpresentability of death, therefore they tried to find proper methods, techniques and tools for readers and spectators to imagine this experience. Modern thinkers found this relationship between language and death as crucial for human being, as expressed by Martin Heidegger: "The essential relationship between death and language flashes up before us, but remains still unthought" (1971: 107). This observation is consequently developed by Giorgio Agamben, who notices that "If the relationship between language and death 'remains still unthought' it is because the Voice – which constitutes the possibility of this relationship – is the unthinkable on which metaphysics bases every possibility of thought, the unspeakable on which it bases its whole speakability" (1991: 88). Theatre can and should try to make spectators feel and imagine what is invisible, unthought and unspeakable as death is, however, as Rosenzweig observes: "Tragedy created the form of the dialogue in order to be able to represent silence" (Rosenzweig quoted in Agamben 1991: 89); and what Agamben continues "It is in this silent *non liquet*, rather than in positive reconciliation, that we should see the essence of tragic dialogue" (*ibid.*).

Keeping in mind various practical and theoretical approaches to the acting out death scenes in Antiquity and the above outlined theoretical approach to the unpresentability of death, we can now look at contemporary procedures employed to stage death scenes from ancient dramas. According to the postmodern aesthetics, along with the postmodern philosophy of being that often meet each other on contemporary stage, the act of artistic creation arises from the desire to express the unpresentable that cannot be signified in rational description (Lyotard 1984: 81). Forasmuch modern aesthetics just alludes to the unpresentable, simply missing content while the form retains its recognizable consistency, postmodern aesthetics considers the unpresentable both in content and in form, putting an emphasis on its elusiveness (*ibid.*). Such philosophical-like approach affects the postmodern act of creation and, consequently, the reception of a piece of art. Significantly, the main goal of so defined art is not to offer pleasure, but evoke the discomfort caused by the longing for the unpresentable. Therefore, artists create their own private language for their works, a language which is provisional and evanescent, such as the unpresentable appears. Thus, postmodern aesthetics shares the field with postmodernity as defined in philosophy of being where "[O]ne may say that in this world of ours signs float in search of meanings, meanings drift in search of signs (…)" (Bauman 1997: 170). However, each found meaning has only the status of a proposal, wherein the nature of postmodern art is just a simulation of the process of searching for meanings, because, paradoxically as it seems, its main goal is, by evoking discomfort, "to act as a sort of intellectual and emotional antifreeze, which prevents solidification of any half-way finding into an icy canon arresting the flow of possibilities" (*ibid.*: 171).

So defined philosophical and aesthetical nature of postmodern artistic creation expresses itself by "crossing borders of art; recognition of what is incidental and fragmentary; heterogenic forms intentionally created (…); constructions which are inconsistent, generically and stylistically blurred, double-coded (such as parody, pastiche, collage), of intensified, conspicuously disclosed intertextual dimension, simultaneously ludic and critical" (Nycz 2000: 165; trans. M.B.). Although the postmodern trend in art was initiated and developed in the 1950s and 1960s of the twentieth century in USA and Western Europe, its overwhelming and still vital impact on contemporary art is undeniable. Fully developed into different continual or critical branches and rhizomes, postmodernism supported (or not) by postmodernity, changed all fields of contemporary art, including theatre with its main concern of presenting the unpresentable and invisible.

In theatre, the main change seems to have happened in relation to physicality and, consequently, to the phenomenal presence of bodies on stage; bodies which become not only a medium for meanings, but which are inhabited by meanings. Mimetic nature of theatre is then exposed more directly (by corporeality) and, at the same time, more blurred (by inconsistency), more inclined towards mimesis of the process than mimesis of the product.[30] In processual mimesis, theatre imitates the processes of life and the process of creation itself, and in this creative procedure *natura naturans* is staged.[31] In the context of corporeal mimesis of life processes, stage images of death pretend to be a great challenge for the art of acting that does really intend to express the unpresentability of the experience of death. To find relevant audial, visual or linguistic (or mixed) signs to designate death, and not to be trapped in cliché or platitude, is the most difficult task for staging tragedy today. The problem is intensified if we realise the split nature of contemporary common aesthetics followed by contradicted senses of receptivity. On the one hand, we are constantly exposed to the "gore" aesthetics of violent language, images and sounds employed extensively in cinema and video games. Furthermore, similar scenes containing blood and violence became a steady element of the news shown in the media. The recipients familiar with this kind of imagery become desensitised and could hardly be shocked seeing or hearing any violence

---

30 Cf. Hutcheon 2013.
31 Cf. Arist. *Poet.* 1448a1: μιμοῦνται οἱ μιμούμενοι πράττοντας ("imitators/artists imitate/represent people doing something").

on stage. Then again, in today's absurd world we are predominated by an aesthetics of beauty, defined by the criteria of physical perfection and youthfulness, which refuses to acknowledge the existence of ugliness, disease, senility or death.

> Our culture is dominated by a craze for youth, slimness, and fitness. Bodies that blatantly contradict this ideal are stigmatized as abnormal and banned from the public sphere as far as possible. Likewise sickness and death, though not a taboo, represent an anathema in our society. Sick and dying bodies trigger resistance, loathing, disgust, fear, and also shame. By putting these very bodies on stage without specially justifying their deviation from the expected norm (…) they left the audience "defencelessly" exposed to the sight of these bodies. The force of social convention produced corresponding emotional responses in the perceiving subjects, which they articulated physically and which then were perceived by others. The meanings were undeniably culturally predetermined and thus adopted and shared by its individual members, guiding their perception and inducing strong emotions. (Fischer-Lichte 2008: 152–153)

Current notion of *decorum* seems to suffer from a schizophrenic split of mind, mainly because art lags behind life. In reality, people can find violent death scenes in everyday news on TV or on-line, especially in the last years with the increase of terrorist attacks and staged executions of hostages. People are also subjugated by the aggressive campaign of a highly stylish and artificial vision of life identified with external beauty. Theatre, trying to fulfil the task of mimetic art, becomes confused what exactly should be represented to stimulate spectators' emotions. To *re*-present death in the context of current realities is to represent the process without defined emotional protocol and as such eluding from any stage framework. However, as Fischer-Lichte aptly observed above, the image that can indeed evoke strong emotions concerns the "backstage" of death – sickness, pain, ugliness, deformity, decomposition. Performing death in the manner of "wet" theatre, when "the actor gets wet feet, literally and figuratively, taking risks, breaking a sweat, externally and internally, producing an excess of energy that leads to an overflow of bodily fluid, of residue, of detritus and of filth" (Pavis 2013: 234), is the most common in contemporary theatre. This aesthetics corresponds with the violent images of death flashing towards people everyday and everywhere. In contrast, death can be also enacted in the "dry" manner, using Pavis' terminology, in which the stage "stays dry, linked to the word alone, to pure language: the symbolic replaces the literal, the cerebral neutralises the visceral, dry convention takes the place of realities" (*ibid.*). This type of acting traces the path of culturally established conventionalities repressing physical literality of life, and it involves into intellectual, more diegetic descriptions of death. Apparently, "dry" theatre remains in accordance with the ancient Aristotelian *prepon* devoted to verbality and Horatian *decorum* forbidding cruelty on stage. Paradoxically, Senecan aesthetics can be seen in both types of theatre, depending on the way in which his pictorial language is taken on stage. Postmodern theatre plays with these clichés, both "wet" and "dry", bringing them to the extremum, blending together or mocking at them. Death scenes come to be a great opportunity to employ each form of postmodern heterogenic procedures to verify spectators' reactions, as will be traced in the following sections of short case studies of death scenes from different productions of ancient dramas in Polish theatre.

Subversive *wet death* – *Phaedra* by Maja Kleczewska (National Theatre in Warsaw, 2006)

The most common method of staging death in ancient theatre is announcing it through the messenger's speech.[32] Being "a complex mental picture", it depends "on the pleasure and learning that arises from imitation of what has been seen before" (Chaston 2010: 22). Particularly, Euripidean messenger's speeches are characterised by "visual clarity" (*ibid.*), and they can be compared to the great Senecan *ekphrases*. The status of the messenger figure, however, is of an inconsistent nature, while the role of the narrator, actor and spectator is blended in one character. Although quite often the messenger in ancient drama performs the role of an extradiegetic narrator,[33] in the dramas about Phaedra myth he belongs to the fictional world of the play as a companion and friend of Hippolytus. Thereby, his report is not emotionally neutral, and Maja Kleczewska took this fact under consideration. Kleczewska based her production on both (survived) ancient dramas regarding the Phaedra myth, by Euripides (*Hippolytus*) and Seneca (*Phaedra*), and she completed her textual basis by including two contemporary plays adapting this myth, by Hungarian playwright István Tasnádi (*Phaedra. The Therminal Act*) and by Swedish poet Per Olov Enquist (*To Phaedra*). Creating such a dialectic framework between ancient and (post)modern versions of the myth, she employs the form of "wet" theatre with strong language disrupted by more stylish ancient parts, psychedelic, provocative acting and clean, sterile scenography which becomes more and more dirty with human fluids, clothes, leftovers and rubbish. On this dirty stage, at the end of the play, the director enacts the messenger's report of Hippolytus' death. Kleczewska uses the fragment from Euripides' play, however, she extracts from the Euripidean "mental picture" some phrases to make

---

32 About messengers' speeches in ancient drama cf. Green 1996 and 1999.
33 Zanobi (2014: 148) noticed that Greek tragedies' messengers are deeply emotionally involved in the report they deliver, while Senecan messengers are mostly extradiegetic narrators, being outside the fictional universe.

them literally visual. In this death scene she subversively connects visuality and verbality, making a "dry" report "wet". What is seen on stage is the character of the messenger – Theramenes (Paweł Tołwiński) – who is naked and wholly covered in blood (*Fig. 1*). He reports Hippolytus' death to Theseus (Jan Englert) with Euripides' words screamed expressively and dreadfully, and his bloody figure reflects the description of Hippolytus' body: "(…) and the poor man himself, entangled in the reins, bound in a bond not easy to untie, was dragged along, smashing his head against the rocks and rending his flesh (…)" (Eur. *Hipp.* 1235–1236).[34] This juxtaposition of visual and audial signs refers both to Euripides' great *ekphrasis* and to Seneca's aesthetics of disgust, however, it paradoxically preserves the ancient principle of *prepon*, in which death itself is absent, but its signs are so striking that image of death is intrusive. By the messenger's speech itself, the mimetic effect is achieved through evoking the spectators' real experience. However, "this memory material, fashioned by descriptive passages, as Taplin writes, 'only matters in so far as it is brought to bear on the focus of the play on stage'" (Chaston 2010: 28). Kleczewska brings the "visual clarity" of Euripides' language to focus on the visual effect of the actor's body, which seems to be really inhabited by the meanings of the words he speaks. Words, the manner of their expression, and body by which they are spoken create the death scene built simultaneously by phenomenal and semiotic body. Nonetheless, visuality of this scene is so telling that it overwhelms the spoken words. Put simply, the messenger's death report in this production is made of a visual image of a bloody naked body and audial image of quickly shouted words. Spectators can hardly understand their meanings, but it does not stop from understanding of communicated signs.

The subversive procedure employed on stage by Kleczewska when linguistic *ekphrasis* is transformed into the audiovisual sign performed by body adapts ancient *prepon* in a postmodern manner. The messenger's report is visually "written" on his body – signs of death are literally and figuratively shown on stage, underlining its involvement in postmodern aesthetics of heterogenic, blurred form, being a quite cogent scenic translation of the unpresentability of the phenomenon of death.

---

34 All English translation from Euripides' *Hippolytus* I provide on the basis of the edition: Euripides 1995 (ed. Kovacs).

Fig. 1: *Theramenes (Paweł Tołwiński) and Theseus (Jan Englert). Photo by Bartłomiej Sowa*

Parodic *dry death* – *Iphigenia. New Tragedy* by Michał Zadara (National Old Theatre in Cracow, 2008)

Myth of Iphigenia and her death, already in its ancient version by Euripides (*Iphigenia in Aulis*), unmasks the power of public opinion. The image of the leader, created to satisfy the public, is frequently framed within the discourse of science or religion in order to cover any deficiencies. The authority of these both fields of human reflection on the world phenomena is unquestionable, therefore they considerably affect any political narration. The director of the play *Iphigenia. New Tragedy*, Michał Zadara, together with dramaturge Paweł Demirski, wrote the new script based on the Racinian version of the Greek tragedy (*Iphigenia*), confronting contemporary scientistic political discourse of technocrats[35] with the hidden,

---

35 This type of *politics of conduct* is "a new form of governmentality, that is 'the conduct of conduct' (Foucault, 1982; Lemke, 2002), in which a particular rationality of gov-

however still present and extensive, religious narration. Even though the leader himself (Agamemnon – Jan Peszek; *Fig. 2*) describes religion as an "idiotic humbug", he is forced to accept it in order to satisfy the public opinion and maintain his political power – and it does not matter that this "idiotic humbug" demands the death of his own daughter. Death of the leader's child, seen as absolute devotion of the king to the state, is one of the ritual murders performed in order to restore public order. As such, this death needs to be performed as a kind of a public performance, ceremony of sacrifice executed and shown to the people.

Fig. 2: Iphigenia (Barbara Wysocka) and Agamemnon (Jan Peszek). Photo by Ryszard Kornecki

This death in Racine's play is reported by a messenger who, again, is not just an extradiegetic narrator[36] but Ulysses himself, a character deeply immersed in the fictional world. Although the whole performance is intentionally kept in the convention of theatre of words where acting is limited to declamation, the last scene of Ulysses' report breaks this framework. The "dry" form of this production becomes blurred and travestied. Ulysses (Roman Garncarczyk), with the bottle of beer in his hand, reports of Iphigenia's ceremonial death in an informal, joking manner, describing it as a comic spectacle with a surprising end. Liberating this character

---

erning is combined with new technologies, instruments and tactics of conducting the process of collective rule-setting, implementation and often including policing as well" (Swyngedouw 2005: 1992).

36 In Euripides' tragedy the messenger was an extradiegetic narrator.

from the great Racinian-like narration, the director constructs the scene cancelling the whole pompous political and military discourse. From the ideological point of view, Ulysses reduces Iphigenia's sacrifice to the comic incident where both army and religion become the objects of mockery and where the figure of the victim is completely forgotten.

The serious speech given by the messenger from Racine's tragedy is transformed in Zadara's play into a funny story, and by this procedure the director underlines the fact how "the report" can be mediated by the way of its delivery. The object of the report becomes just a product that should be sold in a proper way. Obviously, Zadara mocks at the contemporary media discourse that can – and that really does – sell death as a product. But it seems apparent that he also takes a critical discussion about the messenger's speech as a narrative part of drama, which replaces mimetic action by words. Messenger's speech, as it seems, is here considered just as a rhetorical exercise, a masterful show of verbal description of action instead of the action itself. Death is just an object of language exercise and the director employs it to show that even such substantial experience can be just an impulse to practice artistry of verbality. This self-reflective scene enacted in the form of parody makes us aware of the falsified nature of mediated report and of the power of words employed on stage in place of visuality.

Between *wet* and *dry death* – Oresteia by Michał Zadara (National Opera in Warsaw, 2010)

Agamemnon's and Cassandra's deaths can be the most significant examples of stage death, since the myth of Atreides was well known and extensively commented in Antiquity as the best matrix to muse human cruelty at the very beginning of the statehood. Death of Agamemnon in Michał Zadara's production is performed without words, mainly because it is the staging of Iannis Xenakis' opera. The audial semiotics of the scene is created by stochastic, irritating and worrisome music, however, the director develops the scene from ancient drama dividing its visuality between behind and onstage performance. Initially, the audience can see just splashes of blood expressively appearing on the white big sheet hanging on the stage wall. Immediately after, characters of Agamemnon (Sean Palmer) and Clytemnestra (Barbara Wysocka) appear on stage. Clytemnestra strikes Agamemnon with an axe while he is entangled in the bloody sheet (*Fig. 3*). This gory scene ends with Clytemnestra and Aegisthus (Mariusz Zaniewski) smearing Agamemnon's blood on their faces with triumph. Agamemnon's corpse is taken from stage on small *ekkyklema*, platform used also in ancient theatre for the same purposes. The death of Cassandra (Holger Falk; *Fig. 4*), however, is played oppositely, from a very symbolic perspective. While Cassandra is ending her aria the character of state security service agent appears in the shadow to finally break a stick and simultaneously Cassandra falls down dead. Her body is also taken off stage on *ekkyklema*.

Fig. 3: Clytemnestra (Barbara Wysocka) and Aegisthus (Mariusz Zaniewski) over the body of Agamemnon (Sean Palmer). Photo by Krzysztof Bieliński

In the same performance we can observe different, "wet" and "dry", stage methods to enact violent death, although mainly employing visuality and audial semiotics of music as specific for operatic performance. *Opsis* is here the most important way of tragic expression, while words are displaced by music that remains pictorial even being chaotic and stochastic.[37] In this production, audial performance pretends to repeat ancient tragic melorecitation, that is Aristotelian rhythm and tune of words, as composer Iannis Xenakis admits: "The poetics of the speech is

---

37 The nature of Iannis Xenakis' music is explained by its author as follows: "Instead of starting from the unit element concept and its tireless iteration and from the increasing irregular superposition of such iterated unit elements, we can start from a disorder concept and then introduce means that would increase or reduce it. This is like saying that we take the inverse road: We do not wish to construct a complex sound edifice by using discontinuous unit elements (bricks = sine or other functions); we wish to construct sounds with continuous variations that are not made out of unit elements." (Xenakis 1992: 246)

the most important tradition we have inherited. None of the translations render or will ever render its strength" (Xenakis quoted in Vagopoulou 2005: 3). The intention of the composer, then, was to reflect ancient Greek way of describing life in tragedy, which employed sung, choral or solo, words. Therefore, he created the composition consisting of choral parts with just two long solo arias for Cassandra and Athena.[38] Agamemnon's death, as described above, is performed with the accompanying cries of the chorus and music of drums. Cassandra's death, performed without words and just with symbolic gestures, is also played without music, in complete silence. Drums just foreshadow her death, but the act itself is silent, as it was described in scholia above. An interesting quotation from ancient theatre practice is the use of the *ekkyklema* prop. Usually used to remove dead bodies from stage, in Zadara's production it is employed for the same purposes, yet appears in a miniature form looking like a child's toy. The dead bodies of Agamemnon and Cassandra are removed in silence from the stage on this small *ekkyklema* by two soldiers. Both death scenes are also accompanied by a percussion which is placed directly on stage, apart from the orchestra playing, as usual, from the orchestral pit.

Fig. 4: Cassandra (Holger Falk) singing her aria. Rehearsal. Photo by Krzysztof Bieliński

---

38 Xenakis first (in 1965–1966) composed the *Oresteia* consisting of three parts that reflect three tragedies in Aeschylus' trilogy. After 20 years, in 1987, he created an aria for Cassandra and next, in 1992, an aria for Athena. Both arias he included to the previous *Oresteia* composition. Cf. Vagopoulou 2005: 6.

The audial semiotics of these two scenes is overwhelming, especially when clashed with silence, as it happens in Cassandra's death. *Opsis* in both scenes is used only to express Aeschylean text. The dynamic and cruel scene of Agamemnon's death, with his cries coming from behind the stage and chorus' screams from the stage, is shown here mostly through visual signs of splashed blood and subsequently by the act of the murder itself. Zadara could suffice with these splashes of blood on sheet which were highly suggestive, however, by showing the cruel act of bloody murder before the spectators' eyes he seems to have achieved his main goal of depicting the cruel circle of vengeance in political struggle. The scene literally flooded with blood clearly reminds the aesthetics of "wet" theatre with little shade of self-irony: actress playing Clytemnestra smears blood on Aegisthus' face with smile like it was a child's play. In this production, blood as a sign of death appears many times and mostly as a metatheatrical sign used directly from bottle as it used to be sold for theatrical purposes. In this production Zadara seems to play both with myth, recontextualising mythical index into communist Poland, and with its staging, by employing metatheatrical use of accessories like blood or *ekkyklema*. The fact that both props (blood and *ekkyklema*) are used in death scenes (also in the scene of Clytemnestra's and Aegisthus' death) proves the critical reading of this particular scene from ancient drama.

Conclusion

A recapitulation of this brief overview of stage images of death and rules of their acting can be provided in two perspectives. Bearing in mind the strong ethical aspect of ancient theatre expressed by the notion of *prepon* considered in the wider background of *psychagogia*, two practical tendencies could be recognized. The first one intends to employ mostly the theatre of the spectator's imagination, offering only post-mortem signs, messenger reports or screams from behind the stage, and using verbal semiotics to move imagination (Greek tragedy). The second uses aesthetics of shocking, pure visuality or of extended ghastly *ekphrases* (Latin tragedy). From the theoretical point of view, Aristotle and Horace agree not to show death directly as performed on stage, but they put emphasis on different fields of perception: the Greek philosopher underlines *leksis* in the background of *opsis*, while the Roman poet pays more attention to *opsis* appreciating the effectiveness of visuality.

Within the, originally ancient, belief that mimetic art as theatre is able to infect human soul[39] and even body to alter its state, Antonin Artaud formulated the idea of theatre considered as a plague, "a communicative delirium" (1958: 27)

---

39 Cf. Plato's *Republic* III.

which pollutes the spectators. This emphasis put on the ethical aspect of theatre seems to be a core of both theatrical ways of acting indicated by Patrice Pavis. "Wet" theatre plays with exaggeration, extreme emotions, extreme visuality, and extremely dirty stage, while "dry" theatre acts with fashioned narrations, rhetorical speeches, and stylish, ordered and clean stage. Apparently, there is a difference based on dichotomy between emotional/libidal and intellectual, between two kinds of human expression not only in art, but also in life. Since art imitates nature, this mimesis of processes of life is employed on stage to show the most unspeakable phenomenon – death. As we could notice on the example of a few case studies, contemporary theatre did not forget ancient *prepon*, but it adapts this rule in a critical way. Breaking *prepon* partially, Maja Kleczewska in her *Phaedra* inscribes death signs on the body of the messenger, still letting him to speak emotionally as it belongs to "wet" tradition. Breaking *prepon* partially, Michał Zadara in his *Iphigenia. New Tragedy* mocks the messenger's speech through parody of classicist tradition of theatre of words, which was an extreme adaptation of Aristotelian *leksis*, as it was intercepted by "dry" tradition. Playing with *prepon*, Zadara in his *Oresteia* shows death *in crudo*, in accordance with "wet" aesthetics (Agamemnon's death), and *in sublime*, in accordance with "dry" aesthetics (Cassandra's death). Regardless of how it is shown – whether by "wet", "dry" or mixed way of acting – death remains the most unpresentable phenomenon in theatre. Postmodern theatre, with its tendency to the fragmentary, inconsistent and double-coded form being simultaneously ludic and critical, paradoxically, pretends to be the best way to express phenomenon of death, which is met by humans just in fragments, without consistency and full understanding, in banal, ludic, as well as in very sophisticated form, sad or funny, sudden or anticipated, wet or dry. Still remaining an unspeakable taboo, death is *re*-presented on stage in the *continuum* between emotions and intellect, within felt understanding – the true goal of the mimetic art of theatre.

References:

Aeschylus. 1926. *Aeschylus*. Trans. by Herbert Weir Smyth. Cambridge MA: Harvard University Press; London: William Heinemann, Ltd. Vol. 2. *Agamemnon*.

Agamben, Giorgio. 1991. *Language and Death: The Place of Negativity*. Trans. by Karen. E. Pinkus and Michael Hardt. Minneapolis-Oxford: University of Minnesota Press.

Aristotle. 1926. *Aristotle in 23 Volumes*. Trans. by J. Henry Freese. Cambridge and London: Harvard University Press; London: William Heinemann Ltd. Vol. 22.

—.1932. *Aristotle in 23 Volumes*. Trans. by W.H. Fyfe. Cambridge, MA: Harvard University Press; London: William Heinemann Ltd. Vol. 23.

—.1959. *Ars Rhetorica*. Ed. by William D. Ross. Oxford: Clarendon Press.

—.1966. *Aristotle's Ars Poetica*. Ed. by Rudolf Kassel. Oxford: Clarendon Press.

Arrivé, Michel. 2010. "Langage." In *Dictionnaire de La Mort*. Ed. by Philipp di Folco. Paris: Larousse. 610–614.

Artaud, Antonin. 1958. *The Theatre and Its Double*. Trans. by Mary C. Richards. New York: Grove Press.

Bauman, Zygmunt. 1997. *Postmodernity and Its Discontents*. Cambridge: Polity Press

Beale, Walter. 1996. "Decorum." In *Encyclopedia of Rhetoric and Composition: Communication from Ancient Times to the Information Age*. Ed. by Theresa Enos. New York: Garland. 168–169.

Budzowska, Małgorzata. 2012. *Phaedra – Ethics of Emotions in the Tragedies of Euripides, Seneca and Racine*. Trans. by Adriana Grzelak-Krzymianowska. Frankfurt am Main: Peter Lang.

Cicero, Marcus T. 1902. *M. Tulli Ciceronis Rhetorica*. Ed. by Augustus S. Wilkins. Oxonii: e Typographeo Clarendoniano. Tomus I.

—.1911. *M. Tulli Ciceronis Rhetorica*. Ed. by Augustus S. Wilkins. Oxonii: e Typographeo Clarendoniano. Tomus II.

Coleen Chaston. 2010. *Tragic Props and Cognitive Function. Aspects of the Function of Images in Thinking*, Leiden-Boston: Brill.

Critchley, Simon. 2004. *Very Little . . . Almost Nothing. Death, Philosophy, Literature*. London and New York: Routledge.

Easterling, Pat and Edith Hall. 2002. *Greek and Roman Actors: Aspects of an Ancient Profession*. Cambridge: Cambridge University Press.

Erika Fischer-Lichte. 2008. *The Transformative Power of Performance: New Aesthetics*. Trans. by Saskya I. Jain. London and New York: Routledge.

Euripides. 1995. *Children of Heracles. Hippolytus. Andromache. Hecuba*. Ed. and trans. by David Kovacs. Cambridge, MA: Harvard University Press.

Green, John R. 1996. "Messengers from the Tragic Stage". *Bulletin of the Institute of Classical Studies* 41: 17–30.

—.1999. "Tragedy and the Spectacle of the Mind: Messenger Speeches, Actors, Narrative, and Audience Imagination in Fourth-Century BCE Vase-Painting". In *The Art of Ancient Spectacle*. Ed. by Bettina Bergmann and Christine Kondoleon. Washington, New Haven, London: Yale University Press. 37–63.

Halliwell, Stephen. 2011. *Between Ecstasy and Truth: Interpretations of Greek Poetics from Homer to Longinus*. Oxford: Oxford University Press.

Heidegger, Martin. 1971. *On the Way to Language*. Trans. by Peter D. Hertz. New York: Harper Collins.

Horace. 1836. *The Works of Horace*. Ed. by Christopher Smart. Philadelphia: Joseph Whetham.

—.1863. *The Works of Horace*. Trans. by Christopher Smart and Theodore A. Buckley. New York: Harper & Brothers.

Hughes, Joseph J. 2002. "Kairos *and* Decorum. *Crassus' Orator's Speech* de lege Servilia." In *Rhetoric and Kairos. Essays in History, Theory, and Praxis*. 2002. Ed. by Philip Sipiora and James S. Baumlin. Albany: State University of New York Press. 128–137.

Hutcheon Linda. 2013. "Process and Product: The Implications of Metafiction for the Theory of the Novel as a Mimetic Genre". In Linda Hutcheon. *Narcissistic Narrative. The Metafictional Paradox*. Waterloo: Wilfrid Laurier University Press. 36–48.

Lewis, Charlton T. & Short Charles. 1879. *A Latin Dictionary*. Oxford: Clarendon Press.

Lyotard, Jean-François. 1984. "Answering the Question: What is Postmodernism?" Trans. by Régis Durand. In *The Postmodern Condition: A Report on Knowledge*. Trans. by Geoff Bennington and Brian Massumi. Manchester: Manchester University Press.

Mans, M.J. 1984. "The Macabre in Seneca's Tragedies". *Acta Classica* XXVII: 101–119.

Nünlist, René. 2009. *The Ancient Critic at Work: Terms and Concepts of Literary Criticism in Greek Scholia*. Cambridge: Cambridge University Press.

Nycz, Ryszard. 2000. „Literatura postmodernistyczna a mimesis.". In Ryszard Nycz. *Tekstowy świat. Poststrukturalizm a wiedza o literaturze*. Kraków: Universitas. 161–196.

Pavis, Patrice. 2013. *Contemporary Mise en Scène. Staging Theatre Today*. Trans. by Joel Anderson. London and New York: Routledge.

Powell, Barry B. 2007. *Writing and the Origins of Greek Literature*. Cambridge: Cambridge University Press.

Scholia in Aeschylum. 1976 (vol.1), 1982 (vol.2). Scholia vetera. Ed. by O.L. Smith. Leipzig: Teubner.

Scholia in Euripidem. 1887 (vol.1), 1891 (vol.2). Scholia vetera. Ed. by E. Schwartz. Berlin: Reimer.

Seneca, Lucius A. 1917. *Seneca's Tragedies*. Trans. by Frank J. Miller. London: W. Heinemann; New York: G. P. Putnam's Sons.

—.1921. *Tragoediae*. Ed. by Rudolf Peiper and Gustav Richter. Leipzig: Teubner.

Sifakis, Grigoris. 2013. "The Misunderstanding of *Opsis* in Aristotle's *Poetics*". In *Performance in Greek and Roman Theatre*. Ed. by G. W. M. Harrison and Vayos Liapis. Leiden-Boston: Brill. p. 45–61.

Suzuki, Tadashi. 2012. *Czym jest teatr?* Trans. by Anna Sambierska. Wrocław: The Grotowski Institute.

Swyngedouw, Erik. 2005. "Governance Innovation and the Citizen: The Janus Face of Governance-beyond-the-State". *Urban Studies*, Vol. 42, No. 11: 1991–2006.

Untersteiner, Mario. 1954. *The Sophists*. Trans. by Kathleen Freeman. New York: Philosophical Library.

Vagopoulou, Evaggelia. 2005. "The Universality of Xenakis' *Oresteia*". In *Definitive Proceedings of the 'International Symposium Iannis Xenakis'*. Ed. by Makis Solomos, Anastasia, Georgaki, Giorgos Zervos. Athens.

Xenakis, Iannis. 1992. *Formalized music. Thought and Mathematics in Composition*. Stuyvesant: Pendragon Press.

Zanobi, Alessandra. 2014. *Seneca's Tragedies and the Aesthetics of Pantomime*. London-New York: Bloomsbury.

Burç İdem Dinçel[*]

The Tragic Burst of Laughter in Theodoros Terzopoulos' *Prometheus Bound*

Abstract: To say that there exists a symbiotic relationship between tragedy and comedy would not be an overstatement. As early as in Plato's *Symposium*, the coexistence of the two was not only acknowledged as one of the most vital aspects of dramatic composition, but also deployed to broach philosophical questions concerned with the art of theatre. Moreover, on the performative level, the implications of this correlation between the two genres attract notice, owing to the intricate nature of laughter and the ways in which it is metamorphosed into a tragic component on stage within the context of contemporary productions of ancient Greek tragedies – a *topos* in its own right with which to explore the reception of ancient myths in the performative framework, whose hallmark is mimesis. Taking this basic premise as a starting point, the present paper sets out to scrutinise the tragic function that laughter acquires in the theatre of Theodoros Terzopoulos, specifically in his production of Aeschylus' *Prometheus Bound* that was staged in 2010 as part of the transcultural Promethiade Project. Before going into the details of the production, however, the study will offer an in-depth account of the project itself in order to cast light on the dynamics by way of which the Promethean myth functions as a means to problematise and overcome the notion of borders. This account forms the backbone for the subsequent sections of the article devoted to Terzopoulos' "biodynamic method" that brings the ancient Greek concept of *mania* into focus and the manners through which it finds a mimetic echo in the staging praxis of the director. The study will concentrate on Terzopoulos' conception of "tragic mask" in particular, which is, in essence, nothing but a facial *gestus* that aims to convey the *pathos* of the tragic personae through the explosions of laughter over the course of *Prometheus Bound*.

Keywords: borders, *mania*, mimesis, reception, Prometheus, Promethiade, Terzopoulos

Prologue

Being among the most profound resources that have nourished artistic genres and philosophical discourses since time immemorial, myths not only have the capacity to activate and reactivate themselves whenever they are interpreted and reinterpreted, but also have the potential to carve out a common ground where various people from different castes can meet. As it is, the intellectual and so-

---

[*] Trinity College Dublin, Ireland.

ciocultural facets of myths complement each other so much, that, after a certain point, one can barely reflect on a given *mythos* without taking into consideration its distinctive *logos*. Setting great store on the communicative and transformative powers of myths, this view sets an angle from which to weigh the pros and cons of *mythopoesis*. The fact that world history has a tarnished reputation, insofar as the dire consequences of nationalism, discrimination, fascism, ethnicity, let alone fundamentalism are concerned, illustrates the extent to which mythmaking can become a tool of manipulation. The examples are too many – and too unworthy – to list. Still, shifting the emphasis from myth-making to *mytho-poesis*, and harkening to the broad range of connotations that Antiquity has bequeathed to *poiesis*,[1] it can plausibly be maintained that the creative possibilities offered by myths have the power to counter any form of ideological misuse.

The point is decisive and compels one to place maximum weight on the capability of myths to form a common ground and *hold* that ground between people, albeit temporarily, just before ideology takes its toll and turns myths into a discursive battlefield. This stress on common ground goes very much hand in hand with what Jean-Luc Nancy views as the "interruption" of myth/s. "Once myth is interrupted", notes Nancy, "writing recounts our history to us again. But it is no longer a narrative—neither grand nor small—but rather an offering: a history is offered to us. Which is to say that an event—and an advent—is proposed to us, without its unfolding being imposed upon us. What is offered to us is that community is coming about, or rather, that something is happening to us in common. Neither an origin nor an end: something *in* common" (1991: 69, emphasis in the original). Nancy's take on myths proves to be significant in the sense that it sets measures against the dangers intrinsic to the aforesaid totalizing and manipulative features of myth-making. Additionally, and maybe more decisively, this interruption, this resistant act of breaking the cycle of myths, amounts to an "opening of space" (1997: 37), to quote Nancy once again. This space, in fact, is nothing but the domain of mimesis. Nancy takes a step forward to encapsulate the entire range of nuances of mimesis within the specific context of *mytho-poesis*: "Myth is not simple representation, it is representation at work, producing itself—in an autopoetic mimesis—*as effect*: it is fiction that founds. And what it founds is not a fictive world…but fictioning as the fashioning of a world, or the becoming-world of fictioning" (1991: 56, emphasis added). The manner in which Nancy utilises mimesis is quite appealing, as it concurrently undermines such conventional ways

---

[1] The scope of *poiesis* broadens even more when one thinks of its close association with *techne*. For a comprehensive survey, see Halliwell (1998: ch.2, esp. 56–59).

of understanding mimesis as imitation, realism, or even representation; instead, mimesis *qua* world-making comes into prominence as a prerequisite for *mythopoesis*.

This being said, it is worth bearing in mind that Nancy's remarks draw their conceptual strength from the privilege he bestows on literature. Yet, far from being a drawback, the ways in which he dwells upon the act of *writing* itself vis-à-vis myths intimates the urgency of engaging in a dialogue with him. Drawing on an archaic notion of mimesis and, by extension, on the evolution of myths via the physical performances of the *aoidoi*,[2] is of prime importance for this conversation to commence, simply because it is in this corporeality that Nancy's words find a telling echo: "*Bodies don't take place in discourse or in matter*. They don't inhabit 'mind' or 'body.' They take place at the limit, *qua* limit: limit—external border, the fracture and intersection of anything foreign in a continuum of sense, a continuum of matter. An opening, discreteness" (2008: 17, emphasis in the original). In fact, viewing the body *qua* limit gestures towards a conception of mimesis in which physicality concomitantly precedes and supersedes the conceptual accounts of the notion formulated by Plato and Aristotle in Antiquity.[3] Handed down from generation to generation, these accounts of mimesis have been generated and re-generated – chiefly mimesis *qua* imitation, realism, representation and so forth – to such a relentless degree that mimesis itself has become, as Stephen Halliwell has put it, "one of the supreme myths of modern histories of aesthetics" (2002: 25). The discursive charm of this myth is so powerful that even such a meticulous thinker as Nancy himself is tempted to make use of it when getting to the core of mimesis in highly corporeal terms: "the philosophico-theological *corpus* of bodies is still supported by the spine of *mimesis*, of representation, and of the sign" (1993: 192). While it is true that the discursive burden on mimesis is too heavy to lift, considering mimesis *qua* mimesis alongside with its archaic background, where it basically denoted a form of physical re-*action* to something,[4] dispels the charm around the *myth* of mimesis. And so, it becomes possible to site Nancy's invaluable discussion in a context that is, arguably, much more performative – much more corporeal – than literature: theatre.

---

2   See, Budzowska in this volume.
3   And to some degree by Xenophon, although his accounts of mimesis can scarcely be taken too philosophically, as was cautioned by Havelock (1963: 212–213, fn. 17), Sörbom (1966: 81), Halliwell (2002: 124; 2008: 140) and Puchner (2010: 24).
4   Compare and contrast the discussions by Else (1958: 73–90); Sörbom (1966: 41–77); Keuls (1978: ch.1, esp. 9–23) and Halliwell (1998: ch.4, esp. 109–116; 2002: 15–22), for pre-Platonic occurrences of mimesis terminology.

Keeping in mind that the said basic mode of physical reaction stands, by and large, for a re-*action* to myths within the frame of the oral tradition of Antiquity, reinforces the argumentative basis of the point at stake. Moreover, evoking the idea that theatre is a form of art that can by no means do without an audience and thus requires a social setting to occur, furnishes an occasion to reframe the performative space of theatre as a liminal *topos*, in which the *interruption* of myths provides a *community* – a *body* – of people with the unique chance *to be able to be in common*, however for a brief period of time. And this framework, without a doubt, is supported by the *spine* of mimesis, of re-*action*, and of the corporeality of the theatrical *event*.[5]

(Trans)cultural Prometheus: Promethiade

Despite the fact that (re)workings of ancient myths prove to be a goldmine for examining numerous aspects of their reception over time, the diversity in reproduction of myths comes with a mixed blessing. On the one hand, this multiplicity stretches the scope of research so much that it becomes almost impossible to decide where to begin to probe into the dynamics that sustain the survival of myths in and beyond culture; and on the other, what seems to be a taxing task at the beginning may turn out to be not so punishing at all once one lends a close ear to the subtext of the prologue above. Therefore, it is vital to insist on the significance of myths' potential to (trans)form a community through the medium of theatre in the tangibility of the *hic et nunc*. This deceptively contemporary articulation of the issue, in essence, implies nothing less than an archaic conception of myths, where their physical performances and, by unquestionable necessity, their mimesis played the crucial communicative role in society. Needless to say, with its *own* socio-transformative nature, as well as with its unique capacity to reach wider audiences in a manner that can raise awareness of the burning questions about the ways of the world,[6] theatre suggests itself as the ultimate medium to embody this archaic, if not ancient, notion of myths in the twenty-first century. Indeed, by offering, so to speak, an outlet for the release of the archaic force of myths, the art of theatre functions, in a very energetic sense of the term, as a safety valve in their afterlife in modern culture. This, of course, is the latent power of theatre. What deserves close scrutiny in this regard are the means with which to realise this potential and translate it into a transcultural act that can challenge the generally

---

5   In the precise philosophical sense that Alain Badiou associates the word with intervention. See meditations 20 to 25 in (2005).
6   See Wilmer in this volume.

accepted, yet rarely questioned facts imposed by history – an area that is perhaps most vulnerable to the perils of myth-making.

Fig. 1: Sophia Hill in Prometheus Bound *by Aeschylus, directed by Theodoros Terzopoulos, Istanbul, Rumeli Fortress, 2010. Photo by Uğur Hepdarcan*

In this particular respect, the Promethiade Project comes to the fore as a significant attempt to actualise and exercise this potential on a large scale. As the title indicates, the impetus behind this joint project of the Hellenic Festival, the Zolleverein Foundation, Istanbul and RUHR.2010 European Capitals of Culture was the Promethean myth. The ideational seeds of the Promethiade were sown mainly by the critically acclaimed Greek director, Theodoros Terzopoulos, when he was in in Istanbul in Turkey with his production of Aeschylus' *The Persians* during the 15th International Istanbul Theatre Festival, which also hosted the 4th Theatre Olympics under the title of "Beyond Borders" in 2006. All these details supply the necessary conceptual and historical background of the Promethiade. It is especially because Istanbul, or to be precise, the Bosporus, that is of importance here, as it strikes the right mythical note within the tragic framework of Aeschylus' *Prometheus Bound* – it is via Bosporus that Io reaches Prometheus in her exile, or, in the words of Ruth Padel, "in her wandering by madness externalized as *oistros*"

(1995: 15). Moreover, while passing through the *ford* qua *ox* in absolute *mania*, Io (Fig. 1) leaves her own tragic mark on Bosporus by naming the place.[7] As such, the Promethiade brought the myth to the exact place that it *once* sprouted. Furthermore, thanks to the collective efforts of the artists and intellectuals from Greece, Turkey and Germany, the project generated and regenerated three distinct reworkings of the Promethean myth: *Prometheus Bound* by Terzopoulos, *Anti-Prometheus (How to Forget in Steps)* by Şahika Tekand, and *Prometheus in Athens* by Rimini Protokoll to take place in Athens, Istanbul and Essen.[8]

In the light of this information, the main question – "How will Prometheus face us today and how will we encounter him?" – that the co-organisers of the project – Terzopoulos, Frank Raddatz, Jolanta Nölle, Fabian Lasarzik and Dikmen Gürün – posed in their manifesto, gains additional importance in that it resonates with the entire concerns of contemporary classical studies when it comes to the modern reception of ancient myths.[9] For that reason alone, the declaration of the co-founders of the project deserves attention.

> The Promethiade is the draft of a common mirror, which reflects the complex Prometheus theme in a non-mimetic manner. This mirror goes back to the fountains of the myths and tells about a time before the beginning of history and nowadays. These sources lay in a landscape, where today the states of Greece and Turkey are located. Here the European civilisation is [sic] born. This civilisation has lead mankind to the global world. Prometheus, who brings the fire to mankind, is the first hero of this civilisation. Prometheus, who ignores the forbiddances of the gods and steel [sic] the fire, free up a tremendous dynamic, which continues until our age. This civilisation reveals a double face. On the

---

7   Cf. "ἰσθμὸν δ' ἐπ' αὐταῖς στενοπόροις λίμνης πύλαις
    Κιμμερικὸν ἥξεις, ὃν θρασυσπλάγχνως σε χρὴ
    λιποῦσαν αὐλῶν' ἐκπερᾶν Μαιωτικόν·
    ἔσται δὲ θνητοῖς εἰσαεὶ λόγος μέγας
    τῆς σῆς πορείας, Βόσπορος δ' ἐπώνυμος
    κεκλήσεται. λιποῦσα δ' Εὐρώπης πέδον
    ἤπειρον ἥξεις Ἀσιάδ'/ Next, just at the narrow portals of the harbor, you shall reach the Cimmerian isthmus. This you must leave with stout heart and pass through the channel of Maeotis; and ever after among mankind there shall be great mention of your passing, and it shall be called after you the Bosporus. Then, leaving the soil of Europe, you shall come to the Asian continent" (Aeschylus, *Prometheus Bound*, 729–735, trans. Herbert Weir Smyth).
8   Of these three productions, only *Prometheus in Athens* did not see the light of the theatrical day in Istanbul. In lieu of the event itself, the recording of the production in Athens was shown in the form of a documentary theatre under the name of *%100ATHENS*, thereby hampering the project from achieving the goals that it set at the beginning *in toto*.
9   See the introduction to this volume.

one hand it creates wealth and on the other it destroys nature. The civilisation, which starts with Prometheus on a little part of the earth, determines today the destiny of the whole mankind and the planet. Hence the mirror of the Promethiade shows the shape of Prometheus from an intercultural perspective. (Raddatz 2011: 7).

The excerpt eloquently fleshes out the hints that have been dropped hitherto regarding the nature of the project. With hindsight, it can reasonably be deduced that the Promethiade earns credit for intervening in the hermeneutic cycle, if not circle, of the myth that revolves around the *persona* of "Prometheus as fire-bringer, revolutionary intellect, martyr" (Steiner 1977: 455). Even though the Promethiade derives a great deal of performative benefits from these motifs, the leitmotif of the project turns out to be the emphasis it lays on the geography where the myth sprung forth. Then again, this stress does under no condition designate a return to the hugely problematic notion of origins, as can easily be inferred from the quote. On the contrary, by pivoting the myth around its homeland, the project unleashes its archaic force to embrace the civilisation that Prometheus brought into being as a whole, for what it is worth. The Promethiade thus presents itself as a transcultural act of offering; it forms a common ground and holds this ground temporarily with the history it proposes in the conflict-ridden (geo)political dynamics of the twenty-first century. And that, in a nutshell, is the real value of the non-mimetic mirror of the Promethiade, which is, in fact, a *mimesis* of the Promethean myth from an "intercultural" perspective. Be that as it may, this value, or rather, this formulation of the virtue of the project in view of the above quotation comes along with two problems, one of which can be set aside (at least for now) due to the Platonic insinuations as regards to the concept of mimesis; whereas the other, that is, the "intercultural" viewpoint that the Promethiade pursues, is an issue that is elaborated on further in the manifesto:

> How Prometheus exceeds the boundary, which the gods has established, is how the Promethiade transgress the borders, which are given by the might or power of history. Besides all political tensions and integration struggle this common artistic work about our cultural grounds points to the future. The main point in Promethiade is the presence and the creation of future. How Prometheus will face us today and how we will encounter him? These are the questions of the Promethiade in the beginning of the 21st century. This means to grasp that only a common future will exist in the global framework. This future get [sic] its energy from the common roots. Under this point, the Promethiade is the signal for a decampment to a new common artistic future based on the European culture. This is a new adventure in the long journey of the European spirit, which is not at home in the [sic] postmodernism. The Promethiade will enable us to leave the cycle of eternal present. The message is that the boundary in the time, the walls of time in the historical time, can only be transgressed together. (Raddatz 2011: 7)

The quote is remarkable in the sense that it demonstrates how the Promethiade is an exploration of the "Beyond Borders" theme which inspired the project in the first place. The all-embracing characteristic of the Promethiade, as well as the ways in which the inherent multilingualism of the project buttresses this feature, problematise the existence of borders that nation-states and languages have drawn over the course of history. Nevertheless, the performative language that each reworking of the myth digs out from the common roots, allows the project to transcend not only the linguistic borders that individual languages create, but also the concept of borders as an exclusionary idea. In this sense, borders appear to be concepts that give rise to counter ideas and practices that challenge their own existence. Even so, the unnecessary stress on the European culture and spirit in the declaration appears to be quite disturbing, for with this accent, the reading of history offered by the project predictably imposes a Eurocentric discourse upon aesthetic experience. Still, given the sincerity of the co-organisers in terms of developing an "intercultural" dialogue; given, moreover, that the budget for this large scale project came mostly from the sources associated with the European Union; given, furthermore, the fact that the Promethiade was promoted under the auspices of the European Capital of Culture, this unfortunate statement can be tolerated. What requires immediate attention, however, is the discursive manner through which the Promethiade has been promoted as an "intercultural project", the performances being representative examples of "intercultural theatre" thereof. Actually, this is the case where Erika Fischer-Lichte's caveat/s regarding the subject makes perfect sense: "The concept of 'intercultural' theatre makes the false assumption that cultures are sealed entities—once Japanese, always Japanese; once European, always European", Fischer-Lichte observes, prior to her conclusion that "the concept 'intercultural theatre' implies a sharp division between 'our' culture and 'other' cultures, and should therefore be avoided" (2014a: 130–131).[10] As is known, Fischer-Lichte chooses to align these sort of performative encounters with acts of "interweaving performance cultures", which is, for sure, a much more persuasive way of regarding the issue at stake.

Whatever might be the reasons for this imposition of a highly problematic discourse on performative events, it is obvious that the notion of "intercultural theatre" throws dim light on such an ambitious project as the Promethiade. It seems that, while trying to "leave the cycle of eternal present", the project falls into

---

10 See also the extremely fruitful conversation at http://www.textures-platform.com/?p=1667, where Fischer-Lichte (2011) elaborates on her rejection of the term "intercultural theatre." (Accessed 5 September 2016)

the evident discursive trap of the so-called "intercultural" theatre. Nonetheless, drawing on the fact that the Promethiade does transgress borders with the aid of the overarching nature of the myth while, at the same time, keeping in mind Fischer-Lichte's warnings, the Promethiade can be viewed as a transcultural act, for the lack of a better expression. From this vantage point, one can take a closer look at the theatre praxis of Terzopoulos and Attis Theatre so as to shed light on the staging aesthetics by way of which one of the main initiators of the project aspires to dismantle borders via his production of *Prometheus Bound*.

Attis Theatre and the "Biodynamic Method"

Maintaining this position in the terminological debate on "intercultural" versus "transcultural" is of great importance for an appraisal of the theatrical practice of Theodoros Terzopoulos, even if he is inclined to embrace the former of the two terms. Commenting on the trilingual aspects of his reworking of the Promethean myth in cooperation with actors coming from different cultural backgrounds, Terzopoulos states that "the basic material for intercultural theatre is energy. Body Language. The homogenization of language is reached by energy. The common energy is responsible for the compact result. Common inhaling and exhaling create that depth of energy that makes even the German language sound universal. The principals are always the same: physicality and breath. The body is global. This is the starting point where the intercultural dialogue must begin. At this point zero" (Terzopoulos in Raddatz 2011: 98). Precisely because Terzopoulos gets to the heart of the matter under discussion, this statement can hardly be taken at face value. Without being discouraged by the director's preference of the term "intercultural" theatre, and zooming in on the "point zero" that he so perfectly selects for the "intercultural" dialogue to commence, one can argue that his theatre praxis harbours a potential that lends itself to an examination in "transcultural" terms. Behind this great potential, there of course lies the vast performative geography through which Terzopoulos wanders. Writing, for the most part, in favour of an "intercultural" theatre, Pinelopi Hatzidimitriou maps out the route of the director's performative journey: "From the very beginning, Terzopoulos looked beyond Anatolia to cross borders. In order to break free from the logo-centric Western theatrical tradition, he turned to Noh and Kabuki, to the dances of dark Butoh, as well as the ways of the other civilisations, like the Aborigines in Australia and the Native Indians" (2010: 77).[11] Then again,

---

11 Unless indicated otherwise, all translations are my own.

as Hatzidimitriou concedes elsewhere, "the moment we classify Terzopoulos in this intercultural field of theatre anthropology, we expose him to possible objections over his claims for universality and the political effect of his practice on collaborating cultures" (2007: 65). Whilst Hatzidimitriou chooses to fence off prospective reservations about Terzopoulos' theatrical praxis within the boundaries of the not-so-innocent discourse of the "intercultural" theatre, following Erika Fischer-Lichte (2014a: 113–140) and opting for the usage of "interweaving performance cultures" comes to be a sound safeguard against probable opposition to the claims of a highly rewarding staging practice.[12]

It goes without saying that neither "intercultural", nor "transcultural", or "interweaving cultures" comes without a baggage. Still, taking heed of the issues raised hitherto *pro et contra*, it can be contended that the performative exchange between cultures may take place *inter*, whereas locating the *corpus* at the heart of theatrical practice always gestures towards *trans*. This holds true all the more so when one considers the connotations of these prefixes. *Inter* signifies a situation, in which the involved parties are unavoidably divided by definition,[13] while *trans*, by its etymological nature, invokes a movement that is "across" and "beyond" *by definition*. The distinction is minute, and it underwrites any sincere attempt to cross borders "in the age of supersonic reproduction", to paraphrase Walter Benjamin (2007: 217–251). Terzopoulos seems to think along the same lines: "The actor in antiquity is the definition of the Body, is synonymous with the Body. In the contemporary world the body has been abolished and the man has been turned into a puppet of capitalism, exists merely to serve capitalism. Theatre of today is obliged to restore and cultivate with ethos the idea of the universal body from the start" (2015: 84). Having thus diagnosed one of the most pressing issues of the contemporary theatre, Terzopoulos confronts the problem by summoning the archaic body to the modern stage, so as to be able to *trans*gress its borders, to *trans*form the performative space into a liminal *topos*, wherewith to *trans*mit ancient myths to the *here* and *now* in order to *trans*figure the recipients' perception of ancient Greek tragedies into a tangible experience.

Terzopoulos' diagnosis can be taken quite literally, for the director purports to have found the cure for the modern actor in a medical book that

---

[12] Reminiscing about George Sampatakakis' positive review of Fischer-Lichte (2014b), whose conceptual maxim is "interweaving performance cultures / interweaving of cultures in performance", fortifies the strength of this point. See, Sampatakakis 2014: 387–397.

[13] Cf. The punchline of Fischer-Lichte's above-critique of "intercultural" theatre.

describes the method of therapy at the Amphiario sanctuary in Attica, a hospital site of the god Asclepius, also comprising a wonderful theatre. Patients, who were about to be operated, began walking around naked in a circle on the humid ground at sunset. After the first hour they had to accelerate their step and after the second hour they had to quicken it even more. During the fourth hour they had to bend their knees like in Kabuki. During the fifth hour they had to bend their elbows and, as they kept going around and accelerating this motion with their bent limbs, they proliferated energy similar to that of African performances. They engaged in this exercise for eight hours and their bodily pain vanished. They were in a trance, like the Bacchae, brought on not by wine, not with words, but by the body's wine – their blood. Blood is the wine, and blood that circulates properly in all the veins is happiness. (2000: 50–51)

This therapeutic technique would gradually evolve into what the director calls as the "biodynamic method", whose five phases – "remembrance", "biodynamic charging / *parapraxis*", "deconstruction / isolation of body parts (*ek-stasis*)", "resignification" and "restoration" – are perhaps best studied by George Sampatakakis. He refers to each stage *seriatim* as the five main goals of the method:

To kindle a process of self-discovery, reaching as far as the subconscious reserves of the memory to the extent that they can concurrently transmit the released energy to codify and deposit the required reaction; to obviate the resistances and hindrances (chiefly pain) resulting from the physical and psychical nature of one's organism; subsequently, to resist the idea that the performing body is a centrally controlled unit and afterwards deconstruct the body into lesser kinemes; to be capable of articulating and systematising this procedure into a new memory (anti-memory) and a new body (anti-body) via behavioural overtones; and lastly, to re-locate the new body in harmony with concrete geometrical spaces. (2008: 70)[14]

It is the third phase, namely *ek-stasis* that is of particular interest here, because it takes one straight to the core of the method, where ecstasy proves to be the dynamo behind Terzopoulos' staging praxis which foregrounds the ancient Greek concept of *mania* as the kernel of *the tragic* – an aesthetic motor that would eventually drive the productions of Attis Theatre from the early *Bacchae*, to the middle *Antigone* and the late *Prometheus Bound*, to name just a few.[15]

---

14 See also Sampatakakis (2006: 90–102), as well as Hatzidimitriou (2007: 56–62; 2010: ch.2) and Karaboğa (2008: ch.2).
15 That Terzopoulos revisits almost his every interpretation of ancient Greek tragedies through his "interweaving of cultures in performance" explains why the global impact of the productions of Attis Theatre needs to be taken into consideration from a transcultural perspective. For a recent list of the entire production history of Attis Theatre, see Terzopoulos 2015: 113–117.

It is exactly at this juncture that the ancient bond between *mania* and *menos* comes into full semantic force to disclose the director's conception of the tragic and the corporeal manners through which he *trans*lates it into the dynamics of the performative space of theatre. Ruth Padel, for one, prefers to "use the important association of *mania* with *menos* differently, pointing to the core violence of *mania*, resonant of the bloody force and flood of *menos*. *Mania* has the sudden violence of a 'fit of madness'" (1995: 20, emphasis in the original). As it stands, the semantic bridge that Padel builds between *mania* and *menos* appears to be highly relevant to the theatre praxis of the director due to the fact that it is through the combination of the two that the method distils *energeia* into the performing body. It is no wonder then that Terzopoulos repeatedly refers to the crucial function that the liberation of the pelvic triangle acquires in this process: "The release of the triangle, an area that is comprised of the three main zones of energy (sacrum with anus, genitals, lower abdomen or lower diaphragm with navel) is of utmost significance, because it is pertinent to the release of animal energy" (2015: 24). The energy that Terzopoulos extracts from the plain simplicity of the act of walking – "remembrance" – is noteworthy enough, as the ensuing physical training based on the anesthetisation of the body – *"parapraxis"* – slowly but surely carries the performers to a state of *trance* – *"ek-stasis"* – which, in turn, enables them to transgress (somatic) borders with bursts of *energeia* that are likely to occur in the subsequent stages – "resignification" and "restoration" – of the method. Looking back at the controversies[16] that Attis Theatre's production of *Bacchae* (Fig. 2) stirred in 1985, it can be observed that with the "biodynamic method" Terzopoulos most certainly interrupted the hermeneutic circle around the *myth* of staging ancient Greek tragedies in a fashion that would be faithful to the texts themselves (whatever this expression would mean) and in the presumably appropriate acting style, geared mostly towards realism.

Again, as in the case of the director's soft spot for "intercultural" theatre, his vehement rejection of realism can hardly be taken for granted. According to Terzopoulos, "the performer counteracts the realistic approach to theatre. S/he is neither in search for a form of mimesis, nor a representation of daily life with the familiar behaviours, the open and hidden cards of bourgeois theatre. The performer does not act in a mimetic manner, representing the gestures of everyday life; s/he is not interested in the psychological interpretation of the role" (2015: 45–46). While it is apparent that Terzopoulos militates against such narrow

---

16 Cf. Sampatakakis (2008: ch.2), followed by Karaboğa (2008: ch.2) and Fischer-Lichte (2014b: ch.5).

understandings of mimesis as imitation, realism and representation, his working hypothesis that "the actor in antiquity is the definition of the Body, is synonymous with the Body" gives one an immediate pause. The claims that Terzopoulos makes about Antiquity, about excavating the physical sources of ancient myths, about the Dionysian *mania* as the ontological essence of the ancient Greek tragedies, and so on, encourage one to rephrase his basic premise as "the actor in antiquity is the master of Mimesis, is tantamount to Body". In point of fact, by placing such a momentous emphasis on the primary instrument of the actor with the intention to expel mimesis from his staging praxis, Terzopoulos (instinctively) harks back to an archaic notion of mimesis, whose defining characteristic is nothing short of gestural/vocal physicality that is most corporeally articulated in the choral performances in the *Homeric Hymn to (the Delian) Apollo*, as well as in the two fragments – *Edonians* and *Theoroi* – by Aeschylus.[17] This, in fact, is a case that certifies the validity of Theodor Adorno's prognosis: "Even the rejection of mimesis, the deepest concern of the new matter-of-factness in art, is mimetic" (2005: 145).

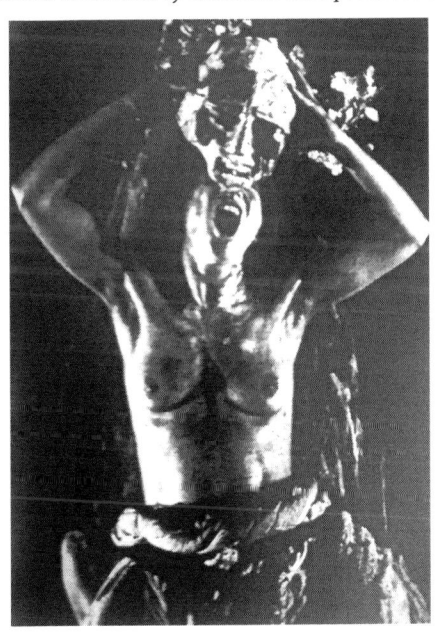

Fig. 2: Sophia Michopoulou in Bacchae *by Theodoros Terzopoulos. Photo by Johanna Weber*

---

17 For linguistic evidence and exhaustive discussions related to the issue, see the sources in the third and fourth footnotes.

It thus stands to surmise that, while Terzopoulos was busy with busting the *myth* of textually oriented approaches to staging ancient Greek tragedies, the *myth* of mimesis lured the director into its discursive trap, thereby impeding one from appreciating what he actually achieves with the always already mimetic material at his disposal. The fact that, apart from the brilliant exception of Sampatakakis (2008), this highly physical yet highly mimetic facet of Terzopoulos' staging aesthetics, based on an archaic conception of corporeality, has been overlooked in the scholarly literature that is literally devoted to Attis Theatre,[18] makes one think that the scholars working under the spell of Terzopoulos' art have also been lured by the temptation of the *myth* of mimesis. The staging practice by way of which Terzopoulos breathes new life into the works of Aeschylus, Sophocles and Euripides on the modern stage certainly has a charm, but it can easily seduce one from doing critical justice to the aesthetics at hand. In this sense, "the icon of charm becomes enigmatic", especially when it turns the performative space of the theatre into a

> **Mirror** of the actor and the spectators. While the actor breaks the time open, sees himself [sic] in the mirror, until he transforms himself into to a mirror that reflects the audience.
>
> The gaze widens to explode his icon, to shatter it into thousands of pieces. The fragments simultaneously dance and re-create his icon, a new icon, the icon of his other self, where the figure of Dionysus, the god of theatre is displayed. The actor looks deep inside the eyes of Dionysus, travels in the labyrinth, driven by his energy. And embarks on a journey towards transcendence along with the fertilising bacchanalia of Dionysus. (Terzopoulos 2015: 76–77, emphasis in the original)

As such, one comes full circle back to the seemingly non-mimetic mirror of the Promethiade. As opposed to the previous situation in which mimesis occurred, the clarity of the context here saves one from exhuming Plato to comprehend the fabric of the looking glass that takes the centre stage now. By conjuring up the archaic body to embody the tragic *mania* on the contemporary stage with total dedication to Dionysus, Terzopoulos – whether knowingly or not – appeals to an archaic conception of mimesis and – whether willingly or not – (re)energises it in such a way that it can break the Platonic mirror which is the *raison d'être* of the traditional understandings of mimesis as imitation, realism, representation, and the like. Hence, the mimetic mirror of the Promethiade destroys the *myth* of mimesis *qua* imitation, only to make it reborn on stage in the archaic shape of mimesis *qua* mimesis, which, in turn, sets the stage for explosions of *energeia* emanating from the Dionysian *mania*.

---

18 Compare and contrast, for instance, the theses pursued in Karaboğa (2008) and Hatzidimitriou (2007; 2010).

Prometheus Bound in Istanbul[19]

Amongst these outbursts of *energeia*, one particular re-action rises to prominence as a vital element of Theodoros Terzopoulos' staging aesthetics: laughter. With this component, the director exposes the ancient bond between tragedy and comedy in a manner that can render the *pathos* and the *mania* of the tragic personae at the same time into the dynamics of the *hic et nunc*. In this respect, Terzopoulos' preoccupation with the *Bacchae* comes as no surprise, since the work itself "not only exhibits the ambiguities of laughter, its involvement in both celebration and cruelty; it transmutes them into the material, the motivations and the disastrous consequences of tragic conflict. One of the supreme, perpetually challenging paradoxes of the play is that Euripides has superimposed the body language of laughter, divine as well as human, onto the bleakest face of tragedy" (Halliwell 2008: 139). Right from the start in his directorial work with Attis Theatre, Terzopoulos has explored the intricacies of laughter alongside with the Dionysian *mania*, so as to melt them in his "biodynamic" pot. Out of this exploration, Terzopoulos ferrets out his individual notion of "tragic mask", which, in the words of Kerem Karaboğa, "signifies the tragic condition depicted by the coexistence of Apollo and Dionysus" (2014: 104). The performers' ability to adopt this "facial Gestus that conveys the terror of the falling subject, expressed either with the tetanic smile and the widely open eyes or with the widening of the eyes and the gaping mouth, all of which are the symptoms of the stricken being" (Sampatakakis 2011a in Raddatz 2011: 116), provides Terzopoulos with the means to cross and go beyond borders with his renovation of the "tragic mask". That is why the director underscores the global value of the human face when meditating upon it as an energy zone: "The activation of the facial muscles is a significant step of the actor towards the universal sense of the body as a landscape of expression and creative expansion of his [sic] material" (2015: 27).

---

19 After Aeschylus, directed by Theodoros Terzopoulos; Space made by Jannis Kounellis; Translations by Eleni Varopoulou, Heiner Müller, Sabahattin Eyüboğlu; Director & Dramatic Advisor Theodoros Terzopoulos; Stage Design by Jannis Kounellis; Technical Advisor / Stage Design Implementation by Eduard Winklhofer; Music by Takis Velliantitis; Costume Design by Theodoros Terzopoulos; Assistant Director Magda Korpi; Light Design by Theodoros Terzopoulos, Konstantinos Bethanis; Production Manager Maria Vogiantzi; Cast: Yetkin Dikinciler, Sophia Michopoulou, Götz Argus, Sophia Hill, Kerem Karaboğa, Statsis Grapsas, Devrim Nas, Christian Holdt, Antonis Myriagkos, Laurens Walter, Thanasis Alevras, Maximillian Löwenstein, Umut Kırcalı, Nazmi Sinan Mıhçı, Savvas Stroumpos, Andree Östen Solvik, Alexandros Tountas.

Needless to say, mimesis, or what George Sampatakakis rightly grasps as the "mimesis of pain" (2008: 72) intrinsic to the "biodynamic method", comes to be the driving force behind this outward expression of an inward chaos that divulges itself in Aeschylus' *Prometheus Bound*; "a tragedy that has traditionally suffered from the realism of the fake rock and the red paint" (2011b: 113), to describe the work in Sampatakakis' words again, since it is precisely at this point that his views gain extra significance thanks to the ways in which he draws the line between mimesis *qua* realism and mimesis *qua* mimesis. This, in turn, brings mimesis *qua* world-making into focus as a conceptual tool with which to single out *Prometheus Bound* in Istanbul as a case where "mimesis of pain" has been metamorphosed into "mimesis of physical pain". Here, lending an ear to Eduard Winklhofer, who elaborates on Jannis Kounellis' unique installations for the *Prometheus Bound*, gives one a bird's eye view of the spatial dimensions of mimesis *qua* world-making that is at work in the *Prometheus Bound*:

> The stone curtains above the industrial ruins in Athens, made up of simple gestures of obsessive repetition and time, looked at the stage and the audience like the day marks carved into prison walls. The installation in Istanbul demanded discipline up to self-abandonment from the actors. Being insects in a splintering world where every movement causes scraping and scrunching, they were doomed to act on a surface that was filled up with thousands upon thousands pairs of glasses. For "Zeche Zollverein" in Essen, Kounellis tested a place of migration. Two locomotives with railway cars which still had their interior lights on stood in a context of industrial ruins and rampant plants, a context that had no centre. (Winklhofer in Raddatz 2011: 18)

Winklhofer's description is notable in that it indicates how Kounellis' *arte povera* turns out to be the *modus operandi* behind mimesis *qua* world-making. In a fashion that is true to the demands of *mytho-poesis*, each specific installation designed for each specific venue gives Terzopoulos' *Prometheus Bound* the opportunity to present itself *anew* by way of pushing back the limits of world-making in Athens, Istanbul and Essen respectively, thereby demanding additional physical effort from the actors. As Karaboğa puts it, "we as theatre performers had to make the audience, without getting lost in the gorgeous artistic narration of Kounellis, to listen to and spectate us. We had to avoid the rock spilled out from one face of the deserted olive oil plant in Eleusina, avoid getting lost in the thousands of spectacles filling the open air strand of Rumeli Hisarı (Rumeli Fortress) in Istanbul and avoid being smashed among the locomotives on the rails of the coal mine in Essen" (Karaboğa in Raddatz 2011: 125). Karaboğa's figurative remarks regarding the physical dangers immanent to the *Prometheus Bound* are very relevant to the topic, as they pinpoint the extent to which mimesis *qua* world-making can go.

Fig. 3: *Clockwise from left: Savvas Stroumpos, Sophia Michopoulou, Yetkin Dikinciler, Christian Holdt,* Prometheus Bound *by Aeschylus, directed by Theodoros Terzopoulos, Istanbul, Rumeli Fortress, 2010. Photo by Uğur Hepdarcan*

Perhaps the reason why these remarks can also be taken in literal terms, as far as the Istanbul production of the *Prometheus Bound* is concerned, resides in Kounellis' installation that involved "50,000 pairs of glasses that make a noise when the actors step on them. This also gives rise to something metaphysical. The glasses scream. They cry. They make a sound. In addition, the sick light of Prometheus is refracted in the lenses. The glasses are not friendly towards the actor who is moving on them" (Terzopoulos in Raddatz 2011: 107). From the chorus' rolling over the glasses with their hands on their back, to Prometheus' rubbing his abdomen with black paint; from the old woman's account of the Greek civil war (Fig. 3), to Io's barefoot embodiment of *oistros*, to Hermes' tyrannous appearance, the performers counteract the "realism of the fake rock and the red paint" throughout the production in which the sounds of sirens, gunshots, not to mention the explosions of bombs, create a soundscape that forms a *counter*point to the screaming glasses. Choosing to discuss the subject within the frame of "abstract art", Karaboğa notes that "Kounellis doesn't build up a 'stage', however the 'space' built up by him is evolved into the 'stage' through human action and it is possible to create an 'abstract space' only when the plastic one can be integrated with the organic one" (Karaboğa in Raddatz 2011: 125). This, in fact, is exactly the issue at stake. The moment when human action or, to be more precise, the corporeal expression of human action takes on the decisive role, mimesis steps in to elucidate the aesthetics that govern the production. And the plastic amounts to mimesis *qua* world-making, whereas the organic stands for mimesis *qua* mimesis epitomised by the performers' rendition of mimesis of physical pain into the *hic et nunc*.

Fig. 4: *Clockwise from left: Antonis Myriagkos, Andree Östen Solvik, Statsis Grapsas, Maximillian Löwenstein in* Prometheus Bound *by Aeschylus, directed by Theodoros Terzopoulos, Istanbul, Rumeli Fortress, 2010. Photo by Uğur Hepdarcan*

Reminiscing further about the production, the chorus' eventual transformation into Prometheus attracts particular attention, for it is here that they grow together into one choral corpus to confront Hermes, who, after uttering threats, leaves the scene with a sadistic laughter, to which the chorus as a whole responds with a sardonic laughter in *mania* (Fig. 4). This prolonged laughter goes *on* and *on* until it culminates in a tragic burst of laughter when Zeus' storm advances towards them. The entire choral corpus, in a *mimesis of tremor* involuntarily salutes the *Bacchae*, where Terzopoulos deployed "the Pontic Dance, in which the hands tremble in a mimesis of flying, while at the same time the feet march steadily on the ground" (2008: 73), to clinch the argument with Sampatakakis again. When the manic light of the *Prometheus Bound* fades away in Istanbul, the echo of the tragic burst of laughter holds the centre stage for an instant, only to trail off in the wake of the day which will come when all borders disappear; a trilingual axiom of the production that can be paraphrased as "Θα Ερθει Μια Μέρα Tüm Sınırlar Werden Ausgelöscht."

Epilogue

In an attempt to reframe the performative space of theatre as a liminal *topos*, in which the *interruption* of myths provides a *community* – a *body* – of people with the unique chance *to be able to be in common*, even if only for a brief period of time, the present article proposed a framework that is supported by the *spine* of mimesis, of re-*action* and of the corporeality of the theatrical *event*. To reflect on the implications of the proposed framework, the study focussed on Theodoros Terzopoulos' reworking of the *Prometheus Bound* for the Promethiade Project, a theatrical event, where the tragic burst of laughter plays the pivotal role.

And so, with laughter the paper is back where it started. "Laughter is the substance of art, the subject of art", says Jean-Luc Nancy in a vein that continues the dialogue, "disappearing in its coming. In laughter, the essence of art bursts—presents itself—as the 'art' of making each of the arts disappear in its own essence, in its own absence of essence. Laughter of infinite mockery, of derision and irony: the subject of art sees itself there *as* what bursts, explodes, is consumed, and disappears" (1993: 388–389, emphasis in the original). It is most probable for Nancy's words to reach out to Terzopoulos, who comments on the socio-cultural dynamics in which the Promethiade Project in general, and his production of *Prometheus Bound* in particular took place: "All that remains now is sarcasm. Laughter" (Terzopoulos in Raddatz 2011: 95).

The burst of tragic laughter that resounds for a few seconds after the lights fade away has a lasting effect whose power derives from Terzopoulos' intention to explore "the small interval, not the moment when the explosion has occurred, when the explosion has taken place, and we see the spectacular result as if it were a fanfare, as if it were very beautiful fireworks" (1992: 168). The director's research on the performative possibilities that this small interval opens up, bodies forth an aesthetics that is likely to alter one's perception of staging *the tragic* on the contemporary stage, one's approach to the study and practice of the craft of acting, one's understanding of the art of theatre. Still, the research trajectories that Terzopoulos' work on the *corpus* of ancient Greek tragedies sets are so broad that even he, at times, does not seem to appreciate their conceptual value. The subject of research on Terzopoulos manifests itself at the precise moment when the figure of Dionysus breaks the Platonic mirror to renovate one's conception of mimesis with all the archaic overtones that the notion brings along to the modern stage. This is what the tragic burst of laughter of the *Prometheus Bound* outbursts. And it is exactly at this point that the "charm" of the director's work starts to become visible.

References:

Aeschylus. 1926. *Aeschylus*. Trans. by Herbert Weir Smyth, Cambridge MA: Harvard University Press; London: William Heinemann. Ltd. Vol. 1. *Prometheus Bound*.

Adorno, Theodor. 2005. *Minima Moralia: Reflections from a Damaged Life*. Trans. by E. F. N. Jephcott. London: Verso.

Badiou, Alan. 2005. *Being and Event*. Trans. by Oliver Feltham London: Continuum.

Benjamin, Walter. 2007. "The Work of Art in the Age of Mechanical Reproduction". Trans. by Harry Zohn. In *Illuminations*. Ed. by Hannah Arendt. New York: Schocken Books, 217–251.

Else, Gerald Frank. 1958. "Imitation in the Fifth Century". *Classical Philology* 53, no. 2, 73–90.

Fischer-Lichte. 2011. "Dialogue: Erika Fischer-Lichte and Rustom Bharucha". http://www.textures-platform.com/?p=1667 (Accessed 5 September 2016).

—.2014a. *The Routledge Introduction to Theatre and Performance Studies*. Trans. by Minou Arjomand, ed. by Minou Arjomand and Ramona Mosse. London and New York: Routledge.

—.2014b. *Dionysus Resurrected: Performances of Euripides' The Bacchae in a Globalizing World*. Chichester: Wiley-Blackwell.

Halliwell, Stephen. 1998. *Aristotle's Poetics*. Chicago: The University of Chicago Press.

—.2002. *The Aesthetics of Mimesis: Ancient Texts and Modern Problems*. Princeton: Princeton University Press.

—.2008. *Greek Laughter: A Study of Cultural Psychology from Homer to Early Christianity*. Cambridge: Cambridge University Press.

Havelock, Eric. 1963. *Preface to Plato*. Cambridge: Harvard University Press.

Hatzidimitriou, Pinelopi. 2007. "The 'Bacchanalian' Body in Theodoros Terzopoulos' Theater: A Case of Interculturalism". In *The Flesh Made Text Made Flesh: Cultural and Theoretical Returns to the Body*. Ed. by Zoe Detsi-Diamanti, Katarina Kitsi-Mitakou and Effie Yiannopoulou. Frankfurt am Main: Peter Lang, 55–71.

—.2010. *Θεόδωρος Τερζόπουλος: Από το Προσωπικό στο Παγκόσμιο*, Thessaloniki: University Studio Press Publications.

Karaboğa, Kerem. 2008. *Tragedya ile Sınırları Aşmak: Theodoros Terzopoulos'un Tiyatrosu*. Istanbul: E Yayınları.

—.2011. "The Journey of a Performer with Theodoros Terzopoulos in Prometheus Bound". In *Promethiade*. Ed. by Frank Raddatz. Klartext Verlag: Essen, 124–127.

—.2014. "Copeau'dan Terzopoulos'a Oyuncu ve Maske". In *Maske Kitabı*. Ed. by Kerem Karaboğa and Oğuz Arıcı. Istanbul: Habitus, 94–107.

Keuls, Eva. 1978. *Plato and Greek Painting*. Leiden: E. J. Brill.

Nancy, Jean-Luc. 1991. *The Inoperative Community*. Trans. by Peter Connor *et all*. Ed. by Peter Connor. Minneapolis: University of Minnesota Press.

—.1993. *The Birth to Presence*. Trans. by Brian Holmes *et all*. Stanford: California University Press.

—.1997. *The Sense of the World*. Trans. by Jeffrey S. Librett. Minneapolis: University of Minnesota Press.

—.2008. *Corpus*. Trans. Richard A. Rand. New York: Fordham University Press.

Padel, Ruth. 1995. *Whom Gods Destroy: Elements of Greek and Tragic Madness*. Princeton: Princeton University Press.

Puchner, Martin. 2010. *The Drama of Ideas: Platonic Provocations in Theater and Philosophy*. Oxford: Oxford University Press.

Raddatz, Frank (ed). 2011. *Promethiade*. Klartext Verlag: Essen.

Sampatakakis, George. 2006. "Dionysus Restitutus—Terzopoulos' *Bakchen*/Dionysus Restitutus—The Bacchae of Terzopoulos". In *Reise mit Dionysus: Das Theater das Theodoros Terzopoulos/Journey with Dionysus: The Theater of Theodoros Terzopoulos*. Ed. by Frank Raddatz. Germany: Theater der Zeit, 90–102.

—.2008. *Γεωμετρώντας το Χάος: Μορφή και Μεταφυσική στο Θέατρο του Θεόδωρου Τερζόπουλου*. Αθήνα: Εκδόσεις Μεταίχμιο.

—.2011a. "Codex Prometheus". In *Promethiade*. Ed. by Frank Raddatz. Klartext Verlag: Essen, 116–117.

—.2011b, "Gestus or Gesture? Greek Theatre Performance and Beyond". In *Receptions of Antiquity*. Ed. by Jan Nelis. Gent. Academia Press.

—.2014. "A Performance History of Euripides' *Bacchae*". *Logeion: A Journal of Ancient Theatre* vol. 4, 387–397.

Sörbom, Göran. 1966. *Mimesis and Art*. Stockholm: Svenska Bokförlaget.

Terzopoulos, Theodoros. 1992. "Theodoros Terzopoulos' Talk". In *Ancient Sun, Modern Light: Greek Drama on the Modern Stage*, by Marianne McDonald. New York: Columbia University Press, 159–169.

—.2000. *Theodoros Terzopoulos and the Attis Theatre: History, Methodology and Comments*. Trans. by Alexandra Kapsalis. Athens: Agra Publications.

—.2011. "Language and Space: Theodoros Terzopoulos in Conversation with Frank Raddatz". In *Promethiade*. Ed. by Frank Raddatz. Klartext Verlag: Essen, 97–115.

—.2015. *Η επιστροφή του Διόνυσου*. Αθήνα: Θέατρο Άττις.

Steiner, George. 1977. *After Babel: Aspects of Language and Translation*. Oxford: Oxford University Press.

Winklhofer, Eduard. 2011. "Breaking up the Bounds of Casualness". In *Promethiade*. Ed. by Frank Raddatz. Klartext Verlag: Essen, 16–18.

Index

actor(s) 21, 34, 37, 52, 99, 135, 137–138, 142, 144, 150, 156, 180, 184, 195, 197, 199–201, 203, 208–210, 212, 218, 221–223, 231, 243–244, 247–251
adaptation 15, 17–18, 23, 134, 150–151, 158–160, 171, 191, 195–197, 230
Adonis 106
Aeacus 96
Aeschylus
    Agamemnon 47, 115–117, 131, 213–214, 216, 230
    The Eumenides 47–48, 113, 117, 131
    The Libation Bearers 47, 116, 131
    The Oresteia 47, 114, 116–117, 131, 207, 226, 228, 230, 233
    The Persians 31, 45–46, 60, 239
    The Suppliants 191, 197
Aeson 17, 89–90
aesthetics 10, 11, 21, 31, 65, 113, 139, 142, 145, 158, 207, 209, 211, 215, 217–221, 223, 229–231, 233, 237, 243, 248–249, 252–254
Afghanistan 197, 203
Agamben, Giorgio 219, 230
Agamemnon 46–48, 50, 116, 195, 213–214, 225–230
Agathias Scholasticus 103, 106–108
    Cycle 103, 108
Ajax 34, 91, 125, 183, 216
Alexandria 42, 57–58
anger 5, 79, 81–82, 84–88, 162, 187
Anouilh, Jean 134
Antigone 20, 79, 81, 83–84, 159–160, 162–177, 192–194, 196, 204–205

Antiphanes 29–31
Aphrodite 104, 106–107
Apollinaire 139–140, 146
    Les Mamelles de Tirésias 139
Arabia 63, 66
archon 43–44, 46–47
Ariadne 107
Aristophanes 30, 56, 68, 72, 91
    Acharnians 30, 68
    Birds 30
    Peace 30
Aristophanes of Byzantium 42–43, 47, 49–50
Aristotle 9, 21, 34, 37, 42, 62, 79–80, 135, 207, 209–212, 214–215, 229–231, 233, 237, 254
    Poetics 34, 79, 207, 233, 254
    Rhetoric 211, 231
Artaud, Antonin 133, 139, 144–145, 229, 231
asylum 191–192, 197–198, 200, 202
Athena 34, 48, 183, 228
Atreus 32, 41, 46–47, 52, 96, 215
Attic comedy 30, 38
Austria 191, 198, 202, 205
avant-garde 10, 19, 133, 135–136, 139, 145
Avignon 181

Barba, Eugenio 179–180, 188
    On Directing and Dramaturgy: Burning the House 179, 180, 188
Bauman, Zygmunt 219, 231
Beckett, Samuel 9, 11, 23, 133–134
Behemoth 68, 74, 78
Belfast 161, 166, 175
Blumenberg, Hans 13–15, 22
boar 5, 16, 55–59, 62–68, 70–72

Borscht, Mirko 198–199
Brecht, Bertolt
Breton, André 137, 139, 146
Brodski, Josif 181, 188
Brutus 97
Burg Theater 198–199, 204
Butler, Judith 192–193, 196, 204
Byzantine 5, 17, 27, 42–45, 52, 103–105, 107–109

Caius Laelius 96
Calderón de la Barca, Pedro 180
Caligula 68–69, 77
Callimenes 105
Calliope 105
Camus, Albert 113–114, 120, 124, 126–129
    The Myth of Sisyphus 124, 128–129
    The Rebel 124, 129
Canada 20, 180
Carr, Marina 21, 194–196, 204
    By the Bog of Cats 194
    Hecuba 21, 194–196, 205
Cassandra 47–48, 195–196, 213, 216, 226–230
Catholic Church 161, 168
Cato the Elder 89–90, 93, 97–99
Catulus 97
choragus 44, 47–48
chorus 34, 43–44, 46–48, 50–51, 80, 122, 127, 150, 162–163, 169, 186, 193, 199, 203, 210, 228–229, 251–252
Christianity 103, 109, 254
Cicero 5, 11, 17, 63, 73, 89–102, 207, 212, 231
    De oratore 98, 212
    De senectute (On Old Age) 5, 17, 89–90, 92–93, 95–97, 99–101
    On Duties 96
    On Glory 91

    Orator 91, 212
    On the Ends of Good and Evil 94
    Tusculan Disputations 94, 98, 100
Circe 107
Classical Reception 11, 17, 18, 21, 23, 113, 130, 177
Claudel, Paul 135
Clio 105
Clytemnestra 116, 226–227, 229
Cocteau, Jean 134
comedy 29–30, 38, 44, 92–93, 95–101, 121, 130, 133–134, 151, 210, 235, 249
communist 19–20, 229
Corneille, Pierre 155
    Horace 155
Craig, Gordon 133, 136, 180
Crassus 97–98
Creon 162–165, 167, 169–172, 218
Critchley, Simon 208, 231
Curiatian 155
Cyprus 120, 122–123, 125–126, 128

Dadaism 114, 139
Daphnis 105–106
death 21, 46–50, 72, 80–82, 84, 90, 92, 94, 105–106, 116, 140–141, 145, 150–151, 153–155, 161–162, 165–166, 170, 172, 176, 181, 193–195, 207–210, 213–231
decorum 21, 89, 96, 99, 102, 207, 212, 218, 221, 231, 232
Demetrius Triclinius 43, 47
democratic turn 23
Derrida, Jacques 192, 204
deus ex machina 154
Devlin, Bernadette 167
Dicaearchus of Messana 42
Dilthey, Wilhelm 13, 119
Doric farce 30
dry theatre 207, 221, 230
Durand, Gilbert 14, 22–23, 33, 38

Egypt 10, 55, 57, 59, 61–62, 66, 71, 77, 104, 120, 122, 197
ekkyklema 226–229
ekphrasis 223
Electra 46, 49–52, 150
Eliot, Thomas Stearns 113–115, 119, 128–131
Endymion 94, 101, 106
Enquist, Per Olov 222
  To Phaedra 222
epigram 11, 66, 103–109
epitome 42
Eratosthenes Scholasticus 104
Erinyes 46, 48–50
Esslin, Martin 134
Eteocles 79–81, 84–85, 87, 162
ethopoiia 96
Euripides 9, 16, 35–36, 38, 42–44, 48–52, 80–81, 98, 106, 113–114, 116, 120–122, 128–131, 138–139, 147, 150, 182, 194, 207, 213, 216, 222–225, 231–232, 248–249, 254–255
  Hecuba 35–36, 48, 192, 213, 216, 231
  Helen 113–114, 120–122, 128–131
  Hippolytus 216, 222–223, 231
  Ion 121
  Iphigenia in Tauris 35, 121
  Orestes 49–51
  Phoenissae 46, 80–81
exile 20, 80, 179, 181, 191, 193–194, 239
existential historicism 113–114, 118–119, 128
existentialism 19, 113–114, 123, 127–130

feminist 166–167, 169, 171, 176
flamingo 55, 67–69
furor 79, 85–87
Futurism 139, 145

Gadamer, Hans-Georg 17, 22
Gambaro, Griselda 193
  Antigona Furiosa 193
German Democratic Republic (GDR) 20, 147–149, 151, 153, 155–157
Germany 148, 191, 196, 198, 200, 202, 240
Gide, André 133
Giraudoux, Jean 134
Glauce 106
Głowacki, Janusz 193, 205
  Antigone in New York 193, 205
Goll, Yvan 19, 133, 135–146
  Mathusalem ou l'Éternel Bourgeois 133
  Le Surdrame 133, 136, 146
Gregorius Corinthius 44
Gregory of Nazianzus 108
grotesque 83, 138–142, 144
Grotowski, Jerzy 179–180, 187–188
  Tu es le fils de quelqu'un 179, 187–188
Guterres, António 192

Hector 91, 195
Hecuba 36, 125, 194–196, 205, 216
Heidegger, Martin 30, 219, 232
Helen 49–50, 120–125, 149
Heliogabalus 55–56, 68–69
Hellenistic 17, 42, 44–45, 50, 52, 103–105
Hermes 30, 105, 120, 251
Hermione 49–50
Hesiod 108
  Works and Days 108
Homer 31, 42, 48, 83, 91, 231, 254
  Odyssey 48, 116, 182
Horace 21, 66–67, 74, 80, 207, 213, 215, 229, 232
  Ars poetica 37, 207, 213, 215

Horatian 20, 147–149, 155–157
Hortensius 97
Hydra of Lerna 149
hypothesis 41, 44, 46–48, 50–52
illogical dramaturgy 140
imitation 18, 32, 79–80, 87, 104–105, 173, 222, 237, 247–248, 254
immigration 196, 198, 204
incipit 27, 33–35
Ionesco, Eugène 134, 141–142, 146
  La Cantatrice Chauve (*The Bald Soprano*) 141
  Rhinoceros 134
Iphigenia 46–47, 225–226
IRA (Irish Republican Army) 161, 166
Ireland 20, 159–161, 163, 165–168, 172–175, 177, 194
Iser, Wolfgang 17, 23
Isidorus Scholasticus 104, 106
Ismene 161–165, 170–171
Israel 180, 183

Jarry, Alfred 135, 145
  Ubu Roi 135
Jauss, Hans Robert 17, 23
Jelinek, Elfride 20–21, 191, 196–200, 202–203, 205
  Die Schutzbefohlenen 20, 191, 196–198, 201–202, 204
Jocasta 29, 79–81, 84–85
Johannes Logothetes 44
Joyce, James 115
  Ulysses 115
Julian of Egypt 104–105
Julianus Antikensor 104, 107

Kennelly, Brendan 20, 159–160, 166–177
  New Version of Antigone 20, 159–160

The Irish: Priests and the People 168, 175
Kerr, Alfred 144
kirchenasyl 200
Kleczewska, Maja 207, 222–223, 230
Kurdi, Aylan 196

Labdacus 32
Lampedusa 191, 197, 200
Lebanon 20, 180–183, 185
Lehmann, Hans-Thies 135–136, 146
Lehrstück 154
leksis 210, 229–230
lemma 27–29, 34
Lemnos 151–153
Leviathan 69, 74, 78
Levinas, Emmanuel 192, 205
Libya 200
Livius 155
  Ab urbe condita 155
Lucullus 97
Lyotard, Jean-François 219, 232

Macedonius Consul 103, 108
Maeterlinck, Maurice 135
Mallarmé, Stéphane 135
manus 79, 81, 84
manuscript 43, 45, 50, 69, 74, 97, 113, 174
Markievicz, Constance 176
mask 19–20, 35, 134, 137–138, 140, 143, 145, 150–151, 156, 199, 208, 211, 214, 235, 249, 255
Medea 17, 90, 92–93, 95, 98, 101, 106, 148, 191–192, 194, 196, 215, 217–218
melodrama 50
Melpomene 107
messenger 47, 80–81, 115, 125, 207, 213–215, 217, 222–23, 225–226, 229–231
metoikos 193

Index   261

Meyerhold, Vsevolod 136, 180
mimesis 15, 207–208, 210–212, 214, 220, 230, 232, 235–238, 241, 246–248, 250, 252–254
Minos 96
modernism 29, 113, 119, 131
Mouawad, Wajdi 20, 179–189
   Blood Promises (*Le Sang des promesses*) 181
Muses 105
Müller, Heiner 19, 147–158, 249
   Cement (*Zement*) 148
   Despoiled Shore Medea Material Landscape with Argonauts (*Verkommenes Ufer Medeamaterial Landschaft mit Argonauten*) 148–149
   Germania Death in Berlin (*Germania Tod in Berlin*) 148
   Herakles 5 148
   Krieg ohne Schlacht (*War without battle*) 149, 158
   Mauser 148
   Philoctetes 20, 147–149, 151, 157–158
   Prometheus 148
   Sophocles: Oedipus the King (*Sophokles: Ödipus Tyrann*) 148
   The Correction (*Die Korrektur*) 148
   The Horatian 20, 147–149, 155–157
   The Scab (*Der Lohndrücker*) 148
   Volokolomsk Highway I–V (*Wolokolamsker Chaussee* I–V) 148
mythographer 45
mythopoesis 14–15, 21, 236

Nancy, Jean-Luc 236–237, 253, 255
Neoptolemus 150–154, 157
New Criticism 17

Northern Ireland 159, 161, 163, 165, 167, 173–175
Nübling, Sebastian 198, 202–203
   In unserem Namen 198, 202

O'Brien, Conor Cruise 163
Odin Theater 179
Odysseus 34, 149–154, 157
Oedipus 20, 29, 32, 79–83, 86–87, 179, 185–186, 191–193, 209
opera 226–227
opsis 209–211, 213–214, 227, 229, 234
Orestes 32, 46–51, 150, 191, 214

Pakistan 197
Palatine Anthology 103, 108
Palestine Liberation Organization 180
palm 16, 55–66, 71, 73, 76
Pandora 108
pantomime 148, 218, 233
Paulin, Tom 20, 159–167, 169, 173, 177
   The Riot Act 20, 159–161, 167, 177
Paulus Silentarius 103, 105–107
Pavis, Patrice 207, 221, 230, 232
Pelasgos 191, 197
Pelias 17, 89–90, 92–95, 99
Pentheus 120
Persephone 106
Petronius 75–76
   Satyricon 55–56, 64–65, 67, 69, 71–72, 74–77
Philippus of Thessalonica 103, 105
Philoctetes 149–154, 157
phoenix 16, 55–57, 63–73, 75, 77
Phrynichus 31, 45
   The Capture of Miletus 31
Pirandello, Luigi 137
Piscator, Erwin 133, 136

Plato 104, 120, 229, 235, 237, 241, 248, 253–255
Plautus 89–101
    Pseudolus 89, 91–95, 97–100
Plaza de Mayo 193
Pliny the Elder 16, 55–56, 60, 66, 72, 76
    Natural History 55–56, 63, 72, 76
Pliny the Younger 72
Plutarch 68
Polydorus 36, 195–196
Polymestor 195
Polynices 79–81, 84–85, 87, 163
Polyxena 213
postdramatic theatre 19, 133–136, 138–140, 144–146
postmodernism 220, 232, 241
prepon 207, 209, 211–215, 218, 223, 229–230
Prometheus 30, 239–241, 251–252
prosopopeia 208, 214
Protestant Unionist 161
Psalms 63, 69–70
psychoanalysis 183

Racine, Jean 225–226, 231
    Iphigenia 207, 224
racism 201, 204
recusatio 151
refugees 20–21, 191–192, 196–200, 202–203, 205
re-occupation (*Umbesetzung*) 14, 16, 18
Rezeptionstheorie 17
Roscius 97
Royal Shakespeare Company 194
Russian formalism 17

Sartre, Jean-Paul 114, 120, 127, 134, 150
    Huis Clos 127

scholia 9, 11, 16, 27–29, 33, 35–37, 43–45, 47, 49–50, 52–53, 207, 213–214, 228, 232
Scipio Aemilianus 96
Seferis, Georgios 19, 113–130
    Book of Exercises 116
    …Cyprus Where it Was Ordained For Me… 120
    Helen 114, 120, 122–125, 127–128
    Letter to a foreign friend 114, 130
    Logbook III 113–114, 126–127, 130
    Monday 116
    Mycenae 116
    Mythistorima 113–116
    On Stage 116
    Salamis of Cyprus 125
    Thrush 113–114
    Three Secret Poems 116
    Wednesday 116
Selene 106
Seneca 9, 16, 67, 77, 79–82, 85–88, 207, 215–218, 221–223, 231–233
    Medea 218
    On Anger (De ira) 85–88
    Phaedra 222
    Phoenissae 16, 79–81, 84, 86–88
    Trojan Women 216
sermocinatio 96
sexuality 166, 172, 174
significance (*Bedeutsamkeit*) 13
Socialism 147, 156
Sophocles 16, 20, 28–29, 35–36, 38, 42–44, 49, 53, 80, 116, 147, 149–150, 154, 158–161, 163, 166–169, 172–177, 179, 182–183, 185–186, 216, 248
    Ajax 182, 216
    Antigone 38, 159–161, 169, 171–174, 176, 182, 192–194, 245

Electra 116, 182
Oedipus at Colonus 16, 38, 49, 80, 182, 191–192
Oedipus Tyrannus 28, 32, 35, 38
Philoctetes 20, 182
The Trachiniae 182
Stalinism 147, 156–157
Stein, Gertrude 136
Steiner, George 159, 177, 241, 256
Stemann, Nicholas 191, 197, 199–204
Stesichorus 105, 120
 Palinode 120
stochastic music 226–227
Stoic philosophy 79, 85, 88
Strabo 58, 77
Strindberg, August 133, 135, 141
Suetonius 69, 71
Surrealism 114, 136–137, 139–140, 145–146
Surrealist Manifesto 140
Symbolism 105
Syria 55, 65–66, 69, 180, 194–195, 203–205

Tasnádi, István 222
 Phaedra. The Therminal Act 222
Theophrastus 58–59, 61
Terpsychora 107
Terzopoulos, Theodoros 21, 235, 239–240, 243–256
Teucer 29, 122–127
Thalheimer, Michael 198–199, 203–204
Thalia Theatre 197, 199, 201–202, 204
The Silent Majority 191, 202–203
The Travelling Community 194
Theatre of Cruelty 136, 139
Thebes 79–80, 193
Theramenes 223–224
Theseus 192, 223–224
Thoth 105

tragedy 15–16, 19, 21, 27–31, 33–34, 36, 41, 44–45, 48, 50, 79–81, 84–85, 88, 98, 113–116, 119–121, 126, 128–130, 133–134, 150–151, 159–160, 162, 165, 172–177, 181–182, 188, 191, 197, 202, 205, 207–211, 213, 215–216, 218–220, 224–226, 228–231, 235, 249–250, 255
tragicomedy 50
translation 18, 23, 159, 160–161, 168, 170, 172–173, 179–180, 223
Trimalchio 55–56, 64–66, 68–70, 72, 74–75, 77
Trojan War 48, 149, 154, 195
Troy 46, 107, 120, 122, 124, 150–152, 154, 158, 195

Ulysses 125–126
Unpresentable 21, 208, 219–220, 230

Varro 58, 93–97
 Menippean Satire 93, 95
verbality 114–115, 118, 221, 223, 226
Vergil 105
visuality 209–210, 214–215, 218, 223, 226–227, 229–230

Wedekind, Frank 233
wet theatre 221–222, 229–230
Witkiewicz, Stanisław Ignacy 136
work of myth (*Arbeit des Mythos*) 13–15, 18, 21–22
work on myth (*Arbeit am Mythos*) 13–14, 16–17, 20–22

Xenakis, Iannis 226–228, 233
Xerxes 45

Yeats, William Butler 160, 174

Zadara, Michał 207, 224, 226, 228–230
Žižek, Slavoy 196